Also by Marc Ostrofsky

Get Rich Click!
The Ultimate Guide to Making Money on the Internet

Word of Mouse

101+ TRENDS IN HOW WE BUY, SELL, LIVE, LEARN, WORK, AND PLAY

Word of Mouse (wurd uv maus): n. a "one-to-one" but more often a "one-to-many" (i.e., broadcast) communications method using the power of networks and the internet to disseminate content. This content can be words, audio, video, games, software, images, texts, or ideas and can be spread to the masses by using an array of technological options including computers, iPads, smartphones, and a host of technologies in a state of constant evolution.

Marc Ostrofsky

Simon & Schuster
New York   London   Toronto   Sydney   New Delhi

Note to Readers

This publication contains the opinions and ideas of its author. It is intended to provide helpful and informative material on the subjects addressed. The strategies outlined in this book may not be suitable for every individual, and are not guaranteed or warranted to produce any particular result.

This book is sold with the understanding that neither the author nor the publisher is engaged in rendering legal, financial, accounting, or other professional advice or services. The reader should consult a competent professional before adopting any of the suggestions in this book or drawing inferences from it.

The publisher does not have any control over and does not assume any responsibility for the author's website(s) or its content, and neither the author nor publisher has any control over (and such parties do not assume any responsibility for) any third party's website(s) or content.

No warranty is made with respect to the accuracy or completeness of the information or references contained herein, and both the authors and the publisher specifically disclaim any responsibility for any liability, loss or risk, personal or otherwise, which is incurred as a consequence, directly or indirectly, of the use and application of any of the contents of this book.

Simon & Schuster
1230 Avenue of the Americas
New York, NY 10020

Copyright © 2013 by Marc Ostrofsky

First Simon & Schuster hardcover edition September 2013

SIMON & SCHUSTER and colophon are trademarks of Simon & Schuster, Inc.

For information about special discounts for bulk purchases, please contact Simon & Schuster Special Sales at 1-866-506-1949 or business@simonandschuster.com.

The Simon & Schuster Speakers Bureau can bring authors to your live event. For more information or to book an event, contact the Simon & Schuster Speakers Bureau at 1-866-248-3049 or visit our website at www.simonspeakers.com.

Manufactured in the United States of America

1   3   5   7   9   10   8   6   4   2

Library of Congress Cataloging-in-Publication Data
Ostrofsky, Marc.
Word of mouse : 101+ trends in how we buy, sell, live, learn, work, and play / Marc Ostrofsky.
        pages   cm
1. Information technology—Economic aspects.   2. Information technology—Social aspects.   3. Technological innovations—Social aspects.   4. Internet—Social aspects.   5. Electronic commerce—Social aspects.   I. Title.
HC79.I55O755 2013
303.48'33—dc23   2013006141

ISBN 978-1-4516-6840-7
ISBN 978-1-4516-6842-1 (ebook)

I want to dedicate this book to my father,

Dr. Benjamin Ostrofsky,

who spent the last fifty years teaching me
right from wrong,
keeping me focused on the endgame,
treating everyone with love and respect,
and teaching me to always do my best at every turn.
He taught me to plan ahead and to always be
more cautious than others
because, as he put it:
"It's hard to make it,
it's even harder to keep it, and yet
it's so easy to lose it."
He has been the ultimate hero in my life
and my mentor for fifty years.
I love him dearly!
Thank you, Dad.

Contents

To be successful, you must know what you know you DON'T know and hire your weaknesses!

Foreword

Clate Mask, CEO and cofounder, Infusionsoft

My world revolves around the success of small businesses. As the CEO of Infusionsoft, I am all about helping small businesses find more customers, get repeat sales, and save time, which means saving money! In today's incredibly competitive world, that's a lot harder than it once was. The Yellow Pages is dead. Print advertising is tougher than ever. As Marc said in his previous book, *Get Rich Click!*, suspects, prospects, and clients are hanging out online. The ultimate competitive advantages are automation and technology tools that simultaneously increase sales and lower costs.

The old world of business has changed dramatically. It's a digital world today. The process of efficiently finding, landing, and serving customers—what our organization calls the "Perfect Customer Lifecycle"—brings with it a host of complexities. SEO, PPC, and blogs. Multiple tools and systems. Technologies that don't work well together. Information overload. It can quickly become chaos for anyone in business, the entrepreneur who simply wants to run a successful business, or a parent who simply wants to communicate with his or her teenager!

So what does all of this mean? It means that along with the digital revolution comes the cold, hard fact that companies today must assign technology the critical role of gaining the upper hand to help all of us succeed in business. If we want more customers, repeat sales, and better efficiency if we want success in our businesses—we've got to embrace technology, not just for our competitive advantage but also for our very survival. The writing is on the wall. Those businesses that adapt will succeed. Those that don't will be left behind.

And that's why this book is so important. *Word of Mouse* helps readers see the impact of internet technology and adapt to the future—in life and in business. Marc shows us the trends, the case studies, and the impact of the internet and its associated technologies in a way that readers can't ignore. He helps readers see how the gradual rise of the internet has changed everything, even though we may not recognize how it is impacting us.

This book will open your eyes to a world of opportunity you probably didn't know existed. In the pages that follow, you'll read about the emerging trends and the ways that everyday people just like you are using technology to achieve breakthrough success. Through Marc's years of experience and his in-depth research, he brings a wealth of expertise that you can apply in your business to achieve greater levels of success or in everyday life to simply stay in touch with your friends on Facebook, via Twitter, or through Pinterest.

The case studies are my favorite part of the book. And that's not just because some of them feature Infusionsoft customers. (See more about their success at www.infusionsoft.com/casestudies.) While it's true that I love to see our customers effectively using our software to find more customers, get repeat sales, and save time, there's another reason why I love the case studies: in working with entrepreneurs for many, many years, I've noticed that most of them struggle to see the "better way" to use technology—until they see that same technology being used by someone like them in a similar business. Marc has done a great job of making these case studies vivid, real, and easy to understand, so that you can see how *you* or *your firm* can employ the same techniques and technologies. In short, Marc teaches the way they do at Harvard Business School: using real-life examples to show you how to achieve greater success in your business through the effective use of technology.

The digital revolution has thrust technology to the forefront of the small-business-success equation. It truly levels the playing field and gives any small or midsized business a huge leg up on the competition. It can be daunting to navigate the waters in this new world, but you can do it! My hope is that you will use this book as a resource in your sales and marketing efforts as you embrace the internet and adopt technology. I am confident that as you study the trends and the examples, your eyes will be opened to new ways that you can achieve small-business success.

Although I gravitate toward the business applications of the content, this book is written for consumers. Marc focuses his "serial entrepreneur" trend-watching lens on the internet-driven changes he observes today and how they will evolve. The book is a wake-up call for consumers who are immersed in technology but are sleepwalking through its impact. Whether voluntarily, involuntarily, consciously, subconsciously, or unconsciously, we have assigned technology a dominant role in our lives. Taking the time to understand the "mind-body-internet connection" is key to ensuring that consumers let that dominance work in their favor, in a way that it is welcome, efficient, productive, and transparent. This book brings readers to that understanding. It gives readers the tools they need to dig themselves out from under the information overload that otherwise paralyzes their use of today's digital delivery systems. It is a brilliantly conceived assimilation of trends, case studies, forecasts, apps, and tips for getting "plugged in" that will put readers in the driver's seat of the world's most powerful, most disruptive force to date. A special bonus chapter guides consumers through the perils of cyber crime, with practical steps on how to avoid becoming a victim. Readers of his book will put it down in an awakened state, feeling smarter, more engaged, and more the masters of the digital world that surrounds them.

Preface

I am a golfer. I just love to go out and play golf. Maybe it's because no one is "the best" at it, or because of the truism of golf: "The harder you swing the club, the *worse* you will do." Golfers will understand that irony, but it's a hard, wonderful, maddening, and perplexing sport. I do love it!

For twenty years, I have purchased my golf clubs, golf shoes, and thousands of golf balls (most of which now reside at the bottom of a lake) at a small local retail golf shop owned by a nice guy named Jim Harrison.

I went in one day about six months ago to find a sign on the door saying STORE CLOSING—NEW LOCATION TBA. I was shocked. Jim had been there for almost twenty-five years! At the register was another note written on a yellow notepad:

> *We lost our lease. We have thirty days to vacate. Please give us*
> *your email address so we can tell you our new address when we*
> *have one. Thanks, Jim*

"What a shame," I thought. "The guy has no clue!" In today's tech speak, what ran through my head was, "OMG! Are you kidding me? He doesn't have a database of his clients and their email addresses?" Sure enough, Jim said he didn't—and never thought he needed one. Jim said something I'd heard a hundred times before:

"Why should I? All of my customers know me, and I know them."

Now that Jim was moving to a new location, he didn't have a quick way of telling everyone where and when he'd be open for business again! Only if someone walked into the store during that thirty-day period and was served by Jim or another employee would he or she know the details of the move. To make matters worse, what was the likelihood that even informed customers would remember that Jim had moved *and* where he was moving to the next time they needed golf supplies? And none of these problems takes into account the fact that, as of my visit, Jim still hadn't found a new location. It was entirely possible that he wouldn't have a new site before he was forced to leave the building—and all his customers—behind.

Jim was in trouble for sure. Can you imagine: twenty-five years of hard work, striving every day to build a business, only to have it vanish in thirty days? It's like having all of your assets in a home with no fire insurance when a fire breaks out and burns everything down to a pile of ashes.

Jim was truly upset over the situation. The truth was, though, he was mad mostly at himself. And he was scared, because this turn of events meant that he had to start over from the ground up—as though he'd never had a customer in his life.

The point of the story? Here are six good ones:

1. Jim is typical of many people today, assuming a mind-set of "I've always done it this way, so why should I change?" Until something like Jim's situation happens, these people continue doing everything the "same old way."

2. Jim never knew that he could get *more* business by communicating with his clients via Word of Mouse: via email, Facebook, LinkedIn, and many other tools of the internet age.

3. Jim "doesn't know what he doesn't know." These days, you must observe what other businesses are doing to stay connected with customers, such as having a database of your clients and segmenting which ones spend the most money with you. You also must determine whether you understand the problems you have in a contemporary context. For example, are you losing out to the competition because they have a better social media strategy than you (if you even have one, that is)? Are you complacent about checking online reviews regarding your business, and have you perhaps missed a single negative review by a disgruntled customer, with the unfortunate impact of lowering your average "star rating"? Finally, you need to find someone to help you fix—or avoid—problems using state-of the-art technology.

4. Jim thought he was merely in a brick-and-mortar business located in a small strip mall, not in the information and/or communications business. He thought word of mouth would suffice, when what he really needed was *word of mouse.*

5. Jim never "hired his weakness," a *key* strategy in my world of teaching others how to be successful, especially in business. The strategy goes hand in hand with "know what you don't know" to help navigate in our new information age. Jim didn't know technology—email, databases, internet marketing, and so on—so he should have hired somebody who did.

6. You can tell from Jim's note that he wanted email addresses only to inform his clients where he was moving. He still had no clue how to use an email address as a *free way to communicate*—quickly—to his prospects and clients. To alert them to the move was the first application. To tell them of great weekly sales and to invite them in for the "Titleist Golf Club Demo Day" were just two of hundreds of other uses for those email addresses.

I have learned a valuable lesson from being in business for the last thirty years. We are in a major shift in the world of business and communications. The way we buy, sell, live, learn, work, play, communicate, and socialize will never be the same again! It's truly a whole new ballgame, and anyone who "gets it" can win and make big bucks. All you need to do is work with the smartest folks you can find to fill in the parts of the puzzle that you don't know. But first you have to know which parts of the puzzle you're missing. This book will help you do that.

Maybe it's best said this way. My dad, a college business professor for more than thirty-five years, taught me this saying: "If you keep doing what you've always done, you'll keep getting what you've always gotten." That was true for many, many, *many* years. It still is when it comes to things such as weight loss. But in today's fast-changing, technology-driven, internet-based climate, it is *no longer* the case! The fact is, if you keep doing what you've always done, you will lose *a lot* of market share or disappear altogether, because your competitors who are using these tools will become faster, smarter, and more efficient than you are and hence will get more business because of it.

As I say in all of my speeches:

- Don't be afraid of technology.
- Know what you don't know.
- Hire your weaknesses!

In story after story, covering one technological innovation after another, this book presents a very clear understanding of what is happening in our world today and how to beat the odds to become successful—personally or in business!

—Marc O.

PS: Remember the new rule in business: Money doesn't grow on trees; it grows in databases! Build your database of friends, suppliers, business prospects, clients, and even competitors. In our information age, I strongly believe that the person or business with the best data will always win the game!

Want to make money online?
Buy Marc Ostrotsky's other book,
Get Rich Click!—a *New York Times* bestseller!

Word of Mouse

Introduction

A recent ad from IBM read:

> *Growing up, Tom Watson couldn't hit a curve ball while playing baseball. Nick Faldo rarely found the back of a hockey net, and Arnold Palmer just wasn't fast enough to make the track team. Isn't it funny how sometimes success begins just by putting the right tools in the right hands?*

Well said! Put an iPad in the hands of a person who can't speak, and with a talking app, she types her words and communicates with the world. Learn a new business skill such as Photoshop or Excel, and you are a more valuable employee to your company! Put a laptop in the hands of an entrepreneur, and he can single-handedly compete with his much larger competitors.

This book is all about understanding the opportunities in the world today and finding which tools are out there to help you get ahead personally and professionally. Once Arnold Palmer was given a golf club, he found his place in life and became one of the greatest golfers in history.

Ten years ago, if you wanted to buy a new television, you headed over to a big-box retailer and prayed for a sale. Today you likely have an app on your smartphone that can tell you who has the best prices at that very moment!

Ten years ago, if you wanted to become a chess champion, you read a book. Today you can learn from a grand master over Skype or from a YouTube video.

Ten years ago, if you wanted to keep in touch with old friends, you went to your high school reunion. Today you simply log onto Facebook.

These tectonic, technology-enabled lifestyle shifts are a subject of fascination to me. In fact, I have devoted my whole life to immersing myself in the world of technology so that I could help people outside the tech bubble understand it all by breaking down the information into easy-to-digest, bite-sized "nibbles." But make no mistake, I'm no inventor; I'm more like an interpreter. When I make appearances on CNN and shows such as ABC-TV's *The View* and *20/20,* I talk about tech products, in addition to internet sites and cool apps that people love—not things I've invented. As you read my book, consider me your personal interpreter, one who's been doing this sort of thing for years. Along the way, I've made a great deal of money by investing in many of these technologies and helping folks like you to understand them, via research reports, trade shows, magazines, websites, and newsletters, as well as books, audio books, and professional speaking engagements.

If you're a parent of teenagers, this book will help you understand their world, one that is dependent upon and integrated with technology we could only dream of when we were growing up. I'll introduce you to the tremendous benefits that can be derived personally and professionally from a variety of technologies, social media sites, apps, educational opportunities, and a host of online resources.

There's no reason to let technology stand in the way of you and your children. I should know, I have five daughters! Alas, while they have not all "friended" me and my wife on Facebook, we keep trying.

Addressing your role as a consumer, this book will show you how to use mobile technology to make smarter purchases for you and your family. Don't set foot in another department store before you've read the "Buy" chapter, which shows you how to save money and outsmart the system using nothing more than your smartphone and an app that allows you to instantly check the price and availability of a particular product from local competitors!

If you're an online marketer, this book will give you real-world examples of how people are using data analytics and intelligent software to locate their audiences, better manage their customer relationships, and tailor their online content accordingly. You don't have to be a big company to do these things. You just have to be a forward thinker.

If you're involved in the operational or financial side of business, I want to show you how to use the internet to lower your costs, increase your revenue, automate, outsource, and even drop ship products directly to your customers, and be more competitive at every level of your enterprise.

Why should you listen to me? I've got the experience to back it up.

I was one of the founders of the competitive telecom marketplace and the prepaid phone card industry, and I was an early pioneer in the voice mail industry. I'm one of the few keynote speakers and authors who actually own a portfolio of highly profitable online business ventures. No, I'm not an author by trade; I'm a businessperson with extensive marketing experience in teaching others how to learn, understand, and profit from the many technologies in this new interconnected world of ours. My current internet companies generate more than $90 million annually and include Blinds.com, CuffLinks.com, SummerCamps.com, eTickets.com, MutualFunds.com, Photographer.com, Consulting.com, TechToys.com, salestraining.com, Bachelor.com, and others. In my previous book—*Get Rich Click! The Ultimate Guide to Making Money on the Internet*—I showed how I've made millions online using practical tools and how you can too. Researching *Get Rich Click!* made something very apparent to me: the internet no longer is a tool to be seized solely by entrepreneurs but, rather, is one that people of every age and with every interest can use to improve the way they harness all that modern life has to offer. That's when I knew a second book, *Word of Mouse,* was in order. The question I intend to answer for you in this book is pretty straightforward:

How will technology and the internet continue to change the way we live? My research revealed an infinite number of answers. My purpose became clear: in order to put the potentially overwhelming possibilities into a usable context, I had to answer the key follow-up question for you, the reader: *"What's in it for me?"*

Like no other force before it, the internet has revolutionized nearly every facet of our professional and private existence, and it's done so in the historical equivalent of a blink of an eye. That's right. Things are changing fast—really fast! Such changes also mean big opportunities for those who understand what is going on and can act quickly to integrate themselves into this new social fabric.

How many of us sit down at our computers each morning and take for granted the fact that we can shop for clothing, chat with somebody on the far side of the world, or take a college course for credit—all online? Don't forget that fewer than thirty years ago, the internet was still being birthed by the National Science Foundation as a niche way to shuttle research between researchers and universities. Yes, the internet, coupled with the changes in technology such as the iPad and iPhone, is creating a furiously fast-paced market full of friction. These developments are presenting better solutions to problems that most of us aren't even aware exist.

How rapidly are things changing? Ask your kids. Or better yet, try having a conversation with them when you sit down for dinner tonight. If your household is like mine, there are times when it seems they're speaking a different language. In some ways, they are. If you're over the age of thirty, you didn't grow up texting and using Skype. Whether it's Facebook or Foursquare, today's tech-savvy young people use those tools and many more. They may not know what an eight-track tape is, but they do know how to become the "mayor" of your local Starbucks on Foursquare.

This is the language of the future. If you're not already fluent, you need to learn it quickly. If you're involved in a business, at any level, and you want to stay employed, move up the ladder, and continue making money, you don't have a choice. It's impossible to compete if an entire segment of your population is speaking Chinese and you're still speaking English.

But you are not alone! For most people, the rapid pace of change elicits feelings of intimidation. After all, learning a new language can seem impossible at times. Before you get discouraged, remember this: you're not the only one who doesn't know the new lingo. We're still in the early stages of the internet and the vast changes in new consumer technologies that affect our every move. Online opportunity is all around us. Fortunately, there's still plenty of time to pick up this new language.

Believe it or not, I often find myself in the same boat as you. I try to use the latest app or try to deconstruct complicated information, but typically I need help from others who understand it better than I do. I don't know how to build a website! But I do know how to find answers to my questions by watching a YouTube video, by performing a Google search, or by talking to someone who knows the answers, typically at my local Apple store.

What continues to surprise me—and what I think will surprise you, too—is the myriad ways in which people are using the internet and innovative technology to make their lives easier, more productive, and more fun. For all of the internet's negatives—such as its ability to expose private information, create distractions, and generate or spread messages of intolerance—most experts believe that its social benefits and the opportunities it offers easily outweigh its potential drawbacks. By the time you finish my book, I think you'll agree.

In the "Learn" chapter, I write about Larry Kahn, a man who managed a data center for a Fortune 500 company. Today he works as the chief technology officer at the Kinkaid School, an elite college preparatory school in Houston, where he oversees some of the radical changes in educational technology.

Touring Kinkaid, I got to see firsthand how our children are adapting to the online world. In a third-grade classroom not far from Kahn's office, students had recently initiated a Skype conversation with a popular children's author, which they featured on a classroom blog. As Kahn noted, the idea of third graders interacting with an author ten thousand miles away and producing original content for a worldwide audience was hardly imaginable, much less possible, a decade ago.

In the "Live" chapter, we hear from Michael Fertik, the founder of Reputation.com, a company that cleans up people's online reputations for them. As Fertik notes, the internet makes it easy for people to compare products and prices, find doctors, and check out real estate listings all over the world. But it also makes it easy for others to find information about you—or to *create* information about you—that may or may not be true. Did you know, for example, that in many cases, a person's name, age, home address, annual income, and mortgage payments are available to strangers online?

Fertik believes that in the future, the ubiquity of social media will lead more people to turn to companies like Reputation.com to quiet rampant rumors or stop them before they start. In fact, the firm recently ran an ad in the *New York Times* with the headline "The Internet can seriously improve your business. If it doesn't kill it first." It went on to say, "The internet's a great vehicle for promoting a business, but it's a great vehicle for trashing one, too. And since people now search companies before doing business with them, bad links showing up in Google can quickly drive away potential business."

In the "Play" chapter, I write about the unexpected figure behind "Tebowing," one of the internet's most popular memes (a meme is "an idea or element of social behavior passed on through generations in a culture, especially by imitation," according to dictionary.com). His name is Jared Kleinstein, and he's a typical twentysomething who lives in New York City, grew up in Denver, and is a longtime Broncos fan. Using little more than a creative spark and a photo posted to his Facebook account mimicking professional quarterback Tim Tebow's kneeling in prayer while his teammates celebrated a victory, Kleinstein single-handedly launched the now popular Tebowing phenomenon.

The next morning, he purchased the domain name Tebowing.com for $10 and sent an email to friends around the world urging them to submit Tebowing photos. The day it launched, the site had 785 views. That ballooned to 10,000 by the second day and more than 350,000 a day later. Although Kleinstein hasn't quit his day job, the last time we checked, he had turned his idea into a full-fledged online business selling T-shirts and he just trademarked the term "Tebowing."

But not every story I feature in this book has grabbed huge amounts of attention. Some of the best online success stories are barely noticed by the public. For example, I write about a small Mexican restaurant whose owners used Twitter to stay afloat. Or Switchboard, a nonprofit organization that uses the internet and cell phones to aid doctors in Africa.

And then there are the apps! Consider *Word of Mouse* your guide to a lot of incredible, wonderful, and helpful apps! Whether you're looking for apps to help you travel in Europe or train your mind, we've included them in this book. One of my favorite apps is Bromance, which was founded by four young male software developers who graduated from college and moved to Chicago, where they struggled to make connections with other guys. Their solution was to create an app that helped guys meet one another to play sports, have a drink at the local sports bar, or just hang out.

In my book, you'll read about countless people who have leveraged the power of the internet to better their own lives, help those around them, or explore their passions. Whether you're a retiree who likes to post photos of your grandkids on Facebook, a single mother looking for simple ways to make an extra $250 a week, or a young entrepreneur who wants to build an online business, there's never been a better time to take advantage of the online opportunities unfolding around you.

Unfortunately, the power of these technologies brings with it the potential for corruption and crime. For this reason, I have included a bonus chapter on cyber crime, coauthored by my friend James G. Conway Jr., who is president and managing director of Global Intelligence Strategies and a retired FBI special agent. The chapter is a must-read for anyone who wants to know how to sidestep the everyday threats of crime via the internet.

Using *Word of Mouse* as your guide, I urge you to delve into the web and find new ways to explore yourself and the world around you. Today's world is different. As I said before, if you keep doing what you've always done, you're just going to fall behind, because your friends, neighbors, and competitors are changing by the minute as they learn how to use the array of amazing new technologies, websites, and apps. Are you ready to take one giant leap forward in understanding how to catch up? Then turn the page.

This Book Is INTERACTIVE!

WHAT ARE THESE?

Watch the video here!
Scan the QR code, or go to http://www.wordofmouse.com.

You've probably seen these in your favorite newspaper or magazine; they're called quick-response codes, or QR codes. In short, let's just say that they are like bar codes but better! The difference is that a QR code will take you *instantly* to a webpage when scanned by a smartphone. It's one of the latest cool technologies that help bridge the virtual world and the physical world.

Why Are They in the Book?

Word of Mouse is the ultimate source for the latest internet trends. The problem is that there are countless new ideas out there, so I thought that incorporating QR codes into the book would be a great way to make it come alive and enhance your reading experience as you discover the latest information on the *Word of Mouse* world.

How Will They Benefit Me?

It's my favorite saying: "Learn more, earn more." The internet changes fast, and I am committed to bringing you the most up-to-date information possible.

How Can I Use the QR Codes—Now?

There are many free apps available via iTunes, the BlackBerry App World, and the Android Market that allow you to scan these codes. Just search for "QR code," download an app now, and try the QR code above.

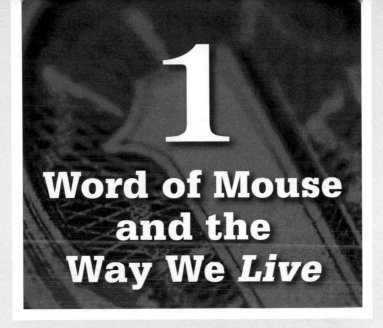

Word of Mouse and the Way We *Live*

It seems that everywhere you turn these days, a new technology springs up promising to transform the way we live. Whether you're a teenager making new connections though a niche social-networking app on your smartphone, a parent using your mobile device to purchase groceries while on the subway, or a backpacker using a revolutionary travel website that allows you to locate and rent living spaces all over the world (even a Slovenian dacha, through an online service called Airbnb), advances in online technology are reconfiguring almost everything we do.

These changes aren't reserved only for consumers. Technology is also changing the way that businesses market themselves to the public, transforming the nature of consumer behavior. These days, when you look at a billboard on the street, in the mall, or in the airport, there's a chance that a camera is looking back at you, tailoring the sign's message to your age, your gender, and perhaps even your shopping history.

But there are drawbacks to the information age as well. A number of problems have arisen from our sometimes knee-jerk willingness—and ability—to disseminate information about ourselves, another person, a company, or a product. "The set of problems has become a lot more complex," said Michael Fertik, CEO of Reputation.com, in a recent interview with *Time* magazine. "As social media and mobile media exploded and data mining has gotten more sophisticated, people have a lot more points of vulnerability."

A lot of the activities that people engage in online can damage their reputation in a heartbeat. Take these examples:

- **posting or emailing drunken photos**
- **blogging details about a nasty divorce**
- **recording rowdy videos to post on YouTube**
- **posting names and photos from a gay pride meeting**
- **blogging about your company's internal matters**
- **tweeting about a disgruntled customer**
- **discussing workplace disputes on Facebook**
- **seeking public opinion about business issues via email or online forums**

Although still relatively new, online-reputation-management firms are becoming increasingly popular resources for people who discover that their "private" lives are increasingly more public and for businesses that understand the detriment of a negative story written about them. Why? Recall the slogan "What happens in Vegas stays in Vegas"? For this book, we'll say, "What goes on the internet stays there forever."

These days, when you look at a billboard on the street, in the mall, or in the airport, there's a chance that a camera is looking back at you, tailoring the sign's message to your age, your gender, and perhaps even your shopping history.

But the benefits of transparency in our society are plentiful, promising to provide more information, accountability, and convenience to people on a daily basis. For example, in many cities, police officers are being outfitted with wearable cameras for the purpose of recording an officer's experience and providing courtrooms with a new source of evidence. Experts believe that we will even be able to vote using our smartphones in the not-so-distant future, creating a more convenient route to civic participation. Whether it's civic or social, the changes in the way we live are only just beginning.

"What goes on the internet stays there forever."

Did You Know?

Mugshots.com is a website that posts photos of people arrested from around the United States. The site gets a data feed from all of the public records and police departments, and then publishes those lovely mug shots for all the world to see and find *easily* online. Check it out for yourself. It's search-engine-optimized, making it especially easy to find muggers, thieves, and child molesters. How does the site make money? This is the really amazing part: the Mugshots.com business model is to *charge people to have their photos* removed *from the site,* and it refers you to a list of authorized Mugshots.com mugshot-removal vendors. The idea of making money this way is something that one must consider undeniably *contemptible* and yet utterly *brilliant* at the same time!

"I registered my dad with an online dating service. They matched him with a recliner and TV."

Family Living

Among the most palpable changes are those occurring at the familial level, where technology is influencing the way we interact with our loved ones. According to the Pew Research Center Internet and American Life Project, which produces reports exploring the impact of the internet on families, communities, work and home, daily life, education, health care, and civic and political life, the vast majority of parents have had serious conversations with their kids about online life, the problems associated with it, and safe ways to navigate those spaces. Not only are more parents monitoring their kids' online behavior, Pew found, but many have become friends with their kids—as well as friends with their kids' friends—on social network sites.

"This is all spurred by the fact that families are saturated with technology," Pew reported. "Tech adoption and tech-usage rates by teens' parents are higher than the general population." Here are some statistics from Pew that illustrate the way that new technologies have inundated our daily lives:

- **91 percent of parents of children ages twelve to seventeen own cell phones, and 86 percent of those cell owners send and receive text messages.**

- **84 percent of all adults have cell phones, and 76 percent of them exchange text messages.**

- **87 percent of parents of teens are internet users (compared with 78 percent of those in the overall adult population), and 82 percent have broadband connections at home (versus 62 percent of those in the overall population).**

- **86 percent of parents of teens own laptops or desktops, compared with 76 percent of those in the overall adult population.**

- **Online parents of teens are just as likely as the general population of adult internet users to use social network sites such as Facebook or LinkedIn (67 percent versus 64 percent).***

Did You Know?

There are cool digital picture frames that connect to the internet.

When you have a new photo of little Johnny that you want to send to Grandma, you upload it to the web, and then the photo is placed directly on Grandma's interactive digital photo frame—without even the slightest effort from Grandma, who may be halfway around the globe! This capability is driven by Ceiva's PicturePlan Photo Delivery Service, which is bundled with each frame and can be purchased for a nominal monthly fee ($6.95, as of this writing).

"MARC" MY WORDS Smartphones and smart tablets aren't just for tech-savvy teens! New (smaller) models of the Apple iPad, more akin to Ama-

---

* Amanda Lenhart, Mary Madden, Aaron Smith, Kristen Purcell, Kathryn Zickuhr, and Lee Rainie, "Teens' Parents and Their Technology Profile," Pew Research Center Internet and American Life Project, November 9, 2011, www.pewinternet.org/Infographics/2011/Teens-Kindness-and-Cruelty-on-Social-Network-Sites.aspx.

zon's Kindle and other more versatile tablet PCs, are going to dominate the media-related discussions for the next few years.

When you think of smartphones, you probably think of teens glued to their mobile devices wherever they go. But the latest demographics behind smartphone use might shock you.

New research concludes that smartphone ownership among moms is higher than in the general population. Surprising, right? Close to 60 percent of moms have a smartphone, and around the same number told researchers that they use the mobile internet frequently, up from 22 percent just a few years earlier, according to research by the parenting website BabyCenter and reported in eMarketer Digital Intelligence.

The survey results revealed that mothers use their smartphones in different ways from most others. For example, mothers are much more likely to use their mobile phones to find games, use social media, and follow up on health information. However, they are only somewhat more likely to check the weather, listen to music, or shop using their phones. And moms are less likely to use their phones to access content such as maps, productivity tools, and financial and business information. This hints at the idea that they're engaging in activities to help families bide their time, according to the research. Smartphone-owning moms spend more than six hours a day using their phones, on average, compared with just two and a half hours among moms with only a standard cell phone or a landline phone. In that six-hour window, smartphone-using mothers are bound to view advertising. BabyCenter reported that just over half—a full 55 percent—of them considered ads linked to nearby deals most appealing, and they were significantly more likely than the general population to feel that way. More than half of smartphone-using mothers claimed to have done more research or talked to other people about an ad.

Fewer mothers—in this case, 31 percent—actually clicked on the ad or went ahead and made a purchase (14 percent). Even so, the study suggests that mothers are more likely to take indirect action if an ad appeals to them.

Facial Recognition:
Billboards Are Already Looking Back at You!

In the 2002 futurist movie *Minority Report,* starring Tom Cruise, there's a scene where Cruise's character runs through a mall while advertisements around him scan his eyes before tailoring themselves to his precise tastes. As a Big Brother–like voice talks to him ominously from all around, one ad encourages him to stop for his favorite beer.

Sounds far-fetched, right? Well, not really. In fact, that "future" is quite *present.* In the introduction to this chapter, I mentioned billboards that "look back at you," delivering customized messages based on your personal traits and shopping history. Such "smart signs" are alive and kicking, thanks to companies such as Immersive Labs. The Manhattan-based start-up has already rolled out its first camera-enhanced smart signs, equipping billboards and retail signage with the ability to tailor advertisements to the person looking at them at any given moment. The signs launched in Los Angeles, San Francisco, and New York, and can gauge a passerby's age range, sex, and even attention level. "In other words," a description on the company's website reads, "the system is smart enough to display a Gillette ad to a male passerby rather than an ad for perfume."

The technology is a combination of anonymous facial detection, sophisticated machine learning, and strategies specified by the marketer. Other factors also will be assimilated in the smart-sign formula, including time of day, location, and tweets that refer to the area. The resulting information will dictate which ad in the inventory appears on the screen at a particular time, Jason Sosa, founder and CEO of Immersive Labs, told ABC News.*

"If a basketball game is letting out at Madison Square Garden, and we have a sign there with both Nike and OfficeMax ads in the inventory, we can choose to use Nike, because it makes more sense," he explained. "If a lot of people are tweeting about taking their dogs for a walk in a particular area, maybe we'll put a Petco ad in that neighborhood."

The signage will be installed in places with heavy foot traffic, including airports, malls, and retail stores. Next time you pass a billboard, give it an extra long look and smile—after all, you just might be on camera!

Did You Know?

Facial recognition software is already being used on Facebook.

Facebook features a photo-tagging suggestion tool called Photo Tagger (acquired from face.com) that has changed the way people tag photos of friends. As soon as a photo is uploaded to the site, Facebook's "Tag Suggestions" feature uses facial recognition to identify that user's friends in the photo; name tags are automatically suggested based on the matches. The benefit for somebody uploading a large number of photos is that it frees users from going photo by photo typing the same individual's name. Facebook is hardly alone in implementing this sort of software. Similar functions can be found with other popular programs, like Picasa, the photo-editing software from Google.

"MARC" MY WORDS I think this is only the first entry in what will be a much more sophisticated tagging concept for photos and videos in the future. Google's "Goggles" project is already on it with its visual search app

---

* "Billboards Recognize Faces," published on September 20, 2011, ABC News, Science.

for smartphones. You will be able to take a picture of any product, place, or person, run the Goggle app, and get search results with information about the photo subject—whether it's a painting in a museum or a box of cereal at the grocery store. It's only a matter of time before you'll be able to similarly obtain information about people using the photos you take of them or find online!

What Do You Want to Do Tonight?

Imagine peering into a bar on a Friday night to see if it's packed before you drag yourself off the couch to check it out in person.

SceneTap, a new app for smartphones, allows you to do just that. It's just one of the small but pronounced ways that technology is changing the way we live. The app uses cameras with facial detection software to scout local bars before posting information about the demographics inside. Though it avoids identifying individual bar patrons, SceneTap can tell users the average age of the crowd and the ratio of men to women, providing bar-goers with a better sense of where to go. In Chicago, where SceneTap is used at dozens of bars, the app even features drink and food specials.

SceneTap can tell users the average age of the crowd and the ratio of men to women, providing bar-goers with a better sense of where to go.

Facial recognition is poised to become the next advance in mobile technology. Even though it will raise a host of privacy concerns, it will allow marketers to tailor their messages to individual consumers as never before. I believe that the definition of the word *privacy* will inevitably change dramatically over time. In the future, your habits, likes, dislikes, and lifestyle quirks are likely to be embedded in databases that connect to you via networked sensors like smartphones. From a practical standpoint, facial recognition, in general, has its benefits. At its most basic implementation, the technology can be used in place of ID cards, thereby sparing users the nuisance of recalling passwords or replacing lost ID cards. Identity fraud will be a greater . challenge for the criminal. And with more specific physical characteristics available to determine a person's legal status, racial or ethnic profiling could well become a thing of the past. Still, the accuracy of facial recognition systems is not 100 percent, and they can be quite easily tricked (by placing another person's image over your own, for example), meaning your image could be linked with the wrong profile, which, at the very least, puts you on yet another mailing list for all the wrong products (like the "John Smith or current resident" mail you get when you move into a new house). Once your false ID gets entered and multiplied across many databases, removing those links could prove daunting, to say the least.

Are You Dating a Serial Killer?

Is something about your date "off kilter"? To be filed under "strange but potentially lifesaving," there is a website called InvestidateYourDate.com that offers workshops that teach you how to:

- quickly analyze an online dating profile and unravel mysteries using Facebook and Twitter
- create your own "date-a-base"
- interpret body language
- verify a date's employment and academic history, gauge income level, and estimate his or her monthly rent payments

The site offers webinars that invite visitors to call in live and join the discussion on ways to determine if the person you're dating is "just too good to be true."

It's fun to talk about the technology tools that change the landscape of our lives, but I think it's just as pertinent—in some ways, more so—to explore the tools that reshape the tiny vignettes of life. In my personal life, it's a rare day when I don't find a cool new gadget or app that helps make the daily grind run a little more smoothly, more quickly, or just plain better. My wife, Beverle, "plugs in" just as much as I do, if not more. I asked her to write about her love affair with cooking apps. (I use them too, but Beverle's culinary judgment carries much more weight than mine.) She's an avid entertainer and an amazing cook, so her thoughts on the topic are particularly relevant.

Answering the "What's for Dinner?" Question Gets Easier

by Beverle Ostrofsky

I am a cook, a good cook. Not a chef striving for perfection, but a cook's cook, making really good food. Food that people remember when we are having cocktails or chatting months later; food that brings back memories and a taste of something they can't put their finger on. And the longer I cook, the more I innovate, tweaking dishes from year to year. Taking my mom's wonderful comfort dishes and adding my own dash of that sumpin sumpin that says, "Hey, this is me in the kitchen."

When I'm looking for something completely new, I increasingly turn to our "old" iPad for my cooking inspirations and know-how. When Marc bought me my new iPad, he set out to sell the older device on eBay. But I had a better idea. Why not put it to work in the kitchen? It didn't take much to convince him; after all, the man likes my cooking. When I explained that I would be able to instantly access all my favorite foodie sites, while planning his next culinary adventure, he happily agreed. (It didn't take long for him to get the idea, too, that not only would we enjoy better meals, but by eating out less often, we'd save enough money in just one year of usage to make up for any money he "lost" by not selling the iPad on eBay.) Now the tablet takes up full-time residence in our kitchen. I use a staggering variety of cooking apps—the choices available these days represent nothing short of a recipe smorgasbord. I've heard that "the first round of cooking apps left much to be desired. They were slow and dull, and besides—who wants to cook using a tiny screen for instruction?" Not surprisingly, they didn't really catch on.

The growth of tablet technology is changing all that, as cooking apps grow increasingly interactive. With step-by-step video tutorials, informational graphics, voice prompts, calorie counters, handy timers, and embedded links that are intuitive and full of great tips, it's as if Martha Stewart, Rachael Ray, and Paula Deen are in the kitchen with me creating our every dish! I can easily see why old-fashioned cookbooks will soon be a thing of the past! Cooking apps make great sense. It's hard to think of a technology better suited to the chaotic swirl of the kitchen, with its combination of physical labor and mental demands.

One of my favorite apps is Culinapp, which was devised by a Houston-based company made up of an entrepreneur, a software developer, an Emmy Award–winning producer for many top cooking shows, and a software development executive. The app lets users choose from four different views of each recipe. For novice cooks, a "step-by-step" view presents each recipe step in full screen, with a chef doing exactly what instructions on the screen say he's doing. After ingredients are measured and the oven is heated, the rest of the process is shown in a flowchart, illustrated with bright images of mixers, whisks, ovens, and ingredients. For the more confident cook who already knows how to cream butter and sugar, say, but needs to be reminded what to do with the chopped apple and grated fresh ginger, the app offers a "Spin-View" video carousel, so she can watch only the steps she needs explained. "Now is the perfect time to introduce new technology into the kitchen," says the text on the company's website. "iPad sales—and the rapid growth of the tablet marketplace—continue to exceed all expectations, generating staggering demand for content. Simultaneously, two culinary trends are driving consumer demand for new cooking apps: the rise of the aspiring home gourmet and the cult of the celebrity chef. In today's highly interactive and fame-obsessed society, diners and home cooks want more than just a good meal—they want a personal connection with their favorite culinary celebrities."

I couldn't agree more. Here are a few other cooking apps that have earned my stamp of approval:

App Name	Device	Description
How to Cook Everything	**iPhone**	This bestselling, first-of-its-kind app of *New York Times* columnist Mark Bittman's bestselling cookbook is enhanced with helpful holiday menus and fun wintertime animation. Most important are the two thousand recipes and four hundred how-to illustrations, plus specially designed features for the mobile user.
The Professional Chef, by the Culinary Institute of America	**iPad**	Known as "the bible for all chefs," the Inkling (an eBook reader app for the iPad, which can be downloaded free from the iTunes app store) edition of this classic textbook by the Culinary Institute of America includes videos, interactive images, shared notes between cooks using the book, and more.
KitchenMath	**iPad** and **iPhone**	KitchenMath is a cooking utility with three main features: cooking unit conversion, temperature conversion, and serving temperature. Do you want to know how many grams are in a cup of all-purpose flour when you're baking? How about a can of coconut milk for Asian food? KitchenMath has data on more than 380 cooking ingredients for converting between volume and weight units. You don't need to figure out the density of your ingredients.

App Name	Device	Description
Fromage	**iPhone** and **iPad** (supports French, Spanish, and German)	With more than 750 cheeses from around the world, this is clearly the best pocket guide to cheeses. Each entry features artistically presented cheese photos, historically narrated flavor descriptions, and suggested best choices for complementary wines. You can add your own cheeses to the standard library and attach personal notes about any of the cheeses.
Seafood Watch from the Monterey Bay Aquarium	**iPhone**	Provides free, up-to-date recommendations with detailed seafood information. Uses your phone's Global Positioning System to load the right regional guide for your location. Enables you to search for seafood quickly and easily by common market names. Allows you to sort seafood by "Best Choice," "Good Alternative," or "Avoid" rankings.

Cooking apps make great sense.
It's hard to think of a technology better suited
to the chaotic swirl of the kitchen, with its combination
of physical labor and mental demands.

JUST HOW ATTACHED TO OUR CELL PHONES ARE WE?

Addiction or Fixation: Fantasy vs. Reality?

When I was married in 2008, the most appropriate wedding cake topper I found was of a bride and groom each talking on a cell phone. When I suggested we choose it because it was "so us," my wife-to-be said—in a way that only a loving, smart, and beautiful wife could convey—"Absolutely not! Not on my wedding cake, you don't! But if you really love it, honey, you can put it on *your* groom's cake!"

So when the big day arrived, there it was. Atop the groom's chocolate layer cake, a man in a tux on a cell phone and a bride clad in her wedding dress, talking on her cell phone. She wanted fantasy; I chose reality!

A recent Harris Interactive Poll of 2,300 Americans sheds some light on just how attached we are to our beloved technology. Respondents admitted that they wanted access to their smartphones and tablets when on vacation. And get this: 17 percent went so far as to say they even wanted access during their honeymoons! The survey was conducted by Harris and TeamViewer, a provider of remote-access software. TeamViewer's general manager, Holger Felgner, said in a prepared release, "These findings show that no matter what the situation, an overwhelming majority of Americans believe they should be able to remotely access all their devices, use applications, and look for data anytime, anywhere."

Here are a few other situations in which respondents said they wanted mobile or computer access:

- **while in bed, 48 percent**
- **while shopping with a spouse, 36 percent**
- **while at a sporting event, 29 percent**
- **while on a date, 11 percent**

My guess is that if they polled only teenagers, it would have been close to 100 percent for three of the four categories!

The research also touched upon the growing number of people dependent upon multiple computers. Almost two-thirds of the respondents use more than one computer, smartphone, or tablet on a weekly basis, with 15 percent using four or more, Harris reported. This number was higher among men, with 35 percent indicating that they use three to five devices, compared with 27 percent of women. Overall, an overwhelming 83 percent of respondents said that they wanted access to their computers while away from home or the office.

DIY HEALTH:
DR. MOM HAS ALL THE ANSWERS

Health Hackers and Citizen Scientists

In a flurry of self-empowerment, everyday people are using the internet to don virtual lab coats. From conducting do-it-yourself health management to running experiments and sharing the data, people are freshly aware that science needn't be restricted to laboratories.

I don't know even one mother who doesn't have an intuitive sense of when her child is sick, and for garden-variety ailments, what over-the-counter medicine can be used to treat the ailment. Mothers also know when the symptoms require a doctor's expert consultation. Note: this is never the case with the first-born child, because *every* sneeze prompts a trip to the doctor's office. This phenomenon seems to begin with child number two and continues with all future little ones after that. By the time child number three hits the scene, if that kid were to fall off the roof, Dr. Mom will ask, "Does anything hurt?" If the answer is no, she'll plant a comforting kiss and then go about her business. Mom knows best. When I say I don't feel well at dinner, my internet- and Dr. Oz–savvy spouse has a diagnosis by bedtime! The information she has learned, be it on her smartphone, on TV, or via the internet, makes her *think* she's a doctor—and most of the time, she's right. Now, if only she could write prescriptions!

"I already diagnosed myself on the internet. I have either three left kidneys, recurring puberty, or Dutch elm disease."

Besides lacking the necessary tools or other expensive equipment, the main reason that people don't fix the car or the sink is usually the lack of information available to teach them how. The free flow of content in today's internet- and app-driven society gives everyone almost unlimited free information to read, learn, focus on, understand, and implement for almost any task du jour. (Incidentally, we saw sales skyrocket on the Blinds.com website once we uploaded content to teach folks how to measure and then install their own window blinds.)

There are thousands of apps that help consumers in the health sector: in preventing illness and in examining, improving, monitoring, and managing their own health, as well as that of their family. As of this writing, Apple's App Store is approaching ten thousand mobile health apps on cardio fitness, diet, stress relaxation, and every other health-related concept one could imagine!

There are apps to test your eyes, your hearing, your back, and your eating habits. And you'll find an impressive array of cool health-related apps can help you to do the following:

- **monitor your blood pressure**
- **count how many steps you take in a day**
- **track your sleeping patterns**
- **manage the calories you take in and the ones you work off**
- **enter your workout data**
- **discover why your back hurts**
- **record your heart rate**
- **analyze a blood sample (for malaria, no less)**
- **monitor and track conditions for diabetes, asthma, and hay fever**

Just about anything you want or need in the form of monitoring, understanding, and testing any subject in the health sector is available as an app or certainly lies just a few clicks away on any internet-connected device.

The global mobile health-applications market will reach $4.1 billion in US dollars by 2014, according to research company TechNavio. This figure is up from $1.7 billion in 2010. One indicator of this change is AT&T's recent announcement that it will begin selling clothes embedded with health monitors able to track the wearer's vital signs (including heart rate and body temperature) and upload them to a dedicated website. Another example comes from the X PRIZE Foundation, which is cosponsoring a $10 million award for the best mobile device allowing consumers to diagnose their own diseases.

Thank you to Trendwatching.com for permitting me to use the above information, which I found on its fantastic website and newsletter—an amazing source of information on consumer trends!

LIVING ROOMS ARE BECOMING LABORATORIES

Why should science be restricted to professionals in closed-door labs, when there's so much to gain by opening those doors to the public? A grassroots movement of "health hackers" and "citizen scientists" is fed up with data derived from blood work and other health-related lab work being locked away in databases accessible only to the scientific community. And they're using Word of Mouse to do something about it.

The Wall Street Journal recently reported on this movement on its website. The article reported that this movement is colored in many shades of involvement:

- **Everyday citizens who post to online sources personal data, family medical histories, and genetic test results— available to anyone with an interest**
- **Everyday citizens who post to online sources the same data—with only portions of it made public**
- **Everyday citizens who post to online sources the same data but restrict access to researchers, provided that they commit to sharing the results of their studies**

The common thread is twofold: all members of this movement are everyday citizens—not doctors or scientists; and members are *sharing* valuable medical data with the public. This is what Word of Mouse is all about: using the power of networks and the internet to post information, including detailed personal information, family histories, and genetic test results directly from the source for direct and immediate use by the information seeker—who, in turn, feeds information back into the network, to be distributed, absorbed, and updated by everyday people, with no middlemen to muck up the process.

Granted, these "middlemen" can be physicians, hospitals, or insurance companies, who have the knowledge to interpret the information; make analyses, diagnoses, and prognoses; or even project trends, costs, etc., related to health conditions. My point is not that laymen can or should be putting themselves in these roles just because they have access to the information. Rather, I rejoice in the fact that we the people now actually do have access to the information, so we can "shop it around" for analysis by professionals, experts, or researchers, whereas in a non-networked system, this information gets incarcerated, is labeled as the property of whoever last had his hands on it (aka, the "middleman"), and is a pain in the neck—if not virtually impossible—to get into your own hands. That said, I would like to restate and reinforce here that the vast majority of people are unequipped to "analyze" the results of, say, their own blood workup. Information is valuable only if it is interpreted by someone educated in the field—and by educated, I don't mean someone who just read a few paragraphs on a questionable website. I strongly recommend that people who want to avail themselves of the internet as a medical resource visit websites that contain reliable physician-reviewed medical info (such as the National Institutes of Health and websites from major medical institutions such as the Mayo Clinic, Johns Hopkins, etc.). If diagnosing diseases is so complex that it often befuddles doctors, it stands to reason that the average person has no business self-diagnosing. Some skills are best left to professionals!

Beyond sharing health data, these people are also performing their own experiments and clinical trials using one essential piece of laboratory equipment: the internet. The experiments run the gamut, from migraine-related studies to testing vitamins and nutritional supplements. One data bank of "citizen health data" sends kits of blood vials and FedEx envelopes to participants, who have their doctors draw their blood and send their samples to a central lab, accessible to researchers who have agreed to disclose their findings.

Furthermore, a cottage industry of companies has appeared on the online landscape with a mission to facilitate the movement's experiments. And trial results are even being published in medical journals. *Scientific American* now publishes on its website a Citizen Scientist project page, updating researchers on the progress of various research endeavors tapping into the data-gathering power of the mainstream public. One such project, called FoldIt, aims to "solve puzzles to design proteins."

Watch the video here!
Scan the QR code or go to http://tinyurl.com/cnuqteh.

The Wall Street Journal reports on one "health hacker," motivated from years of suffering with Crohn's disease. It's a fascinating video that digs deep into one person's approach to health hacking, the apps he used, the obstacles he faced, and the results he derived.

CASE STUDY
Living Philanthropy:
Sharing Cell Phones and Knowledge
to Improve Health Care in West Africa

I can't think of a tougher but more important job than working as a health professional in Africa. It is a continent that suffers more than 24 percent of the global burden of disease but has access to only 3 percent of the world's health workers, according to statistics from the World Health Organization (WHO).

With ratios as low as one doctor per thirty thousand patients, health professionals there can expect to face extreme challenges: high levels of disease, a lack of basic supplies and medicines, antiquated equipment, and, in remote areas, isolation from medical peers.

That isolation is one of the reasons that Switchboard was founded. This nonprofit, dedicated to facilitating communication and collaboration among health professionals, has three components: (1) doctors can call and text one another free of charge; (2) it distributes a printed "doctor directory" so that physicians can expand their support networks; and (3) it helps governments send critical health alerts to health workers, such as news of an outbreak in a certain area.

Fortunately, the organization notes, Africa is the world's fastest-growing mobile phone market, and with nearly five billion handsets worldwide, mobile phones are already in the hands of nearly every health worker.

To date, Switchboard has joined almost 100 percent of the doctors in Ghana and Liberia on MDNet, the free mobile phone network made available to doctors.

Switchboard's chief medical officer, Dr. Brian Levine, conceived the idea of an internet collaboration tool to connect doctors in Ghana. Because internet connectivity levels were so poor, the Switchboard team adapted the collaboration tool to mobile networks. The team partnered with the Ghana Medical Association and Ghana Onetouch (now Vodafone), and distributed SIM (subscriber identity module) cards to nearly every doctor in the country. Doctors were linked to a calling network via the SIM cards, enabling the organization to gather valuable information about the vast majority of health professionals' locations and expertise in Ghana.

Technology Facilitates Civic Responsibility

We live in a society that encourages proactive participation, meaningful interaction, and ongoing development of civic matters. How we contribute to such a society is paramount to living a meaningful life.

ACCESS TO POLICE VIDEOS

An increasing number of police departments are adopting the use of wearable cameras that attach to officers' uniforms, a practice that stemmed from camera use in police cars. The purpose of the cameras is to document the officer's experience accurately. The videos can be used as evidence and can also keep an eye on officers as they interact with the public. A big issue surrounds this implementation: access to the videos. Police officers are concerned that videos will take on Big Brother–like qualities and will be used to scrutinize their daily routines in search of minor infractions. Officers also want ensured access to their own tapes, especially in the event that they are charged with some type of police misconduct. But the door swings both ways when it comes to concerns about access. I recently read about a Seattle resident, Eric Rachner, a cyber-security expert, who demanded to see videos shot from a squad car dashboard camera, in an effort to prove the illegality of his 2008 arrest for drunken "urban golfing" (seriously). The city dragged its feet for months over the simple acknowledgment that the videos even existed. Rachner sued the city and won a $60,000 judgment. He then demanded a log of all Seattle videos shot from police dash cameras over the past three years.

In a true Word of Mouse moment, Rachner posted the videos to the Seattle Police Video Project Website (seattlepolicevideo.com). People can search the online database to check for videos of themselves. The site will be updated continually and will also include footage from wearable cameras, once they are adopted by the city.

"MARC" MY WORDS Expect to see more sites like the Seattle Police Video Project in the immediate future. Citizens' interest is bound to mount and push these developments, so that they can see firsthand what police officers' wearable cameras are capturing on a daily basis. If the use of such cameras is promoted as facilitating trust between police authorities and everyday citizens, online access to the videos will serve only to enhance this outcome.

VOTING VIA SMARTPHONE

The right to decide who governs our nation is the bedrock of democracy. It's a right that citizens fight to earn, preserve, and protect. And yet, it's my opinion, and that of a growing number of impatient citizens, that voting is just too darn inconvenient. As of this writing, at least one state is testing the iPad for its e-voting procedure. This is a step in the right direction, for sure, but why not go all the way? There is little reason for voting to be attached to a physical location.

"MARC" MY WORDS Voting is ripe for smartphone development. If *American Idol* can pull it off, why not Washington? I read an op-ed piece on the website Mashable about this topic (Mashable is a website geared for the "connected generation" and reports on "the importance of digital innovation and how it empowers and inspires people around the world"). The writer, Lance Ulanoff, who is also Mashable's editor in chief, has a pretty plausible plan to make the idea come to life. Ulanoff starts with the point that each phone has one unique phone number. Correspondingly, each phone would be permitted one vote. When the voting period opens, voters would receive some type of alert via their phones. A government-approved app would launch and, voilà! Instant voting booth! He suggests additionally coupling the smartphone vote with an email to verify each voter's selections. Voters would be given until the close of Election Day to delete and/or recast their votes. The issue of registration would still exist in Ulanoff's vision. Voters would register, and their smartphones would be part of that process. The phone itself would be assigned a specific location, eliminating the chance of votes being cast outside a voter's district. Apps could easily be developed to accommodate this relatively straightforward transaction. A voter could even remotely lock his or her phone should it be lost or stolen on Election Day, thereby reducing the incidence of potential fraud. It's a participation solution for an increasingly busy, distracted, but interested and connected society, and it's utterly elegant in its simplicity. Alternatively, if an election is just too close to call after the "tele-votes" are completed, then and only then would voters be asked to go in and cast their vote in the "old" way.

We are, at heart, an increasingly mobile society. Virtually every aspect of our lives has embraced smartphones as a way to let us live, work, learn, and play at any hour from any location. It makes sense that the methods we use to sculpt the governance of such a mobile society be similarly mobilized.

Organizing the Content of Our Lives

Let's face it: the internet is out of control. The sheer amount of data caught in its "web" can often be more overwhelming than it is useful. It's time for a new system for organizing internet information so that it can actually function *informatively* in our lives. "Lifestreams" may be the answer.

Flickr, Facebook, and Twitter are examples of how the internet is evolving into lifestreams. A recent article on the *Wall Street Journal* website defined lifestreams as a system for "organizing digital objects—photos, emails, documents, web links, music—in a time-ordered series. A timeline, in essence, that extends into the past but also the future (with appointments, to-do lists, etc.)."

Lifestreams, as you might imagine, *depict* their data with the past and future running off either side of the screen. Front and center on the screen is the present, the set of life data most relevant at any given point in time. Such content organization is what makes lifestreams more transparent to users and more meaningful in organizing our lives.

David Gelernter, a computer science professor at Yale University, is an expert on—and evangelist of—this much needed Web makeover. "It is impossible to picture the Web," Gelernter told WSJ.com. "It's a big, fuzzy nothing. I sort of tiptoe around tiny areas of it shining a flashlight." Gelernter sees the day rapidly approaching when streaming-based internet business models will be prevalent. He also predicts the evolution of the "worldstream," populated by a mix of public and proprietary information generated by people all over the world. Here's how Gelernter described the worldstream to WSJ.com:*

> I can visualize the worldstream. I know what it looks like. I know what my chunk of it looks like. When I focus on my stuff, I get a stream that is a subset of the worldstream. So when I focus on the stream, by doing a search on Sam Schwartz [a hypothetical student], I do [what would be known as] stream subtraction. Everything that isn't related to Schwartz that I'm allowed to see vanishes. And then the stream moves much more slowly. Because Sam Schwartz documents are being added at a much slower rate than all the documents in the world. So now I have a manageable trickle of stuff.

* "Rethinking a Digital Future," WallStreetJournal.com, December 3, 2011.

"MARC" MY WORDS The dawn of a "visual" worldstream may be a few years away. But lifestreams are neatly winding their way into the cybersphere of our lives. Internet users will increasingly dip their toes in the lifestream waters via a variety of transformed content apps, sites, and "streambrowsers" tied to a variety of visualization options that help them comprehend the data being presented. Once we get used to adding and managing our data in this manner (which won't take long, I assure you), the content of our lives will become organized in sequence, making it more intuitive, more manageable, and—most important—more timely.

With Life . . . Comes Death

Just as the mighty hand of technology touches lives, it also reaches beyond and follows us to our graves. I'm not trying to be morose. Quite the contrary, I want to share with you what a positive and vibrant role Word of Mouse plays in people's lives when loved ones have passed on. Here are three examples.

INTERACTIVE HEADSTONES

Few, if any, tombstones succeed in capturing the essence and the soul of the honored deceased. Who was this person? All you have is a name, a date, and maybe a quote or scripture to go by. The new interactive options in tombstones literally put "memories" back into cemetery memorials. For example, a California company called Interactive Legacy will create a unique QR code that links directly to a mobile website developed specifically as a memorial honoring the deceased. The QR codes can be applied as aluminum adhesive tags for application directly onto the plaque or headstone, on metal stakes for placement in front or on the side of the marker, or as laser etchings "carved" directly onto the marker. The company even offers website design features that optimize the memorial website for mobile devices, so that visitors to the gravesite can enjoy photos, videos, and writings clearly, without the visual compromises typically suffered in viewing standard web pages on a smartphone.

VIRTUAL "LIVING" MEMORIALS

These websites, set up for those that have departed this earth, are extremely tasteful and comforting, complete with photos, videos, online testimonials, guest books, final "tweets," blog posts, and so forth.

FINAL FAREWELLS

In some instances, people suffering from a fatal illness or injury have adopted the internet as a delivery mechanism for sharing their stories and life lessons— and for saying good-bye. One notable example was that of an eighteen-year-old boy named Ben Breedlove, from Austin, Texas, who had suffered his entire life from a serious chronic heart condition called hypertrophic cardiomyopathy. In

December 2011 Ben posted on YouTube an incredibly moving two-part video of himself telling the story of how he'd cheated death three times. There are no words; instead of speaking, the teenager holds up handwritten cards. It begins, "Hello, I'm Ben Breedlove" and ends "Do you believe in angels or God? I do." One week later, on Christmas, Ben had a fatal heart attack. The powerful video went viral (meaning it has gained widespread popularity through internet sharing), and hence all the deeply penetrating messages this young man wanted to share were shared—and received. As of this writing, there were almost five million views of his video on YouTube! And they were shared directly from him—as if he were sitting in your living room, handing you a book—in his own words, with all his facial expressions. And they were shared not just with family and friends who had access to a privately stored and shared video but also with the whole world. In the time it took this young man to write his carefully constructed thoughts on a collection of index cards, then hold each card up to the camera long enough for the viewer to read it, and for him to convey the deeply personal meaning of each card via his facial expressions, and then upload that video to YouTube—a world was changed. Not in an earthshaking volcanic way. But in a gently sweeping way. In the way that a person is changed by simply knowing another person and by knowing the *truth* of that person. There were no flashy graphics. No distracting music. No props. Just a person and his words. The words of a lifetime. And Word of Mouse gave those words, and that person's life, global reach. It is, quite simply, one of the boldest and most understated examples of the power that technology and Word of Mouse offer a civilization. (Source: All info from ABC and from watching the referenced video.) To see this moving video and truly understand the incredible power of this medium, look up Ben Breedlove on YouTube.com and watch it or click on our QR code below. Have a box of Kleenex at the ready; it's quite moving.

Watch the video here!
Scan the QR code or go to http://y2u.be/tmlTHfVaU9o.

Ben Breedlove's moving video was posted to YouTube just seven days before the teen's untimely death. The video took the internet—and the world—by storm.

INFUSIONSOFT VIDEO SERIES CASE STUDY
Three-Person Company Changes People's Eating Habits with Online Food Delivery Service

Topline Foods delivers all-natural and organic food, meat, and wild-caught seafood. The company's foods are free of antibiotics, added hormones, pesticides and herbicides, nitrites and nitrates, steroids, additives, and man-made chemicals. The nutritional information is easily accessible via the friendly Topline website, which features videos, menus, and recipes, along with sign-up procedures for its food delivery service (which delivers to the Phoenix metro area and ships to other parts of the country). But as founder Jeff Liesener discovered early on, that isn't always enough to make a prospective shopper open his or her wallet.

"For us," he said, "it's about changing people's habits and getting them to plan ahead a little bit. When you're hungry, the last thing you think of doing is going online and ordering food and waiting a couple of days for it to get there. That's a hurdle we had to overcome."

One of the ways Topline addressed that problem is by using automated marketing software for small businesses from Infusionsoft. Liesener's team discovered that, after finding Topline Food's website, potential customers typically spend a few minutes browsing without making a purchase. In fact, he noted, it takes an average of twenty-seven days between a customer's first visit to the website and the initial purchase.

"Email marketing has been key for us to develop relationships and trust with our customers," he said, "so that they feel comfortable coming back and making purchases."

In order to build rapport with potential customers, the company needs to capture their email addresses. Once it has that—usually through one of two forms that customers must fill out if they want to buy something or receive a discount coupon—Topline begins reaching out to those who haven't made a purchase. Liesener described the initial email that prospective customers receive this way: "Hey, we noticed you were on our website and were wondering if you have any questions. Is there anything we can help you with? We're here for you. Let us know what we can do."

If the customer doesn't reply, he or she gets another email a few days later, asking for feedback. Liesener said it goes something like this: "Hey, we're a small Arizona business that wants to improve. We have a couple questions for you. Can you give us some feedback?"

If the first two emails fail to find an audience, prospective customers are placed in the company's long-term "nurture" campaign, which amounts to a weekly email that might include something like Topline's "The Top 10 'Dirty Little Secrets' of Grocery Stores." The series sheds light on the reality of what kind of food is found at your average grocery store, educating prospective customers while reminding them that an alternative exists in Topline's all-natural foods. It's a savvy bit of marketing dressed up in an educational costume.

Watch the video here!
Scan the QR code or go to http://www.wordofmouse.com/qr/3/index.htm.

Chapter Summary Points

- New technology is transforming the parent-child dynamic, presenting challenges and opportunities for both sides. More parents are monitoring their kids' online behavior as a way of keeping them safe and strengthening family relationships.

- The era of the physical cookbook is drawing to an eventual close. Apps tied to smartphones, iPads, and laptops that show step-by-step videos are the new way to cook!

- The definition of privacy is changing in a big way, and current notions may someday be a thing of the past. In the meantime, reputations still matter. If required, consider hiring an online-reputation-management firm.

- These days, taking ownership of your own health data is smart. There are so many tools, websites, and apps out there to help you, your family, and your friends learn, understand, and help manage health issues. Take charge of your own health!

- Voting via smartphones may be fast approaching.

- Lifestreams are an upcoming internet overhaul that will make the data in your life easier to manage, understand, and make relevant. It will make the internet, as a whole, a more transparent technology.

- Get used to the idea of ads looking back at you. The first camera-enhanced smart signs are already out there looking for potential customers and tailoring their content accordingly.

- If you have qualms about a police officer and you're headed to court, make sure you find out whether the incident was recorded.

BONUS SECTION:
PERSONAL AND BUSINESS BRAND MANAGEMENT

In a world where more people are telecommuting than ever before and traditional jobs are falling by the wayside, it has never been more important to exercise your personal branding power so that you can stand out from the crowd. Using true Word of Mouse, you have countless means by which you can and should create, spread, and inform others about you—your mission, your message, who you are, what you stand for—and why others should think of hiring you.

I know what you're thinking: Why the heck do I need a personal brand? Most of us really do, especially if our careers force us to interact with the public on a regular basis. You might think that personal branding is reserved for the Kim Kardashians of the world, but the world is changing faster than you realize, and personal branding is a route that many people are taking toward faster advancement in their careers and more fulfilling social lives.

Personal branding is the way we communicate our marketability to other people. Thanks to the rise of social media, anyone can maximize his or her "brandability." The same strategy that makes any TV star a compelling brand for women's clothing lines and perfumes can also be harnessed to make you an attractive seller, employee, businessperson, creative, or advocate. You can build brand equity, too. The playing field has, in effect, been leveled.

This doesn't mean that you should brand for the sake of branding. Take the time to do it right and learn how you can truly invest yourself in your brand. The goal is to create a personal brand that is believable because it is real. Building a personal brand is about finding who you really are, creating a vision, and then using that vision to create a plan with clearly defined goals. As with a résumé,

"For a good relationship, I need someone who shares the same taste in music, movies, and TV...so I've started dating my iPod."

most people strive to put their best foot forward. They play up their strengths and play down their weaknesses. They know what they are good at and partner with others to "fill in the blanks." It's all in the planning. If you want people to turn to you as an expert on a particular subject, they have to see, learn, and understand that you are the go-to person for that subject! Sometimes you can hire a public relations firm to help your cause, but for the majority of us, it's what we say, what others say, and what we do that teach others who we are and what we stand for. It's Me.com.

Remember that there are downsides to making your mark online. These days, a simple search is all it takes to find customer complaints and fiery opinions that have the potential to mar someone's personal brand forever. This section is all about helping you to develop a personal brand that accurately reflects your passion and personality.

DEVELOPING YOUR PERSONAL BRAND: YOUR ME.COM!

How do people perceive *you*? Are you smart? Funny? Maybe you are the person in your office whom everyone goes to for help with a complicated task? Believe it or not, these qualities are all part of your personal brand. Think about these qualities when you are brainstorming a name for your blog, your business, or any other personal brand you want to develop. Make sure that your personal brand fits within its own niche and is relevant to people involved in that niche. The more easily defined the niche is, the easier it will be for people to interpret your brand.

Once you've developed an idea for your brand, it's time to advertise it. The brand should be an extension of yourself that you're ready to talk about wherever you go. Here are a few tools you can use to get people's attention and help them remember you:

Ten Tools to Help Build Your Personal Brand!

1. Business card: It doesn't matter if you're a college student or a big-shot banker; everyone should be ready to whip out a business card whenever he or she meets someone. At a minimum, you need the name of your firm, your name, and your email address and phone number. The card could contain your picture, your personal brand statement (something that identifies your unique selling proposition, like *A driven, inquisitive, analytical, and articulate journalist*), and other contact information. Some people even include logos and QR codes that whisk you to their websites or videos they want you to see. Create your own business card and share it through your mobile phone using any of several online social networks for creating and distributing your personal business card, like BusinessCard2 (which recently joined with Workface). A personal note: I love business cards and for many years have been collecting really cool cards that stand out from the crowd. My card is made of metal and is shaped like a razor blade for my company, Razor Media Group. Remember, this is your personal billboard—create a card that people will remember!

2. Résumé, cover letter, references document: Even in the twenty-first century, the basic documents for applying for a job still matter when you go on interviews. Tailor your documents to the particular job for which you're applying. Don't forget to add your personal brand to the résumé, with links to social networking sites where people can get a better sense of who you are and prospective employers can experience your brand and get a better sense of who you are.

3. Facebook profile: The world's largest social networking site remains an amazing way to generate brand appeal and connect with people. "Fan pages" allow businesses and people to brand themselves and be shared. Remember to keep your page friendly and accessible if you want it to appeal to the masses. No beer bottles or scantily clad friends, for example. Don't forget to fine-tune privacy settings that keep people from tagging you in pictures and videos that you might not want associated with your personal brand. I assure you, potential employers do go to your social sites and look you up online to find out as much as they can about you! So know this before you post something that you don't want others to see. Remember: what happens in Vegas stays on the internet— *forever*!

4. Blog/website: Don't hesitate to start writing a blog or a website, especially if you plan on updating it frequently. The more you blog, for example, the better chance your blog has of standing out, because it will rank higher on search engines. Insert photos, videos, and links to other sites or friends' profiles—they just might return the favor! If you take on this task, please accept the importance and responsibility of thoughtful, accurate, and grammatically correct writing, or risk leaving the impression of someone who produces sloppy work.

5. **LinkedIn profile:** Founded in 2003, LinkedIn connects the world's professionals to make them more productive and successful. With more than 175 million members worldwide, including executives from every Fortune 500 company, LinkedIn is the world's largest professional network on the Internet. LinkedIn is still a great place to post your résumé and create your own personal advertising. It also remains a good way to search for jobs or meet people.

6. **Twitter profile:** Twitter is a real-time information network that connects users to the latest stories, ideas, opinions, and news about what they find interesting. Users find the most compelling accounts and follow the conversations. At the heart of Twitter are small bursts of information called Tweets. Each Tweet is 140 characters long, and it's really quite amazing what can be communicated in that space. Twitter is another great way to build (and monitor) a brand. Start by creating a profile that is distinctly *you*. Include links to blogs, websites, or LinkedIn profiles, too. Twitbacks.com has templates that you can use to create a unique Twitter background. The site also helps you promote your Twitter profile.

7. **Video résumé:** To stay competitive these days, you should have a short video résumé in which you discuss your skill set and why you're the best candidate for a job. (But don't ramble!) You may want three or four: one for each position you're seeking. The video represents you, so make it as professional as possible, taking into account good lighting and use of a tripod to prevent shaking. Upload your final product to YouTube and put a link on your résumé or by your email so that it can be easily accessed by hiring managers. Note: It's okay to be creative in your video, to set yourself apart from the crowd, but just be sure you consider the possibility of the video going viral. If you don't like the idea of your friends seeing the video, that's a good clue not to submit it online.

8. **Email address:** Yes, email addresses are actually important! Try to give out or create an address that includes your brand or name. It's just one more way to say you walk the walk and talk the talk. Many people use Google's Gmail addresses because of the acceptance of Google and because Google Chat or Gchat gives you an opportunity to converse with people online, which is another avenue for networking.

9. **Portfolio:** Many jobs require portfolios: graphic designer, model, architect, and copywriter, to name a few. In the past, this was done on paper. But employers are increasingly expecting your portfolio to be online, too. It's a great opportunity to showcase your skill set and give people a taste of the creative side of you and your personal brand, which should be easily digested. Sites such as FigDig and Carbonmade are social networks that allow users to showcase creative talent.

10. Photography and style: Never underestimate the power of layout, design, and aesthetics in your personal branding. Whether it's striking photos on Facebook or the clean lines and simple text on your résumé, people notice when your brand looks good. If you don't have a particularly good eye, find a graphic artist (try Guru.com) or maybe a professional friend who does.

How to Monitor Your Brand

In the past, a brand was talked about in private. Good or bad, it spread mouth to mouth, not unlike the flu. Today a brand, whether it's an individual or a business, is at the mercy of the web, and its reputation can change by the hour and might best be compared to a wildfire! Monitoring your brand is a vital component of keeping it alive and healthy. Getting feedback is the key to learning and changing for the better. If you don't know or care what others are saying, that's certainly your choice. Large businesses hire companies to monitor their brand names, but here are a few tools that anyone can use.

1. **Google Alerts:** This is a free notification system that arrives via email. The service tracks blog posts, news articles, videos, and even groups that match a set of search terms selected by the user and stored by the Google Alerts service. Set a "comprehensive alert," which will notify you of stories, as they happen, for your name, your topic, and even your company. I have alerts set for "Marc Ostrofsky," "Get Rich Click," and "Word of Mouse." If you blog or mention this book to your friends on Facebook, I should see it in my Google Alerts!

2. **Yahoo! Pipes:** This web application aggregates web feeds, web pages, and other services, creating web-based apps and publishing those apps. The application works by enabling users to "pipe" information from different sources and then set up rules for how that content should be modified (for example, filtering).

3. **Technorati:** This is the largest blog search engine in the world. When you register, Technorati tracks "blog reactions," or blogs that link to yours. Search for your brand on Technorati and subscribe to RSS (Rich Site Summary), a format for delivering regularly changing web content. Many news-related sites, weblogs, and other online publishers syndicate their content as an RSS feed to whoever wants it. When someone blogs about you, you find out. (RSS feeds share headlines and news items across websites.)

4. **BackType:** This is a tool for monitoring blog comments as well as a search engine. It allows users to find out if someone has cited their name in a blog post. The service also lets you monitor comments from readers of

your blog. It even lets people "claim" comments via a URL. To claim a comment, you need to tell BackType which URL you've left a comment in. Any comment in BackType's database with that URL in the comment is linked to the profile. Note: During production of this book, BackType was acquired by Twitter.

5. **Discussion boards:** Discussion boards join blogs and traditional news stories as vehicles to community gatherings. They provide another channel for people to talk about you. Although a lot of people don't tune into discussion boards until they notice other sites commenting on their content, it's a good idea to stay on top of what's being said about you, your company, or organizations of interest to you. Use BoardTracker to get instant alerts from threads citing your name. BoardReader offers similar capabilities.

6. **FriendFeed:** This is a social aggregator (sometimes referred to as lifestream). Compile all of your social accounts, such as YouTube, Delicious (which lets you save, sort, and search through your own personal collection of links), Twitter, and Flickr, into a single friend feed. Using the search function, you can track your brand across numerous social networks. You can subscribe to updates from individuals and groups, such as your family or a team of coworkers. On FriendFeed, you can contribute to a shared stream of information that you care about, because it's from your friends. You can also receive alerts to your desktop with AlertThingy, which culls information from blogs, comments, news, videos, and micro-blogging sites.

7. **Social Mention:** This social media search engine searches user-generated content such as blogs, comments, bookmarks, events, news, videos, and microblogging services. It allows you to track mentions of your brand across all of these areas. The results are aggregated from the top social media sources such as Flickr, YouTube, Digg (a site that lets you find, read, and share current, interesting, and talked-about stories on the internet), Delicious, Twitter, and more. As with the other services, you can subscribe to your results by RSS or email.

8. **Twitter:** Don't forget about Twitter Search! With this tool, you can find out if your name has been tweeted and decide whether you want to tweet back or ignore the tweet. You can also conduct a search for a company's name or a topic you care about before subscribing to it via RSS. For other sites with similar functions, Twilert and TweetBeep are additional tools you can use to receive email alerts.

Nine Golden Rules for Maintaining Your Personal Brand

Companies go to great lengths and make significant investments to develop, nurture, and protect their brands. Your personal brand should be no different. You have two options: contract with a brand manager or do it yourself. If you choose the latter, here are some rules to get you on the right track.

1. Be the go-to person for something. For example, among my friends, I am the one most of them turn to regarding domain names and online business questions.

2. Don't overdo it. Sending tweets or posting three times a day is just too much for most people. We all get a ton of emails, tweets, Facebook posts, and other inbound marketing hits already. Limit your communications accordingly.

3. Don't post unless you have something important to say. Telling your "followers" that you ate a chili cheese dog at the game today just isn't important. If you must do it, don't do it often. You don't want folks to turn you off. Remember, the sad truth is that most people want to know what's in it for them.

4. Don't just talk to your list. Interact with it, ask questions, and create a dialogue with everyone.

5. Work at creating your lifelong brand—not just your fifteen minutes of fame! You don't want to be the actress who said "Where's the beef?" and currently resides in the "where is she now" files. Rather, you want to be Wendy's, whose brand was strong then and only continues to gain recognition.

6. Be honest! Don't ever inflate your résumé or any other post. It's too easy to prove it's not true via the internet.

7. Be consistent. Talk with your followers on a consistent basis. But . . .

8. Be clear and specific with your target audience. Don't talk about cooking to a list of friends or followers who want and/or expect you to discuss hunting or travel.

9. Remember that your brand is a commitment. Steve Cannon, vice president of marketing for Mercedes-Benz USA, says, "The brand is your promise that represents real things that you deliver."

Large companies should consider hiring one of the new online-reputation-management firms. These firms are worth the price, as they seek out and destroy any negative material about your company that could do serious damage, either immediately or down the line, including unfair news articles, disparaging blog posts, exaggerated reviews, hostile forum comments, outdated legal issues, and blatant smear campaigns.

Go from Profile to Fan Page

One of the most basic ways to market yourself or a business is to turn your personal Facebook profile into a Facebook fan page. While profiles are reserved for individuals, fan pages are ideal marketing tools for businesses, brands, and people in the public eye. After I published my first book—*Get Rich Click!*—I started a fan page, which is located at www.facebook.com/getrichclick. This allows followers to have a more interactive relationship with me, where I can send messages out in "bulk," and they can send me a direct response. Truly a new Word of Mouse way to communicate. Besides, Facebook won't allow you to have more than five thousand friends. For more information, please see Who Should Create a Fan Page? below.

The most important branding distinction between fan pages and profiles is that Facebook users can simply "Like" a page, whereas they must "Friend" (establish a mutual relationship with) a profile. This characteristic makes fan pages a much more effective and efficient branding tool for businesses and public figures.

Once you've created a fan page—let's say, for your new jewelry line—people can connect with your page by "Liking" it, which provides a link to your business on their page, where others can see it. This is an example of Word of Mouse at its best. Convert your profile into a fan page by going here: www.facebook.com/pages/create.php/migrate.

Want to be a fan of Word of Mouse? Find us on Facebook!

**The future is ONLINE learning . . .
What will happen to colleges and universities?**

Create Your Own QR Code

Watch the video here!
Scan the QR code or go to http://www/qurify.com/en/.

I cannot overstate the powerful extension that QR codes bring to any communication effort. And I highly recommend that companies and individuals alike use them to further extend their brands. Did you know you can create your own QR codes (this is called "qurifying") and easily make anything more interactive? Try qurifying your business card, block party flyers, or promotional posters. Qurify your household items, CDs, keys, and tools, so that you can organize them or know how to use them. Many apps let you easily qurify any text or website URL, slap the QR code on an item, and instantly turn a passive medium into an interactive one!

Who Should Create a Fan Page?

You know the time is right to create a fan page if:

- **You're a public person who expects to exceed five thousand friends, which is the largest number you can have on a Facebook profile.**

- **You want to "professionalize" your Facebook use, so that you can link prospective clients, friends, and employees to the page from your website without having to worry about incriminating photos or inappropriate posts by family and friends.**

- **You are not concerned with being able to connect with people on Facebook socially. Once you have a fan page, you will not be able to send individual messages or leave posts on your friends' walls if they make that feature available only to "friends."**

Remember!

- **Migrating your Facebook profile to a fan page is irreversible.**
- **Your Facebook profile pictures will be transferred, and your current Facebook friends will be converted from friend status to people who like your page.**
- **Before making the switch, back up your Facebook profile content because photos, wall posts, messages, and friend lists will not be transferred. For a good Facebook backup try SocialToo, at http://socialtoo.com.**

Ten Ways to Maximize Google+

Although Facebook still dominates the social media landscape, Google+ is gaining ground quickly. If you're looking for a new way to leverage the power of the most popular search engine on earth for your own marketing strategy, check out Google+ for an additional profile. Shama Kabani, CEO of the Marketing Zen Group (www.marketingzen.com), composed a brilliant tutorial on this powerful tool. We are reprinting the piece here, with Shama's permission (and with my thanks to her and her full-service digital marketing agency).

1. Set up a solid profile. Your entire Google+ experience starts with the profile. Just as on Facebook, your profile is key, so spend some time building it correctly. Start with a good headshot. And, if you think this advice is commonplace, just look at some of the pictures on Google+ now. When you show up in people's streams, all they will see is a thumbnail. So choose something where you really stand out. Craft your introduction well. Make it so that people would want to add you to their specific "group" known as "circles" on Google+ (see number 5 below). And Google+ allows for live links in the introduction itself, so make the most of it. Add links to your website, blog, LinkedIn profile, etc.

2. Add relevant and remarkable images. My hunch is that Google will index the pictures you share (unless you've kept them private). So use images you want found in the search engines. If you are a speaker, add pictures of you speaking. An author? Add pictures of you at your book signing. The idea is to convey the right brand image.

3. Make sure your profile is *open* to search. This is key; since Google reigns supreme in the search world, the chances are that your profiles will be indexed *very* quickly. When you hit "Edit Profile," the very last item on your profile is "Search Visibility." Make sure you have checked the box that says "Help others find my profile in Search Results."

4. Optimize the links to the right of the profile, using keywords. Again, a great search engine optimization (SEO) feature. What are the chances that Google will value these links highly? Pretty good, I'd say, if only to encourage people to use Google+. On the right-hand side of your profile, you can add links and any text that goes with them. Make sure you use the *right* keywords to connect to your website. For example, our link to the Marketing Zen home page uses the phrase "online marketing."

5. **Use "Circles" to communicate with clients, prospects, media, etc.** This is perhaps Google+'s greatest selling point. Most people's lives have layers: professional, personal, acquaintances, etc. And Google Circles allow you to make the most of the layers. For example, you can create a circle for your friends, a separate circle for your family, and another circle for your prospective clients, and then cater specifically to them with industry news, a solid case study, etc. (Tip: although Google will inform people that you have added them to a Circle, it won't tell them *which* Circle.)

6. **Use +1, Comments, and Share to boost relationships.** At the heart of all good social media marketing and networking lies the power of relationships. As you interact with others, show support for their ideas. The "+1" on Google is akin to Like on Facebook. You can also +1 and comment when you see fit, and you can also share within your own stream.

7. **Add videos to your profile.** If only from an SEO perspective, the chances of your videos being indexed into Google's search are higher. So if you have an online video, share it.

8. **Add your industry or business name as a "Spark."** Sparks is a new Google+ feature and still in development as of this writing. But something tells me that this technology will also tie into search results or affect them in some way. For now, use it as you would a Google Alert, and set up Sparks for your name, company name, and industry terms. You can also always follow industry news using Sparks. For example, I have technology and business as my Sparks, and I follow the top articles in those areas.

9. **Market research: ask questions and use "Google+ Hangouts" as needed.** Google+ is a hotbed of market research right now. People are *a lot* more engaged there because it is a fairly new playground. It reminds me of Twitter in the early days. Google+ Hangouts incorporates video chat with Circles. Want to invite all your salespeople for a quick Monday morning meeting? How about a Hangout?

10. **Get a custom URL to share your Google+ profile.** Just as in the early days of all social networks, there will be a huge rise initially as people try to fill up their Circles. And, as time goes on, this will slow. To make it easy for people to follow you, get a custom URL. You can do so at www.gplus.to.

How to Use Social Media to Create Buzz About Your Passion!

Let's say that you want to make a film, or maybe you've already made one and need to market it. It's never been harder to become the next Steven Spielberg. These days, we are all pinched for cash and dealing with more competition than ever before. Newly affordable equipment and a plethora of online marketing strategies are creating opportunities for amateur filmmakers to make credible work that grabs people's attention. Forget the big production house budget. These days, you can go it alone! Here are a few strategies.

SOCIAL MEDIA

There has never been a better time to create buzz for a person, a film, a product, or a service than now. Social media can be used to market your work, help find funding for your work, or hook you up with other people who are experts in your field. Start by doing the following:

- **Set up a Facebook fan page—not a profile—for your film. This will provide you with a link to send people as well.**
- **Drive traffic to your page by getting your friends to Like your page, which creates a link to your film on their page that other people will see.**
- **Drive more traffic to the page using Facebook ads, one of the most cost-effective forms of online advertising out there these days. One of the things I like about Facebook ads is that you're able to niche-target unique groups of people based on their interests. Let's say that your film is a documentary exploring butterflies. You can target your ads to butterfly enthusiasts, for example.**
- **If you have a YouTube trailer, this is the perfect place to post it to create even more buzz.**

FUNDING

This might seem like an even more daunting challenge, but don't be intimidated. The last couple years have seen an enormous growth in "crowdfunding" platforms, which can reach the masses and give anyone an opportunity to fund projects of all kinds that others deem worthy. (Read more about crowdfunding and crowdsourcing in chapter 5, "Word of Mouse and the Way We *Work*.")

THE BATTLE FOR PRIVACY

Between blogs and social media sites, the internet has virtually assumed the role of town square, with "citizens" sharing every aspect of their lives, from snapshots of the night you hardly remember to hot family-feud exchanges. In this Word of Mouse world, public figures are no longer the only ones who find themselves vulnerable to rumor.

The internet makes it easy for people to compare products and prices, find doctors, and check out real estate listings all over the world. But it also makes it easy for others to find information about you—or create information about you—that may or may not be true. Online-reputation managers specialize in making damaging information harder to find by altering the results produced by search engines such as Google. For a few hundred dollars, they might remove risqué photos left on a blog posting or make a negative website more difficult to find.

As the internet becomes nearly ubiquitous on smartphones, and damaging information becomes easier to find, more companies will take a cue from Reputation.com. And while many futurists argue that privacy as we know it will eventually become a thing of the past, the battle for transparency is just beginning to brew.

Here's how the Reputation.com website explains its interaction with customers: It "will monitor the web 24/7 for your private data, finding and removing it from dozens of people search sites. And we'll keep monitoring it, to make sure that the information stays private. Our publishing team will create custom profiles and other content for you or your business to build a positive online presence, and our expert reputation advisors will work with you to push down or suppress any negative content that shows up high in your search results."*

Special Section Summary Points

- Almost anyone can create a personal brand.
- Social media have made it easier than ever before to advertise your marketability.
- You don't have to be Kim Kardashian to have a brand.
- Monitoring a brand is an important part of keeping it healthy.
- When it comes to branding, your online reputation is all you've got!
- There are a variety of new crowdsourcing (crowdsourcing is the practice of obtaining needed services, ideas, or content by soliciting contributions from a large group of people and especially from the online community, rather than from traditional employees or suppliers) platforms that can help anyone launch a creative project that is part of his or her personal brand.
- Everyone is susceptible to marred reputations and privacy invasion on the internet. Several tools and services are available to help you protect yourself.
- Even in our electronic world, everyone should have a business card ready to hand out.

Sign up to be a fan of Word of Mouse on Facebook.

* Reputation.com website.

2
Word of Mouse and the Way We *Learn*

Shabbir Massih is a twenty-eight-year-old father of two who grew up in a gritty slum on the outskirts of Lahore, a dusty metropolis of ten million people on the eastern border of Pakistan. When he was growing up, his family found that each day was a struggle to make ends meet. They spent their days looking for odd jobs and their nights squatting in abandoned buildings, where power and running water were infrequent at best.

After dropping out of school as a teenager, Shabbir worked for years as a dishwasher at a local restaurant, barely making enough money to keep his family fed. Unable to land a higher-paying job because he didn't speak English, in 2008, Shabbir eventually found a job serving tea in a private office. That's when he discovered Google.

Suddenly, a young man whose only sense of the outside world came from periodic images he'd seen on television and in movies had the most powerful source of knowledge the world has ever known at his fingertips. As Shabbir quickly realized, Google was more than a search engine; for him it was a tool of escape.

He began listening to his English-speaking coworkers, writing down new phrases and words in a small notebook that he kept with him at all times. When the office cleared out each evening, he'd log onto Google Translate, where he'd type phrases in Urdu and memorize their English translations. Facebook and YouTube allowed him to connect with people around the world and watch instructional videos about language and money management. For the first time in his life, Shabbir was learning from experts, and he was doing it free of charge.

Perhaps most effective in his quest to learn English was a tool that most of us associate with overly social teens: online chatting. Shabbir opened a Gmail account and—after making connections with native English speakers—would force his new friends to chat with him late into the night. His drive paid off. Within months, Shabbir had single-handedly taught himself rudimentary English, enough so that he was able to get a job as a waiter at an upscale restaurant that catered to foreign workers who tipped well and made for good contacts. These days, he is married, speaking English fluently, and hoping to enroll in a local college and one day work for the government or move abroad.

Twenty years ago, a story like Shabbir's would not have been possible. But in the age of the internet, learning is no longer confined to the classroom. So long as you have access to the internet, it is a process that has no boundaries, hierarchy, or barriers to entry.

In the United States, students who look to the classroom for learning don't always need to set foot in one, either. An increasing number of universities are offering accredited online programs that allow students to learn from their laptops. Websites such as Blackboard have become transformational forums where students can exchange ideas, check their grades, and gather information about assignments, projects, and tests.

What they will learn in those classrooms is less about memorization and more about how to navigate the endless sea of information that is the online universe. Like the printing press that changed the way our minds needed to memorize essential information, the internet promises to become a powerful extension of our minds themselves.

When growing up, many of us had to memorize large chunks of poetry, biblical text, and scientific laws. I spent years learning how to do long division and remember conversion tables and the periodic table of elements. I offer to you a radical idea: it was often a waste of time! Instead of cramming our brains with rules and recitation, the internet offers *access*—access to that information and much more—all of it with the click of a mouse, freeing up our brains to creatively engage with the pressing challenges of the coming century. For better or for worse, instead of learning the data itself, so many are learning how to access the data. As Shabbir would tell you, the internet hasn't merely changed the way we learn, it has also changed why we do it in the first place.

For the purposes of this book, learning is not restricted to the educational process that occurs in a classroom setting. Rather, it takes on its true definition: acquiring knowledge, skill, instruction, or experience. As such, I will address social learning, lifelong learning, personal growth learning, professional development, lifestyle learning, and educational learning.

"It's called 'reading'. It's how people install new software into their brains."

Social Learning from Unlimited Sources

One theory has it that the more people learn about each other, the longer they're willing to wait to get married. As a result, we're seeing lower divorce rates. People today are immersing themselves in social networks and other avenues of social learning to the extent of earning what I would call an MBA in humanity. After all, people with MBAs aren't necessarily smarter than those without. They just learn to make fewer mistakes about a given subject. As a researcher and the son of a college business professor, I was taught that people make fewer mistakes via more research on *any* given subject—be it marriage, dating, buying a product, or researching the lowest price to pay for a given hotel. Research these days comes from a plethora of online sources, as well as from friends, friends of friends, and bloggers, all of whom are more accessible, in a real-time and non-real-time capacity, whenever they're needed, thanks to social networks. Add to that the benefits of mobility brought to us by smartphones, tablets, and laptops, and you've got the best of all worlds for social learning that we've experienced to date. The funny thing is, we've just begun the process. The changes coming in the next twenty years will be fast and furious.

People with MBAs aren't necessarily smarter than those without. They just learn to make fewer mistakes about a given subject.

MEDIA IMMERSION

I recently came across some shocking data from a study conducted by the University of California, San Diego. It really put this dramatic evolution into perspective: we ingest about 100,500 words daily from various forms of media and take in about 350 percent more data than we were swallowing just three decades ago.

And to show you just how far we've come from the golden age of radio, check out this chart illustrating the digital platform landscape, as defined by users and owners of various media devices:

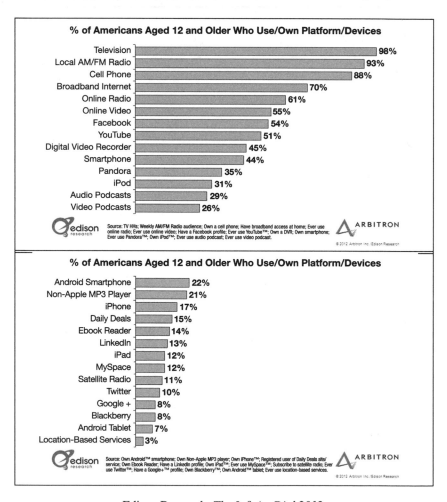

Edison Research, *The Infinite Dial 2012.*

Besides showcasing all the different forms of media we're using these days, the report goes on to estimate that *Americans are spending almost an hour and a half more time per day with media than we did in 2001.*

Information Transparency: Are We There Yet?

I once asked Nobel Prize laureate Arno Penzias to give the keynote speech at a trade show I was running. Penzias's book *Ideas and Information* had just been published, and the man was nothing short of a visionary on the topic of managing information in a high-tech world. He proposed that society will have reached a state of information transparency when we are *actually happy* to receive all the information with which we are presented.

From high school kids to senior citizens, people are learning how to relearn *how* they learn.

I don't think we've reached this ideal state yet. But, obviously, technology is past the point where it's a barrier. It's approaching transparency. Now technology is enabling us to do whatever we want. Not only are we embracing all the media forms cropping up all around us, we're also changing our ways to adapt to the media. We've learned how to use media as a natural extension of our learning toolbelt. So much so that we're able to multitask with more than one form of media at a time. I swear, my teenage daughters can multitask ten different ways at a time! From high school kids to senior citizens, people are learning how to relearn *how they learn.*

And there's more relearning to come. As more and more of the data we seek end up cataloged in online databases, we are going to have to adjust the way we learn to mimic the way that databases think.

As more and more of the data we seek end up cataloged in online databases, we are going to have to adjust the way we learn to mimic the way that databases think.

Lifelong Learning Is the New Norm!

You probably remember your elementary school teachers telling you that we all have five distinct senses: sight, touch, smell, hearing, and taste. In the not-so-distant past, these modes of perception were the only tools available to help us learn about the world around us.

The internet seems to have added what I would call a sixth sense, one that is transforming the way we gather information and turn it into useful knowledge: *experience.* For the first time in history, people's ordinary experiences—

whether they're captured on videos uploaded to YouTube, recorded on iTunes podcasts, seen and heard over Skype, or communicated over Gchat—can be broadcast around the world and onto your personal computer, forever altering the way we learn from one another. The consequences of this change are nearly impossible to overstate.

When I was growing up, I was considered a poor reader. I still am, actually. I was diagnosed with dyslexia in third grade, but even into junior high school, my father had to read my textbooks to me because that was the only way I could comprehend the material fast enough to keep up with my classmates. Imagine if I'd been born a few decades later. Imagine how radically different my approach to learning would be if I were a kid with dyslexia today. Instead of slogging my way through course work that read like a foreign language, I could be watching courses on TV and learning from the internet—hearing, seeing, and interacting with others on a daily basis—with no one else in the room but me! In the old mode of learning, knowledge was stable and hierarchical. In the new way, it is fluid and interactive. But what does this all mean?

In the past, learning required a library card, a ticket to a seminar across the country, or taking up a hobby in your free time. And while those outlets for growth remain invaluable and will never disappear entirely, today's interactive media have rewritten the rules for learning forever!

Let's say that you're nearing your fortieth birthday and want to lose weight. While the "old" way of seeking out a dietitian or a personal trainer is still a practical answer, these days you can simply log onto YouTube, where you'll find thousands of professionals who are offering their expert advice on diet and exercise free of charge. You can watch any number of network and cable TV shows discussing the topic. You can download one of a hundred apps for your smartphone, desktop, or laptop to help you count calories, measure your intake, and monitor the calories burned in any exercise you can imagine. You can even turn to Nike's smart shoe, which monitors the number of strides you take in a given day and allows you to then download the data to your computer.

Whether it's making travel plans or learning the two-step, learning is no longer the domain of the young. The young have a big advantage over those of us above the age of forty. They are growing up digital, while the rest of us must relearn how to play the game and stay competitive.

The young have a big advantage over those of us above the age of forty. They are growing up digital, while the rest of us must relearn how to play the game and stay competitive.

Today social media, e-learning, and interactive media make it easier than ever to revamp your résumé with an online consultant, learn a new language using videoconferencing tools, or drop in on an internet-based college course full of twentysomethings—even if you are well into retirement.

Learning Communities: The New Learning Model

Sometime around 1997, I read some fascinating new ideas on learning by Shanna Ratner, who is the principal of Yellow Wood Associates, Inc., and holds a master of science degree in agricultural economics from Cornell University and a bachelor's degree in value systems from New College in Sarasota, Florida. Back then, Ratner was already tuned into the idea of learning communities, and she got me thinking about the remarkable changes we'd be seeing in our learning methods.

Ratner described two models of learning: old and new. Here's how she defined them:

Old and New Answers to How We Learn

Old Answers	New
Knowledge is a "thing" that is transferred from one person to another.	**Knowledge is** a relationship between the knower and the known; knowledge is "created" through this relationship.
Knowledge is objective and certain.	**Knowledge is** subjective and provisional.
We all learn in the same way.	**There are** many different learning styles.
Learners receive knowledge.	**Learners create** knowledge.
Knowledge is organized in stable, hierarchical structures that can be treated independently of one another.	**Knowledge is** organized "ecologically"; disciplines are integrative and interactive.
We learn best passively, by listening and watching.	**We learn** best by actively doing and managing our own learning.
We learn alone, with our minds, based on our innate abilities.	**We learn** in social contexts, through mind, body, and emotions.
We learn in predictable sequences from simple "parts" to complex "wholes."	**We learn** in wholes.
Our "intelligence" is based on our individual abilities.	**Our intelligence** is based on our learning community.

Citation to Shanna Ratner's report *Emerging Issues in Learning Communities,* published by Yellow Wood Associates in 1997. Adapted from: citation to John Cleveland and Peter Plastrik's paper in the book *Total Quality Management: Implications for Higher Education,* Allan M. Hoffman, Ed.; Daniel J. Julius, Ed., published by Prescott Publishing Co., Maryville, MO, in 1995.

These "new answers" to learning eliminate the separation between teacher and student. The distance is replaced by a dialogue in which each party is responsible for growth and learning.

We all learn at different speeds and require different texts or contexts for how we do so. While I may learn better interacting with a small group, my friend may learn faster by looking at and interacting with a computer!

CHARACTERISTICS OF THE NEW DIGITAL LEARNER

With all the changes in delivery vehicles for information and learning, it makes sense that learners, themselves, will have undergone dramatic changes. The Pew Research Center Internet and American Life Project tracks these and other changes that have unfolded as a function of the internet's increasingly pervasive role in our lives. Lee Rainie, director of this project, has outlined seven characteristics of the newly defined learner. I've added the last three, which I deem significant.

Ten Characteristics of Online Learners*

1. More self-directed
2. Less top-down
3. Better arrayed to capture new information inputs
4. More reliant on feedback and response
5. More inclined to collaboration
6. More open to cross-discipline insights and creating their own "tagged" systems of classification
7. More oriented toward people being their own individual units of production
8. Learning how to search and find the data we need—quickly and easily as opposed to learning the actual information itself
9. Class is in session 24/7
10. Provides access to the very best and brightest teachers on the planet. Why learn from anyone but the best?

* Lee Rainie, "Learning in the Digital Age." Pew Research Center Internet and American Life Project, May 10, 2012, http://www.pewinternet.org/Presentations/2012/May/Learning-in-the-digital-age.aspx.

Personal Growth Learning:
Free, Accessible, and Top-Notch

As the first baby boomers have begun to retire, this notoriously youthful generation shows no signs of slowing down or giving up a quest for personal growth that began to take shape back in the 1960s. Thanks to e-learning, many baby boomers won't be lounging by the pool or playing bingo on Friday nights. They'll have access to more outlets for personal growth than any generation before them.

Take, for example, the nearly two thousand courses available online from the Massachusetts Institute of Technology. Called the OpenCourseWare project, MIT's classes come complete with syllabuses, assignments, exams, and, in many cases, audio or video lectures.

Subjects run the full gamut. Curious about globalization? Check out a course taught by leading political scientist Suzanne Berger, who built her reputation in the 1970s by studying French peasants. The course examines such issues as: Is globalization really a new phenomenon? Is it irreversible? What are its effects on wages and inequality, on social safety nets, on production, and on innovation? How does it affect relations between developed countries and developing countries? How does globalization affect democracy?

The whole lot of OpenCourseWare lessons is nothing short of a personal growth gold mine—one that is completely free!

But let's say that your learning aspirations aren't quite so heady. Maybe you just want to learn how to change the oil in your car or get tips on training your misbehaving dog. Or maybe you want to brush up on your French or learn how to play the flute? E-learning allows you to do all of these things on your own time, at your own pace, and in the way that *you* want to learn: via audio, video, interactivity, distance learning, or any number of e-learning institutions! Even via free courseware on your local YouTube channel. No, you won't receive academic credit for your efforts, but you won't receive a bill in the mail either!

"MARC" MY WORDS I expect that many more "learning" channels will surface for the benefit of all, offering subscribers a video-on-demand option for any subject they want to learn—when they want to learn it! For baby boomers with years of professional experience, free time on their hands, and decades left to live, the exciting thing about e-learning is that you don't know where it will lead. It's easy, fast, efficient, and often free of charge!

After a three-year initiative to enhance courses offered to community college students ages fifty and older, the American Association of Community Colleges reported that schools are offering more certificates aimed at current job openings in cities across the country. For many people considering a new career—or those on the cusp of beginning one—e-learning courses such as those posted online by MIT are the perfect entrees into personal exploration. Spend a few hours on YouTube learning about a new subject. You will be shocked at how much knowledge you retain—and it's only one click away.

FUTURECASTING

Universities are already adapting to a future in which content will be delivered via devices such as computer tablets or laptops, or even mobile apps. According to the National Association of College Stores (NACS), campus booksellers recently netted $10.2 billion in total sales. Of that, $5.8 billion came from the sale of course materials, with the remaining $4.4 billion taking the form of soft goods. E-books, meanwhile, are quickly gaining in popularity and already causing headaches for college bookstores. According to the NACS report, electronic titles currently account for just 2 percent to 3 percent of college bookstore sales but are projected to reach 10 percent to 15 percent in the next few years.

> ## For families with limited funds, "YouTube University," as I like to call it, may increasingly become a more attractive alternative to the typical four-year plan.

Now let's take this trend a step further—a very big step, in fact. With the rise in electronically supported learning, or e-learning, I believe that universities will increasingly find themselves in big trouble. People want to learn from the very best, and as more universities put their course work online, there may come a time when applying to college is no longer necessary or financially feasible for the majority of high school graduates. Keep watching the numbers of e-learning participants go up and the numbers of kids heading to colleges go down.

Why would you shell out an average of $35,000 a year, much less $60,000 a year for a top private college institution, when you could go online and cherry-pick from the best professors at Harvard, Stanford, and MIT—much less the best professors in London, India, or Australia—especially when getting an expensive degree no longer guarantees you a job? For families with limited funds, "YouTube University," as I like to call it, may increasingly become a more attractive alternative.

"MARC" MY WORDS In the world of e-learning, where anyone can learn from the best in their field, mediocre teachers will be phased out as the workforce caters to the best and brightest in a given field of specialization on a global basis! My father had an expression along these lines, one that I've fallen back on during uncertain times: "Become an expert in a growing field, and you should always have a job."

LEARNING VIA SOCIAL NETWORKS

One of the best ways to pursue a new interest or hobby is by connecting with groups of people who are already involved in that arena via social networking sites. Think social networking is just for your kids or grandkids? Think again.

Social network usage is spreading at an unfathomable rate. And research from the Pew Research Center Internet and American Life Project confirms it. The nonpartisan nonprofit organization found that 65 percent of adult internet users in the United States use social networks. That translates into 50 percent of the entire US adult population. Compare this with Pew's data from five years ago, and you'll see that this usage marks an increase of more than 40 percent.

> ## "Become an expert in a growing field, and you should always have a job."

You just can't ignore these numbers. Social networks are here to stay, and they continue to implant themselves in our lives cross-culturally, cross-generationally, and cross-professionally. And as more and more people embrace social networks as an integral component of mainstream online life, the form of these networks continues to change. People are learning from their social networks—and their peers are learning by giving and getting feedback on that same knowledge. We are creating a society of informed niches—where our groups of friends become increasingly specialized in their areas of interest, learning more and more about the same subjects over and over. People of similar interests gather virtually online both to stay informed and to inform. And a whole new professional and hobbyist title of "content curator" has surfaced as a result, with avid, driven, and well-connected enthusiasts collecting links to the most current ideas, some of which are expanded upon by a subject matter expert (SME): another new title in the social media world. An SME has current experience and knowledge well beyond that of his or her peers. In a traditional sense, SMEs can be contracted by organizations to consult on projects or serve on advisory boards. Their body of knowledge commonly dates back to the origin of their area of expertise, which rounds out their depth of knowledge on a topic. The more you drill into a topic, the more complex and intricate it becomes, and the more precisely knowledgeable the site contributors tend to be.

You are the average of the five people you hang out with; choose your friends wisely.

Professional Development and Social Learning Business

For businesses to get on the social business learning bandwagon, they need to leverage their collective knowledge over time. Harold Jarche, a prolific blogger, is an expert in this area. He recommends gathering this collective knowledge using personal knowledge management (PKM), by telling stories, showing examples, and modeling behavior.

I have to confess, I had to look up PKM—it was a new term, and it sounded really important. The most comprehensive definition I found comes from Wikipedia: "a collection of processes that an individual carries out to gather, classify, store, search, retrieve, and share knowledge in his/her daily activities and how these processes support work activities."

Of course, Jarche, doing what he does best, boils the idea down to three words: "Seek. Sense. Share."

However you define it, PKM addresses the notion that professionals need to assume control of their own professional development. The learning model for knowledge has been flipped from a traditional top-down paradigm to a bottom-up tackling of knowledge.

This is where social learning comes in.

Social learning may sound like a foreign concept in the business world, but you probably rely on it already without even knowing it. I know I do. I like to learn about a potential business partner by playing golf with him. If you've ever played golf, you know that its rules are considered sacrosanct. Without referees, it's one of the only games around in which players are trusted to police themselves.

Next time you're on the green with someone, observe how he behaves. Does he play fairly and honestly? Does he throw clubs when angry? Does his behavior change when he thinks you're not looking? In business, the more you can learn about someone, the more informed your decisions involving him will be.

This is all social learning, and, just as on the golf course, you can get it in spades from today's online social networks. Of course, sometimes the biggest challenge is just getting buy-in from some corporate executives who see social networks as a flagrant waste of employee time and tantamount to stealing from the company. Convincing them otherwise takes a little time, a little patience, and some strategic talking.

Here's a list that Jarche came up with in his blog, *Life in Perpetual Beta,* and was generous enough to let me reprint here; it's what he calls an "elevator pitch for social learning." Try pitching it to a decision maker at your company the next time your find yourselves sharing an elevator:

- **The increasing complexity of our work is a result of our global interconnectedness.**
- **Today simple work is being automated (for example, bank tellers).**
- **Complicated work (such as accounting) is getting outsourced.**
- **Complex and creative work is what gives companies unique business advantages.**
- **Complex and creative work is difficult to replicate, constantly changes, and requires greater intuitive knowledge.**
- **Collaborative knowledge is best developed through conversations and social relationships.**
- **Training courses are artifacts of a time when information was scarce and connections were few; that time has passed.**
- **Social learning networks enable better and faster knowledge feedback loops.**
- **Hierarchies constrain social interactions, so traditional management models must change.**
- **Learning among ourselves is the real work in social businesses, and management's role is to support social learning.**

LIFESTYLE LEARNING, FROM TRAVELING TO NEWS CONSUMPTION

Virtual Tour Guides

The age of backpacking through Europe holding an unwieldy guidebook full of confusing maps and poor translations is almost a thing of the past. These days, you'll find that many of Europe's most popular tourist destinations have added multimedia components to their tours, some of which can be downloaded on your smartphone.

These apps are sophisticated, fun, and often free, meaning that you can learn wherever you are in the world. They are often available on both smartphones and tablets. Here are a few examples of what I call a virtual tour guide.

- **Palace of Versailles:** This app lets you wander the gardens of the seven-teenth-century French palace with an aerial-view zoom based on InterAtlas's (an interactive, rich media atlas for travel) photos, distributed by Spot Image (the worldwide distributor of geographic information products and services derived from Earth observation satellites). Or you can enjoy audio commentary on the fountains, statues, and gardens positioned on your smartphone. With geopositioning, you can navigate your way through the gardens and receive interactive information. For example, as you near the Colonnade fountains, your mobile phone starts to vibrate, and a film shows you the underground hydraulic network, narrated by the Versailles fountain keeper (www.chateauversailles.fr).

- **Experience free audio tours** for the Roman Baths in England, Prague's Charles Bridge, and other sites all over the world (www.acoustiguide.com).

- **Drop by the tourism office in Padua, Italy,** where they offer tours of five walks guided by MP3. You can download these for free from its website (www.turismopadova.it).

- **Check out Rick Steves's Audio Europe, which he describes as an extensive free online library.** The "library" collection includes audio tours of Europe's key tourist sites. It also features interviews with travel experts, all categorized by destination (www.ricksteves.com).

- **Need to translate Spanish, French, or Italian to English or vice versa—in real time?** Try Word Lens, the most amazing app I have ever used! Period. Download the app (you can upgrade the free app to the $9.99 version), open it, point your phone to any English words, and watch them show up translated on your screen (http://questvisual.com/us)! Source: Word Lens.

Watch the video here!
Scan the QR code or go to http://y2u.be/h2OfQdYrHRs.

- **Finally, don't forget to download Google Translate,** an app that translates words and phrases between more than fifty languages. Perfect for travelers!

Changing the Way We Learn

While speaking to a group of college students at the University of Houston Entrepreneurship Program, I asked how many of them watched TV. Of the approximately 175 students in the room, fewer than 20 raised their hands! OMG! Just 10 percent watch TV? I asked the next logical question: "Where do you get your news from?" As expected, the answers were:

- **Internet**
- **Facebook**
- **Twitter**
- **Email**
- **Friends/chats**
- **Cell phone**
- **YouTube**
- **Blog posts**
- **Podcasts**
- **Texts from friends**

I would bet that this isn't drastically different from the experience of most college students. My own daughters don't watch much TV at home, as they are tweeting, Facebooking, and Skyping most of the time. If they want to watch a movie, Netflix on their laptops is their viewing medium of choice. News consumption has become a socially driven activity, especially online. No longer is the learning process provided by just a journalist. This dual role the public plays as both news consumer and content provider completely changes the dynamic of the consumer-to-news relationship. News and information are now instant, portable, personalized, and participatory.

Consider these facts:

- **Portable:** 33 percent of cell phone owners now access news on their cell phones.

- **Personalized:** 28 percent of internet users have customized their home page to include news from sources and on topics that particularly interest them.

- **Participatory:** 37 percent of internet users have contributed to the creation of news, commented about it, or disseminated it via postings on social media sites such as Facebook or Twitter.*

---

* Source: Kristen Purcell, Lee Rainie, Amy Mitchell, Tom Rosenstiel, and Kenny Olmstead, "Understanding the Participatory News Consumer," Pew Research Center Internet and American Life Project, March 1, 2010, www.pewinternet.org/Reports/2010/Online-News.aspx?r=1.

Furthermore, people are becoming controllers of the news they receive, by filtering, assessing, and reacting to news via any number of social networking technologies. And they use traditional email and other tools to swap stories and comment on them. Among those who access news online, three-quarters receive their news from forwarded emails or posts on social networking sites. And more than half use these same media to share links to the news items they've read.

Online, the social experience is widespread. People are absorbing the news as a social "happening" of sorts. They are no longer reading it at the breakfast table, and then packing up for work and moving on with their day. They are taking what they read and posting it, sharing it, or adding their own comments—instantly, all day long, and *all online*. They're debating hot news topics in their tweets, even uploading their own firsthand accounts onto community news sites that thrive on such consumer reporting. We are learning, absorbing, interpreting, sharing, and elaborating. When others share their own comments and reply, we learn all over again. It's a potentially never-ending cycle when you consider the number of people throwing ideas into the mix.

> **We are learning, absorbing, interpreting, sharing, and elaborating.**
> **When others share their own comments and reply, we learn all over again.**
> **It's a potentially never-ending cycle when you consider the number of people throwing ideas into the mix.**

Personal Growth on Steroids

- Twenty years ago, you might have told someone face-to-face or over the phone about something interesting you'd learned.
- A decade ago, you probably would have told him or her through email.
- Five years ago, you might have posted it on a social networking site.
- Now you can use a smartphone to do all of the above and a whole lot more—faster than ever!

The point is: it has never been easier to gain access to information and use it to your advantage. In business, we'll call it "competitive advantage." This means that it has never been easier to achieve personal growth. That's because the traditional barriers to becoming an expert—namely, training and time—have been eliminated or dramatically reduced by the democratization of information. For the first time in history we can:

1. Access information faster. Thanks to faster internet connections, mobile access, and twenty-four-hour connectivity, we spend far less time researching information. Podcasts, educational apps, e-learning, and smartphones that stream video make it possible for you to learn anything almost anywhere. And you can access the information you need when and where you want it. Because answers are delivered on the spot, you're more likely to learn from them and use them accordingly.

2. Create information faster. Flickr, Instagram, Twitpic, YouTube—there are dozens of photo- and video-uploading apps from which to choose. Or you can write an article for Wikipedia (the online free encyclopedia that lets users add to, modify, or delete its content via a web browser) and have it span the globe in seconds. You can generate all this content, with no "personal connections" or technical know-how, regardless of your location, thanks to the mobility of connected devices. No longer must we be tethered to an internet connection. Because of all these factors, we have an exponentially growing catalog of content to consume.

3. Communicate more. These days, you can get in touch with—or closely follow—just about anyone using Facebook, Twitter, blogs, YouTube channels, teleconferences, video conferences, and live chats.

Simply put, if you don't participate in this new era, you are in danger of becoming a walking anachronism.

Personal Health Management Changes the Doctor-Patient Relationship

I've said it before and I'll say it again: the internet has changed people's relationships with information. One relationship that continues to evolve is the one between health professionals and their patients. Doctors, nurses, and other health care professionals continue to be the first choice for most people with health concerns, but online resources, including advice from peers, are increasingly gaining ground as a major source of health information.

As broadband expands, and with the increased mobility afforded by modern devices, more people can—and do—share what they are doing and thinking. And these days, they're doing so as a matter of habit. Whether it's managing workout routines, or reviewing medical professionals, or contributing to knowledge bases of health conditions, people are sharing personal information online (family health history, weight, age); and they are eager to use that information as a source for learning about their health.

These data points from the Pew Research Center help illustrate this personal knowledge base evolution:

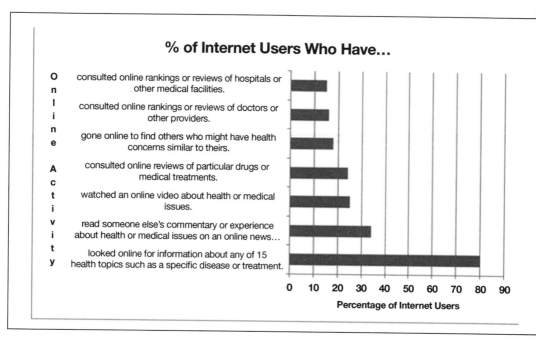

Source: Pew Research Center Internet and American Life Project.

Give Your Brain a Workout!

Like a weight room for your brain, the website Lumosity leverages cutting-edge neuroscience to create games and exercises that are said to improve core cognitive abilities and help users remember more, think faster, and perform better at work and school. The site's team works closely with a scientific advisory board of leading researchers from institutions such as Stanford University and the University of California, San Francisco. With more than fourteen million members, the Lumosity site boasts thirty-five games, some of which can be completed in as little as twenty minutes. Check it out, at www.lumosity.com!

Education: From Books and Soda Cans to Apps and Facebook

If you want to experience technology at its most disruptive—that is, technology that is changing the rules and making old processes obsolete—look no further than today's evolving schools. They definitely "ain't your grandfather's classroom," or even *your* classroom, for that matter. Just to "keep up," schools today *must* have:

- smart whiteboards
- internet access with broadband speeds
- websites that allow parents, students, and teachers to all communicate on everything from homework assignments to progress reports, discussions, and so on
- tablet, laptop, and/or desktop computers for all students to use while in school

Consider the following "then and now" scenarios. They offer just a glimpse of how technology is changing the face of education and redefining how we learn and teach:

IN THE PAST, a teacher in a high school put together her own source book of African-American poets for a course she was teaching to seventh, eighth, and ninth graders during Black History Month. She photocopied poems, short stories, and newspaper articles for the students; bound the documents; and handed each one of her thirty students a folder. This process was time consuming and expensive. But the benefits of the content she offered—tailored to her students—are undeniable.

TODAY this same teacher would offer the same content digitally, making the information up-to-date and diverse, as well as easy for students to access.

IN THE PAST, students lugged heavy book bags around campus and then back home to complete homework assignments. In addition to being cumbersome, books were expensive, were subject to damage, and had to be replaced every few years.

TODAY teachers can post a homework assignment on a platform such as Blackboard Mobile. Using this app on a smartphone, for example, students can access course materials, check grades, and participate in discussions without ever having to crack open a book.

IN THE PAST, teachers used household items—rubber bands, exploding Coke cans, and bouncing balls—to demonstrate physics concepts.

TODAY students can perform an entire classroom lesson around the physics principle of acceleration using only an iPad, free online apps, and PDF files from the classroom textbook. Need to calculate acceleration? Try Touchcalc, a free app that provides a scientific calculator. Want to record actual acceleration? Just shake and wave your tablet computer, and use the SPARKvue app to graph its acceleration along an axis. Log your results on the device's default Notes app and then use a web browser to complete an online quiz that your teacher has prepared.

IN THE PAST, your teacher might have paired you with another student on the first day of school and asked you to write a brief biography of each other as a rapport-building exercise.

TODAY students are being asked to interview and record each other to create digital stories using Adobe Photoshop Elements and Premiere Elements, and other free online digital tools.

CASE STUDY
The Kinkaid School:
Teaching and Growing Up Digital

Before Larry Kahn started working as the chief technology officer at the Kinkaid School, an elite college preparatory school on the west side of Houston, he managed a data center for a Fortune 500 company. And while he doesn't have to go to bed each night holding his pager anymore, Kahn finds himself in the midst of another race, one that seems to accelerate between the time he goes home from work and the time he shows up the next day. Like most of his peers across the world of education, Kahn is racing to keep up with changes in educational technology.

"The last fifteen years have been truly transformational," he told me as we sat down in his light-filled office on a crisp fall day. "Kids today have grown up in a world where they were not just content consumers but also content creators."

With titles such as *Growing Up Digital, "Don't Bother Me Mom—I'm Learning,"* and *Disrupting Class,* the bookshelf in Kahn's office speaks to the educational establishment's attempt to come to terms with what role it should be playing in the current digital revolution, which is revealing itself to be historic in magnitude.

In the past, that role was easily defined, if not utterly simple. Information was somewhat finite. Years of experience and training meant that teachers had it and students didn't. A student doing late-night homework requiring additional research might browse an encyclopedia (assuming her family owned one), peruse a potentially outdated textbook, or call a knowledgeable friend or relative. Barring those options, she'd be forced to wait until the next day to head to a public library.

To be sure, times have changed. In a third-grade classroom not far from Kahn's office, students recently initiated a Skype conversation with a popular children's book author, which they featured on a classroom blog. As Kahn noted, the idea of third graders producing original content for a worldwide audience was hardly imaginable, much less possible, a decade ago.

"Knowledge is no longer scarce, it's everywhere," he said, noting that even today's third graders utilize and understand the benefits of Google, Wikipedia, and collaborative, multimedia slide shows such as VoiceThreads (which hold images, documents, and videos and let people navigate slides and leave comments using voice, text, audio file, or video; VoiceThreads can be shared with other people for them to record comments, too). "What you do with it and how you add value to it—those are the questions for schools today."

While schools such as Kinkaid continue to wrestle with these kinds of questions, walking through the school's hallways provides a glimpse into the future. Peek into the computer lab, and you'll find students bent over rows of shiny iMacs, blogging for homework assignments or creating multimedia presentations using iWork applications. Duck into almost any classroom, and you'll find students glued to laptops, smartphones, iPads, and e-readers. In addition to avoiding trips to the chiropractor, from not having to lug those heavy book bags, students use these tools to add informed content to online forums, make short movies, chart physics problems, create podcasts (digital video or audio recordings, usually from an episodic series), and watch TEDx videos (TEDx events present a short talk, demonstration, and performance—either live or via TED recorded video—on a variety of subjects with the objective of educating, inspiring, and creating conversation on the topic).

One of the most transformative tools they use, administrators said, is Google Docs, which allows teachers to monitor collaborative projects long after the final bell has rung. With Google Docs, instructors can monitor progress in close to real time, making suggestions and providing feedback to students—who receive email updates about schoolwork on their phones—twenty-four hours a day. Teachers are no longer authoritarian figureheads but guides who wander among their tech-savvy students, offering insight and advice.

Teachers are no longer authoritarian figureheads but guides who wander among their tech-savvy students, offering insight and advice.

"As a teacher, you can watch your kids create a study guide using Google Docs that is superior to anything else because everyone has created it," said Kinkaid Upper School principal Patrick Loach. "This really is anytime, anywhere learning."

In May 2009 the US Department of Education released a report entitled *Evaluation of Evidence-Based Practices in Online Learning: A Meta-Analysis and Review of Online Learning Studies*. Among the key findings: "(1) Students who took all or part of their class online performed better, on average, than those taking the same course through traditional face-to-face instruction; (2) instruction combining online and face-to-face elements had a larger advantage relative to purely face-to-face instruction than did purely online instruction."

The ubiquity of online connectivity and the temptations it creates are reasons that Kinkaid relies on the website Turnitin, an internet-based plagiarism-detection service that compares submitted papers with several databases using a proprietary algorithm. Although Kinkaid has a strict honor code, Turnitin is a welcome resource for teachers in a school where 80 percent of the 1,400 upper-level students have laptops and students have significantly less discretionary free time than they did in the past, Kahn said. Besides presenting students with temptation and opportunity, the influx of readily available information is also altering the responsibility of teachers who are flipping the traditional classroom on its head, said Loach.

(1) Students who took all or part of their class online performed better, on average, than those taking the same course through traditional face-to-face instruction; (2) instruction combining online and face-to-face elements had a larger advantage relative to purely face-to-face instruction than did purely online instruction.

"In the land of the blind, the one-eyed man is king," he said. "The one-eyed man used to be the teacher. Now students are no longer in the land of the blind, and for a teacher, the job is to decide what is important and how students should learn it. It's about taking knowledge that's all around you and teaching your students how to make meaning out of it."

Loach and Kahn said that today's administrators face a choice when it comes to embracing technology in the classroom. Administrators can build fences around the pool that is the online world, to borrow Kahn's metaphor, or they can teach kids to swim, knowing full well that their students will pick the locks either way. At forward-thinking schools like Kinkaid, where teachers and students are rewriting the traditional rules of learning, it is clear that administrators are signing up their students for swim lessons.

"In a world where content shifts incredibly fast, becoming a lifelong learner is no longer optional but required if you're going to be a fully engaged twenty-first-century citizen."
—Larry Kahn, CTO, Kinkaid School

CASE STUDY
Turnitin: We Can Prove If You Cheated!

"Prevent plagiarism. Engage students." That's the Turnitin mission. And with more and more students and writers turning to online sources for their work, the mission is relevant and aptly timed.

Specifically, Turnitin's OriginalityCheck feature helps instructors check students' work for improper citations or potential plagiarism by comparing it against an accurate, monstrously huge text-comparison database. Turnitin serves over 10,000 educational institutions in 126 countries, including leading colleges and universities, high schools, distance learning institutions, and middle schools. Here are some more stats that lend credence to the product's viability:

- more than 150 million archived student papers
- more than 90,000 journals, periodicals, and books
- more than 1 million active instructors
- more than 14 billion web pages crawled
- more than 20 million licensed students

For more info, check out www.turnitin.com.

"Yes, I did the book report myself. I found it on eBay myself,
I bid on it myself, I paid for it myself, I printed it myself..."

Did You Know?

That iTunes Has a University?

The Florida Department of Education has created a service called iTunes U, which brings together teaching, professional development, and cultural resources for educators and students. Through podcasts, videos, and digital lectures, students can learn about the Pythagorean theorem or hear a professor of anthropology at the University of South Florida describe aspects of excavating an archaeological dig in South Florida. The digital possibilities on iTunes U (http://etc.usf.edu/floridaitunesu/index.html) are endless.

Apple offers 350,000 free lectures, videos, books, and podcasts from learning institutions all over the world on iTunes U. It's like an untapped library at your fingertips, and you don't even need a library card! Universities such as Yale, Stanford, University of California at Berkeley, Oxford, Cambridge, MIT, Beijing Open University, and the University of Tokyo, as well as broadcasters such as the Public Broadcasting Service (PBS), offer stunning educational content, ranging from lectures and presentations to syllabuses and campus maps.

Mobile and Internet Apps for Education

As iPhones, iPads, and iPod Touches become as commonplace as textbooks and flash cards in classrooms, the demand for new educational apps will continue to increase. Whether students need help translating Spanish homework, practicing math drills, or organizing their demanding homework schedule, there are thousands of interactive educational apps available to students and teachers alike on iTunes alone.

The Apple Volume Purchase Program allows schools to buy apps and distribute them to their students. I've assembled a list of apps for Apple devices and smartphones that can help to automate the classroom curriculum and present new ways to learn. Although many apps are free to download, the majority are a couple dollars each. Here are five great apps:

1. myHomework: Focused on making student life easier, myHomework lets users easily know what's due and when, so they will never forget a homework assignment again. This app has a clear calendar display and even sends users notices when assignments are due.

2. US States (Match 'Em Up History & Geography): Fun for younger kids or adults looking for a memory challenge, this app helps users learn the names, capitals, and shapes of US states in a memory matching game that incorporates a point system and sound effects.

3. Everyday Mathematics Baseball Multiplication 1–6 Facts: Two players play a three-inning baseball game as they practice their numbers 1–6 multiplication facts. Players take turns at bat for three innings, until the player with the most runs wins.

4. Star Walk: Named one of the best apps of 2010, Star Walk lets you point your iPad or other device at the sky and see what stars, constellations, and satellites you are looking at in real time.

5. No Fear Shakespeare: For those of us who would love to understand Shakespeare—but just haven't been able to—this app offers modern translations, side by side with the original text, on your iPhone or iPod Touch.

SOCIAL MEDIA'S ROLE IN THE CLASSROOM

In the past, students shared class notes, test questions, and homework over the telephone. More recently, they used email. But these days, the proliferation of social media and digital technology has created a culture in which students communicate primarily online by way of sites such as Skype and Facebook or via their cell phones! In many cases, the online environment has supplanted teacher instruction altogether as a source of informational sharing. Fortunately, in classrooms across the country, teachers are starting to take notice and use social media to their advantage.

In the National Education Technology Plan *Transforming American Education: Learning Powered by Technology,* the US Department of Education calls for "applying the advanced technologies used in our daily personal and professional lives to our entire education system to improve student learning."

In her many conversations with teachers, Linda Fogg Phillips, a mother of eight and Facebook expert who consults for the site and travels the country holding seminars that teach educators how to use Facebook, has learned that many educators are eager to learn how to integrate the social media giant into their curriculum.

> ## Many educators are eager to learn how to integrate the social media giant Facebook into their curriculum.

Phillips says that Facebook can provide students with the opportunity to more effectively communicate their ideas, facilitate online discussions, and collaborate. She's also a big believer in social networks' enabling educators to "tap into the digital learning styles" of their students. Her rationale is simple: as long as the kids are all using Facebook, why not communicate with them where they are the most comfortable?

INFUSIONSOFT VIDEO SERIES CASE STUDY
Veterinarian Offers Post-Op Info and Bedside Manner via Web, Email, and Social Networks

The weeks after a pet has surgery can be stressful ones for the animal's owner, who, despite oral or written post-op instructions from the vet, may feel intimidated and a little overwhelmed by his or her lack of knowledge regarding the proper care during the precarious recovery period. "You take your pet to have surgery, it costs forty-five hundred dollars, and wham, bam, you're out the door!" said Dr. James St. Clair, a veterinarian in central Connecticut. "If you're lucky, you might get a sheet that reminds you to walk your dog on a leash for the next ten weeks, and usually that's pretty much the only follow-up."

Dr. St. Clair wanted to change that. His goal was to find a way to empower pet owners and make them feel as if he was there throughout their animal's recovery process. After opening his TopDog Animal Health & Rehabilitation facility (http://topdoghealth.com) in 2004, St. Clair began the process of writing and detailing every aspect of postoperative care that pet owners needed to help their dogs heal after various orthopedic surgeries. His writings eventually became educational booklets called *TopDog's Home Therapy Guides: A Step-by-Step Guide to Post-Surgical Home Therapy for Pet Owners*. St. Clair's guides take pet owners step by step from the day the dog gets home through its twelve-week recovery. The guides include detailed instructions with pictures about how to perform the different therapies at home.

Over the years, St. Clair's guides have helped fifteen thousand dog owners aid their pets recover from surgery. It's a feat he says he couldn't have accomplished without the help of today's technology.

"It has dramatically changed who I am as a vet and who I am interacting with and helping as well," he said. "Without my Infusionsoft database marketing system, I would never be able to reach and help that many people."

TopDog also has a very strong Facebook community and a regularly updated blog that draws people to the business and provides a support network of current and former clients who form the backbone of Dr. St. Clair's business.

Using database marketing, the doctor offers booklets to customers who are rehabbing their pets. He pairs those booklets with a twelve-week email series that provides them with additional tricks and tips.

PLUG IN:

Get Social with Your Teaching

Teachers: Students are already using social media apps on their mobile phones while at home or when riding the bus. Study questions posted on these sites can reach these students almost anytime and anywhere, because these days, they are always logged on, whether online or via their smartphones.

According to the US Department of Education's National Educational Technology Plan, "Technology should be leveraged to provide access to more learning resources than are available in classrooms and connections to a wider set of 'educators,' including teachers, parents, experts, and mentors outside the classroom. It also should be used to enable 24/7 and lifelong learning."

So why not leverage open educational resources? You can promote innovative and creative opportunities for all learners and at the same time accelerate the development and adoption of new open-technology-based learning tools and courses.

And why not accept that it might not be so important anymore to memorize facts and tables? With open access to unlimited resources for information, why not accept that the better thing to teach today is *how* to learn? How to think creatively to make something new based on something old? Something for the future, based on things that occurred in the past—or that are occurring right now? How to find resources? And how to use those resources effectively? Keep in mind that technology alters not only *how* we teach but also *what* we teach!

It's not as if affordable learning didn't exist before the internet. Anyone willing to sign up for a library card can attest to that. The difference is that the online library is vastly larger and more engaging than your local library, regardless of how helpful your librarian is. The virtual library also accommodates every type of learning style for people of all ages. If you have kids, you can use the internet to help them learn a new language on YouTube or learn just about any skill, from photography to woodwork. If you're an adult or a recent retiree, there has never been a better time to continue your education. Some of the country's most prestigious universities offer countless courses online—free. Newly improved mobile apps can do everything from helping your kid learn his or her multiplication tables to providing your family with a series of educational tours on your next vacation abroad. Closer to home, when it comes to managing your pocketbook, the same tools can help you learn to become a smarter buyer.

Instead of sending a more branded-looking series of emails from his business, St. Clair uses Infusionsoft's automated sales and marketing system to email customers directly from the "Desk of Dr. James," with messages that are tailored to the animal's recovery timeline. "It doesn't make a difference whether I'm truly there or not," St. Clair said. "It's important that customers have the *feeling* that I'm there. It's a sense of security."

Watch the video here!
Scan the QR code or go to http://www.wordofmouse.com/qr/6/index.htm.

Chapter Summary Points

- Technology is changing how we teach and learn. It is likely, as well, to affect *what* we teach and learn.

- Apps for education are being developed at an explosive rate. Stay on top of the latest offerings to boost your teaching and/or learning efforts in ways you never imagined.

- Learning is no longer about memorizing; it is about gaining the skills that allow us to access accurate information.

- People with an MBA aren't necessarily smarter than those without one; they just learn how to make fewer mistakes by doing more research about a given topic.

- Getting older doesn't mean you have to stop learning. The internet is the perfect tool for a lifetime of learning.

- Keep in mind that as the number of e-learning participants goes up, the number of kids heading to college may go down.

- If you're planning to travel, don't forget your apps.

Be sure to visit Marc Ostrofsky's other website:
www.GetRichClick.com.

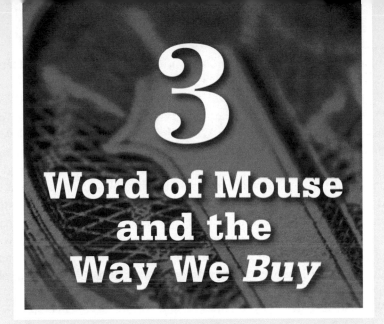

3
Word of Mouse and the Way We *Buy*

To understand how buying has evolved in recent years, allow me to introduce you to two Saturday morning shoppers perusing the television aisle of your local electronics megastore. For convenience's sake, we'll call the first shopper "Progressive Paul" and the second shopper "Laggard Larry." Both men are in the market for a new television, and, after doing some basic online research, each has a budget in mind and a list of key features that he considers important.

In this game of shopping, however, only one man will come out on top. Paul comes out of the gate strong. He's equipped with a smartphone that is chock-full of consumer information apps. Before he ever glances at a television, Paul uses his phone to check Foursquare and Facebook Places to determine if the store is offering any loyalty points or discounts.

Not finding any, he uses his smartphone to read reviews of models before scanning television bar codes to compare prices and specs. After using his phone to search for in-store deals, he finds out that the television he was leaning toward is sold out. He checks the retailer's stock online and comes up empty-handed. Having exhausted his online research, he decides to speak to a salesclerk to get a second opinion about all he's learned. For the next ten minutes, the clerk walks him through various options, prices, and alternatives and is surprised to encounter such a well-informed shopper.

By the end of the conversation, the clerk has unwittingly confirmed what Paul already suspects: he could purchase a significantly better model at a lower price from another retailer altogether. When the conversation ends, however, Paul doesn't leave the store. Whipping out his smartphone once again, he launches his RedLaser app (a multifunctional tool that lets you buy products, find prices, scan ingredients, and compare prices). He points his camera phone at the bar code on the shelf label, and then uses the phone to go online and buy the new television from a different, more competitive retailer. With the information at his disposal to make a more informed purchase, Paul gets a brand-new television at much less than his original budget. The big-box retailer, meanwhile, which provided Paul with a free television tutorial that made him a more informed consumer, strikes out.

What about Larry? Despite his half hour of online research and his vague sense of what he's looking for, his phone remains in his pocket as he strolls the store's aisles looking at new televisions. He doesn't find the forty-two-inch model that he thought was on sale, but Larry does find a handful of suitable alternatives that fulfill his original requirements. A salesclerk swoops in after he catches Larry ogling an even larger model that is a couple hundred bucks beyond his budget. Being a savvy salesman, he feeds Larry a spoonful of justifications for forking over the extra cash, polishing off the sale with an extended warranty that takes an even larger bite out of his customer's weakened wallet. For a mo-

"I guess it's been a while since you've shopped off-line.
It's not necessary to double-check my nose!"

ment, Larry considers postponing the sale to go home and compare this model with similar televisions online, but he has already invited a few friends over for an NFL football game the next day and has become quickly overwhelmed by big-screen visions. He walks out of the store blissfully ignorant, never considering the fact that a much better deal was available somewhere else.

The moral of this shopping parable is that in the current consumer climate, the educated shopper is the empowered shopper. It reminds me of those television ads for SYMS clothing stores, where, the announcer proclaimed, "an educated consumer is our best customer." This is so true! (Great tagline but the SYMS stores needed more. They filed for bankruptcy after fifty years of being in business.)

Back to our hypothetical shoppers: it's safe to say that Paul is already looking for the next great deal, while Larry's feet are planted firmly in the past (and he does not qualify as a "best customer" in anyone's book, if you go by the SYMS definition of the word).

"MARC" MY WORDS Over the past few years, we've grown accustomed to the idea of using our smartphones to access the internet while we're on the move. In the years to come, we will begin to think of our smartphones as networked sensors. Not only will our phones know where we are and where we've been, but they'll also know where we are heading, what food we need in the fridge, and where our family and friends are at any given moment.

Here are a few other smartphone offerings coming down the pike.

Coming soon to a smartphone near you, the ability to do the following:

- **Buy groceries via your phone and have them delivered.**

- **Pay a road toll and reload your toll card via your cell phone— maybe using one of several debit options coming soon.**

- **Pay for food, gas, coffee, groceries—anything—using your phone as a mobile wallet. (The Japanese have been doing this for years.) Riding the subway or buying a bottle of water will be as simple as tapping your smartphone to a sensor. The phone will trigger, store, and tally all your coupons and loyalty programs, so that you can use them later.**

- **You're watching TV, and you see your favorite Hollywood starlet wearing a hot pair of the latest gotta-have Prada sunglasses. You use your phone as a wireless mouse and click on the shades. They will be charged on your cable company bill and arrive on your doorstep forty-eight hours later.**

- **After reading an interesting article, you connect with the journalist one-on-one, to discuss the article or participate in a follow-up chat with the experts that were quoted.**

Are You Using All the Tools in Your Shopping Toolbox?

So you're aware of the useful apps out there, but are you using them—all of them—to their fullest extent? This list of questions will test what I like to call your Internet Shopping Intelligence Quotient (ISIQ).

What Is Your ISIQ?

- **Are you taking advantage of loyalty points?** Starbucks, Macy's, and other stores are using location-based networks such as Foursquare and Facebook Places to identify when potential customers are in the area. The businesses then send discounts and rewards to their smartphones, giving these potential customers an added incentive to drop in. This is smart marketing at its finest!

- **Are you using the Yelp app, as so many of us do?** If so, are you aware of its "Monocle" feature (one of many)? If not, check it out; it's amazing. Monocle uses GPS coordinates and augmented reality to tell you what is near you (restaurants, banks, gas stations, bars, drugstores, whatever). The app can show you the various eateries' "star ratings" and prices directly on your screen as you hold up your smartphone and point it north, south, east, or west! I used it recently after dinner to find the nearest ice-cream store while in Los Angeles. I simply clicked on the app, held up my iPad, and pointed in each direction. I chose the closest one, walked about two blocks, had a double dip, then walked back to the hotel. A very cool app, but I'm not sure I walked off even half of the calories I consumed!

- **Are you using your smartphone to research your purchases?** You can turn to your smartphone to compare competitors' prices on the spot or turn to an app such as ShopSavvy. This app actually lets you scan the bar codes of thousands of products to do price checks. You can even read product reviews, create wish lists, and compare prices at local brick-and-mortar stores. Now, that is savvy shopping!

- **Are you *asking* for the best price?** Use your smartphone to find the best price out there and then ask the retailer to match the lower price you found online. Some retailers actually post signs saying, "We'll match internet prices." Even those that don't might accommodate you—but only if you take the initiative to ask.

Digital Footprints—with *Your Food*

I love to eat at a variety of restaurants, especially at lunchtime. But sometimes business gets in the way, and I don't have much time to peruse a menu or ask my waitress for suggestions. No problem. With Foodspotting, an app that I've downloaded onto my smartphone, I can see food recommendations from my friends or from the Foodspotting team before I arrive at the restaurant.

These kinds of apps are examples of how we're beginning to leave digital footprints of data everywhere we go. Without our even realizing it, these footprints capture what we like, where we go, what we eat, and what we buy.

Mobile devices will continue to grow more and more like digital shopping sherpas that analyze our driving styles and show us quicker, more efficient paths to get from point A to point B. Sure, it's augmented reality, but as smartphones get smarter, they'll get better at revealing things about the world that we wouldn't have seen otherwise.

Mobile Payment Systems: The Next War for Your Wallet!

First there was bartering, and then paper and coins. Next came credit cards, and then debit cards, and now we have smartphones that will come with built-in mobile payment systems! The next big revolution in the way that money is exchanged, already well under way in other countries, involves your phone, with mobile apps such as Google Wallet, which stores on your phone virtual versions of your existing plastic cards.

"MARC" MY WORDS Mobile payment systems represent the *biggest* trend in the cell phone industry we've ever seen. I predict that this development will have the potential to change or even eliminate the entire business model of the credit card and banking industries. Matt Galligan, cofounder of SimpleGeo, a location services company, summed it up by saying, "The 'future of mobile' is the 'future of everything.' "

Google says that its new system has been designed for what it calls an "open commerce ecosystem" using near field communication, or NFC. Akin to what we know as Bluetooth technology, NFC is a wireless technology that enables data transmission between two devices when they are brought within a few inches of each other. Smartphones enabled with NFC technology can exchange data with other NFC-enabled devices—like cell phones, refrigerators, or any household appliance—or read information from smart tags embedded in posters, stickers, and other products.

And because Google Wallet is a mobile app, it will be able to do more than a regular wallet ever could, such as storing thousands of payment cards, coupons, and Google Offers (the company's local deal-finding service), "but without the bulk," as it says on the company's website. Using your smartphone as your credit card (or to accept someone else's credit card) may seem complicated right now, but it's easier than you probably realize. Many of us now download our airline boarding passes onto our smartphones. Coming soon to a smartphone near you: you will download the "key" to your hotel suite so that you can avoid the long lines and go directly to your room.

The Google website advertises that "eventually your loyalty cards, gift cards, receipts, boarding passes, tickets, and even your keys will be seamlessly synced to your Google Wallet."

Here's an example of how I use my smartphone to make a purchase almost every day. I love mocha Frappuccinos from Starbucks. So the other day, I downloaded the Starbucks app and then uploaded a $100 prepaid card onto it (this took all of twenty seconds to do). A few years ago, I might have kept a $100 prepaid card in my wallet. Not anymore. Now when I want to pay for my mocha Frappuccino, I simply open the app, and the debit code with my $100 on it pops up. Next, the digital reader at the counter subtracts the $4.95 from my debit balance, and I'm on my way. No card. No signature. Nothing. It just can't get much easier than that!

Turning Consumers into Merchants

One of the benefits of the tech revolution is that it has taken some incredibly complicated issues and made them simple. The Square is by far one of my favorite products that allow average consumers to become merchants. This simple, small adapter attaches to an iPhone, iPad, or Android and lets its owner instantly accept a credit card anytime, anywhere, from anyone. Card owners simply "sign" their names on the device's screen—using their fingernail! Funds are deposited into the owner's bank account the next day. It's cool, and it works, without all the setup fees and other fuss and muss associated with establishing yourself as a traditional credit card merchant!

Here's an example: my wife likes to buy and sell vintage costume jewelry. She recently held a sale at our home for her friends and clients. But she didn't have a way to accept credit cards. While she has taken PayPal in the past for online transactions, I told her that she could accept Visa, MasterCard, and American Express with the Square. I paid $9.95 to purchase the device at the local Apple Store, and within ten minutes, she was processing her first Amex card ever!

This technology extends a big helping hand to participants in the "maker movement": weekend warrior craftspeople such as artists, farmers, and gardeners who set up shop at local flea markets. And let's not forget garage sales! Anyone whose hobby-based revenue streams have suffered because interested buyers don't carry enough cash can now fulfill those sales. The makers can also use sites such as Etsy (www.etsy.com), one of the most established and popular venues for selling and buying handcrafted items and vintage clothes and goods.

With sales mechanisms and marketing mechanisms that are geographically ambivalent and extremely affordable, anyone has a shot at turning his or her peripheral interests and hobbies into viable businesses.

Watch the video here!
Scan the QR code or go to http://y2u.be/u7DHO_HK_OA.

"MARC" MY WORDS These examples are only a passing way of showing how our smartphones are becoming digital wallets. Soon our phones will have specific chips in them—the same chips that are embedded in "hard-to-jailbreak" smart debit cards. These chip sets will contain all of our data, including a host of debit and credit features that make our phones even *more* attached to our arms.

Will Our Wallets Go the Way of the Eight-Track Tape?

The day is fast approaching when we will no longer need to carry a wallet. Look in your wallet and find something that cannot be digitized or wouldn't be in your smartphone (other than a condom???).

Technology platforms, commerce, communication, and all types of content can and will be streamlined into a single mobile device. Then, what if that device could deliver highly personalized content, specific enough to tell you how many calories you've consumed that day, week, or month? Or tell you how old the milk sitting in your fridge is or if you are out of eggs? Imagine that you are at the grocery store, and you receive an automated text from a digital notification system in your kitchen saying that you are suddenly out of Oreo cookies and milk (because your teenager just polished off the bag). Those technologies are real, they work, and they are about to hit the market with a vengeance. I promise one thing: we've only just begun, and none of us can predict how many smart products will be tied to our daily lives in the not-so-distant future.

Futurecasting

More than a decade into the new millennium, consumers find themselves adapting to strangely divergent forces. On the one hand, years of economic uncertainty have forced Americans to do more with less. Going to thrift stores, shopping for used items on eBay, and buying in bulk at—gulp!—Costco is now stigma-free for many Americans who would have shunned the idea of bargain hunting just a few short years ago. And while many people can afford to throw down a few hundred bucks for a plasma screen TV at the local department store, they're reluctant to do so as long as they have to worry about being laid off the next day.

At the same time, advances in mobile technology and online shopping have made it easier than ever to spend your money. No need to load up the kids in your minivan and spend three hours at the local mall. Whether you want to buy groceries or that new iPod, these days, you don't have to get off your couch to do it. Fortunately, in our current economic climate, it's never been easier to spend your money intelligently.

According to a recent study released by Arc Worldwide (the marketing services arm of Leo Burnett, specializing in digital communications, direct and database marketing, promotions, and shopper marketing), 50 percent of Americans use a mobile device to navigate their fast-paced, sporadic shopping journey. Whether it's comparing prices of TVs, ordering a morning latte before you arrive at the local coffee shop, or reading restaurant reviews, mobile shopping has become a way of life for Americans.

> Companies who want to stay on the newly unfolding shopping map are facing the reality that they will either need to present valuable mobile destinations or risk falling off the map forever.

In the study, William Rosen, then president and chief creative officer of Arc, talks about how mobile shopping has created "multiple paths to purchase." The result is nothing short of a complete transformation in how people inform themselves and subsequently buy an array of products and services.

And yet retailers have only just begun to tap into revenue from mobile sales. At the time of this writing, eBay was on track to generate almost $4 billion in mobile sales. But at this point, experts say that many major retailers have yet to develop advanced sites that cater to mobile phones or apps that can be downloaded on smartphones. The Acquity Group—a strategy, design, and technology consulting firm—released a study reporting that only 12 percent of the top five hundred US online retailers had websites compatible with mobile browsers, while just 7 percent had apps.

The growth of mobile shopping is coinciding with a trend in which more people are becoming discerning shoppers. Entire websites are devoted to the art, science, and economics of label reading. And I'm not just talking about ingredients. Some sites offer a form where you enter the inventory composing your lifestyle, and, in return, you get a world map representing the likelihood that the products you use were made using slave labor. The purpose of the site is not to boycott manufacturers but rather to generate a base of consumer knowledge that leads to grassroots campaigns against these production environments.

As consumers grow more informed, companies will have to become increasingly transparent about their practices and products, but especially their prices.

As consumers grow more informed, companies will have to become increasingly transparent about their practices and products, but especially their prices. Why pay more money if a company can't tell you how it justifies a higher price? In this economy, you can bet its competition will. Whether a product is used or new, the consumers are able to access prices, product reviews, inventory, and bargains from multiple streams of information. And they are able to do all of it on the fly, giving themselves more access to real-time information that will enhance their knowledge and inform their decision making.

Today's retailers must learn to play the game with a whole new set of rules that are being written by the customers daily—if not hourly via Twitter! People don't look at shopping the same way they did before the recent recession hit. And for retailers to grab the brass ring of customer loyalty, it is imperative that they understand their newly defined roles, so that they can meet—or exceed—customer expectations.

Five Tech-Savvy Tips for the Word of Mouse Consumer

1. Wanting something *now* is no reason to buy something that's not well priced. Convenience has its value, but a purchase driven by impatience is never a good thing.

2. Go for the price match. Sometimes store managers will honor a competitor's price, so don't hesitate to point out that your app is showcasing a better price at another store. You just might save yourself a trip—as well as the money you would spend on gas driving to the better deal.

3. Why learn the hard way? Be informed and avoid buyer's remorse. The internet is chock-full of reviews and user ratings. Use them to your advantage.

4. When you decide to buy that new handbag, use the map feature on your smartphone to find a nearby ATM that doesn't charge you $2 to get access to your own cash.

5. Now that you're ready to make the long drive home, fill up on gas using GasBuddy.com, an app that shows you where the cheapest gas prices are in your neck of the woods.

PLUG IN:

Download the App Before You Pull Out Your Wallet

Before making a significant purchase from a big-box store, you should download the store's app, if it has one. These retail apps can give you access to the store's online prices, which many retailers will match or beat if you're lucky. For an example, try Home Depot's app, which offers a product search that features a list of video tutorials and a novel tape-measure function.

By the way, wouldn't it be great if big-box stores placed a QR code on any product that must be put together, showing you via video how to set the darn thing up? For instance, that massive TV storage unit from Ikea.

In our highly competitive digital business environment, where new clients come to you in so many different ways, success goes to the business that knows these three values for a new client:
- Short-Term Value (1–12 months)
- Long-Term Value (12–36 months)
- Lifetime Value

"Recommerce": Trading Versus Buying

Resale is no longer limited to thrift shops and used cars. These days, it's not only acceptable but also absolutely chic to show off one's swapping smarts. In fact, there are entire TV shows devoted to the subject that show how folks "trade up" from a microwave oven to a used car! The motivation is multifold. Obviously, we all seek out the things we want. Or perhaps we can't afford something we want at retail prices, or we receive a gift that doesn't suit our fancy. Second, an increasingly pervasive eco-oriented (or green) conscience has warmed consumers to the idea of "recycling" unwanted goods. These two organic drivers initiated an interest in what we'll call recommerce, and the idea proceeded to work its way into general buying habits. The result is that now consumers welcome the bragging rights that come along with trading in and trading up. Today we are all empowered with a host of technologies, websites, and apps that make selling or trading your unwanted goods as easy as posting them on eBay. Using these sites' apps, we can stay on top of auction-site bids, communicate with buyers, and be apprised of shipping details the moment that such data are entered.

The website Trendwatching.com identifies these same trends and describes them as follows:

- **Nextism:** Consumers craving new and exciting experiences promised by the "next."

- **Statusphere:** The growing status boost that comes from being savvy and shopping (environmentally) responsibly.

- **Excusumption:** Cash-strapped, recession-stricken consumers embracing creative solutions to spend less and still enjoy as many experiences and purchases as possible.

Trendwatching.com offers examples of this recommerce trend:

• **Decathlon, the French sports apparel and equipment store, launched Trocathlon for a week in October 2011. Stores bought back any used equipment in return for coupons valid for six months.**

• **US outdoor-gear brand Patagonia's Common Threads Initiative partnered with eBay in September 2011 to launch an official marketplace where customers could buy and sell used goods.**

• **Levi's Singapore offered customers $100 (in Singapore dollars, which is around $80 in US currency) when they brought in their old jeans and bought a new pair: a $50 discount and an additional $50 in vouchers.**

• **US-based MyCabbage allows users to resell and buy past Groupon, LivingSocial, and other daily deals.**

• **The Amazon Student membership program lets students scan the bar codes of books, DVDs, games, and electronics they own, and see the trade-in price. If a trade-in is accepted, a shipping label is generated and the funds are awarded as an Amazon gift card.**

• **StubHub, the secondary ticket marketplace, added mobile ticket functionality to its app in August 2011, meaning that users can resell and buy tickets right at the event, even without access to a printer.**

Smart retailers don't miss a beat! Competition demands that they squeeze every dollar out of their clients. Some are making money on the buy, the sell, or the exchange. Case in point:

I bought a laptop for my daughter. Two days later (maybe a coincidence), I received an email asking if I wanted to recycle my old PC or Mac in exchange for a prepaid card good for other Apple products. The email came complete with a downloadable prepaid Fed Ex bar code that I can attach to the old, unwanted computer, allowing me to ship it free.

Did You Know?

The Houston Rockets basketball team doesn't print "physical" tickets any longer, having migrated to a new system called Flash Seats (flashseats.com). Unless you request a physical ticket, all buying, selling, and trading of Rockets tickets are done on this website. The ticket owner simply scans his or her driver's license or credit card that was used to purchase the ticket in order to gain access to the arena at game time. This system makes it really hard to give my virtual tickets to employees and friends, and that is a big drawback of the new tech-driven system. Easier in some ways, harder in others.

CASE STUDY
Getting the Cheapest Phone Plan

Komparify, an Indian website, provides its visitors with an online tool that lets them view the best available mobile data plan from across the range of networks available in the country. The site also allows users to download an application that, based on personal data and call usage, computes the best available mobile plan for them.

The Reason

Currently, the entire market is flooded with a plethora of mobile operators providing extremely competitive rates on data usage and calls. Often there are various schemes and plans that eventually end up leaving the user utterly perplexed and unable to decide which plan suits him or her the best. Also, more often than not, some mobile plans are deceptive in that, at the end of the month, users are presented with extremely steep bills for usage of which they aren't even aware. The actual costs were "in the fine print." All over the world, 3G mobile plans have been an expensive affair so far, so users feel a tremendous peace of mind in knowing they've selected the cheapest mobile plan available to them.

The Plan

The Komparify team created an online tool using an algorithm that computes data on a real-time basis and aggregates them. After assimilating the data, it adds up the various schemes, add-ons, and plans (that are not part of the core plan but are simple "packs" intended to make your plan cheaper). Number crunching of all the available data is done, and the user is presented with the best possible plan. Consumers wanting plans from a particular network operator simply uncheck the other operators. Those wanting more data usage can type the same at the input screen. The whole thing is completely user customizable.

The mobile application works in a similar fashion. Based on your calls, texts, and data usage, the app communicates with the remote server and recommends a better plan for you.

The Result

The main benefit of the website and the application is streamlining. Getting all the data into a single format, assimilating them, and providing them to the user makes things extremely easy from the user's point of view. Also, having a built-in application on your mobile phone eliminates the need to check your current usage cycle on the internet, as all your data get computed on the phone itself.

The Implications

That being said, the app does have some negative implications at this point. Some mobile operating systems aren't known for their security and privacy features, and there are lots of applications out there that have the potential to get ahold of your personal data. This particular app requires core access to the phone, and that, in essence, can be its biggest drawback. Also, as of this writing, the app is not available for all the mobile operating systems. For example, iOS doesn't invite third-party application access, so the app definitely won't work there. Third, the app communicates constantly with a remote server, something that a lot of users might find unsettling.

There is room for improvement with this concept, but I applaud any initiative such as this that attempts to simplify complex buying decisions. Big points for giving consumers something they really need and want.

Internet Payments . . . as Security Gets Better, Growth Will Skyrocket

According to Forrester Research, a global research and advisory firm based in Cambridge, Massachusetts, almost 30 percent of American consumers who browse online do not purchase on the web. Safety concerns such as entering credit card information present the main obstacle, along with personal information issues.

Another study, by Javelin Strategy and Research, revealed trends related to consumers' fears of online shopping and identity theft. Here are some highlights:

- **Of those surveyed, 39 percent believed that online stores will sell their information.**
- **50 percent believed that they will receive junk mail and spam if they shop online.**
- **12 percent of fraud victims reported that they no longer shop online at all.**
- **25 percent said that the frequency of their online purchases has decreased.**

"MARC" MY WORDS As security gets better and online theft issues diminish, online buying will skyrocket. As things stand, it is no wonder why cart-abandonment rates are still high nowadays, with more than half of all visitors leaving the order process and never coming back. While we wait for these security enhancements to evolve, Multichannel Merchant (a company that covers all aspects of marketing, management, and operations for companies using catalogs and direct and digital/e-commerce channels) suggests steps that merchants can take to ease shoppers' concerns and encourage online shopping:

- assurance that information is secure (83 percent)
- offering zero liability against identity theft (81 percent)
- stronger security at the store website (80 percent)
- a guarantee that the purchase will match the quality expectations of consumers (80 percent)
- a guarantee for the best price online (79 percent)

WU Pay (formerly eBillme), a Western Union company that lets you shop online and pay with cash, claims to be the safest way to buy on the internet. Members will never be asked to enter their Social Security numbers, bank accounts, credit cards, or birthday details. Instead, WU Pay enables secure transactions through each individual bank's website.

Since most, if not all, online banks have full protection against hacking and phishing attacks (phishing is trying to get financial or other confidential information from internet users, typically by sending an email that looks as if it's from a legitimate organization, but ends up linking to a fake website that replicates the real one), customers transact securely and safely through WU Pay's gateway, directly at their own bank, whether they are shopping online or paying their bills.

PayPal offers a secure payment system, but it stores customers' information on the PayPal server, increasing its vulnerability to hackers. WU Pay, on the other hand, says that it is set up so that only the consumer and his or her bank have access to private financial details.

E-commerce retail shops and companies might consider WU Pay a merchant account alternative worth considering and a strong mechanism for attracting the population lacking credit and/or debit cards. Around fifty million adults in the United States still do not own credit cards (as stated by Card-Web, a leading publisher of information pertaining to the payments industry, including, but not limited to, credit cards), but they are probably bank account holders. For businesses, this is a notable segment worth tapping into.

With rising processing fees and security concerns and/or fraud rates, online retailers and web sellers of any kind overlook consumer worries and industry facts at their own risk. A study by CyberSource on more than one hundred leading online retailers found that offering three payment options converted 11 percent more browsers into buyers than a single payment option.

And there is a logical reason behind these stats. Let's pretend that 30 percent of our consumers are not cardholders. They are going to leave a credit-card-based online store and never come back. If we offer them an alternative payment option, one they can trust, 30 percent will buy, increasing online revenues dramatically.

Twenty Best Mobile Shopping Apps for Your Phone*

Finding the best deals is a breeze with mobile shopping apps. They allow you to compare prices, research reviews, and activate coupons without ever leaving your house. Out of the thousands of great apps out there, here are the top twenty recommended by Wise Bread (wisebread.com), an informational website:

1. **ShopSavvy.** The most accurate shopping comparison app, ShopSavvy scans bar codes to find the lowest prices from thousands of retailers (available for iPhone, Android).

2. **Amazon Mobile.** Check the latest prices and read customer reviews of over a million products featured on Amazon.com (iPhone, Android).

3. **Coupon Sherpa.** Coupon Sherpa finds the latest available coupons for in-store deals. Cashiers can scan coupons directly from your phone (iPhone).

4. **Google Shopper.** Google Shopper uses bar codes to help you find local and online deals. You can even take a photo of items or type in the name of a product to find deals (iPhone, Android).

5. **Shopkick.** The Shopkicks reward program lets you earn points for scanning bar codes of featured products with your phone and for opening the app at the entrance of a store. Redeem your rewards for gift cards, restaurant vouchers, and Facebook credits (iPhone, Android).

6. **TheFind.** Set up price alerts for your coveted items with TheFind. This app shows you the lowest price available and lets you set target prices, so that you get alerted when the price drops (iPhone, Android).

7. **RedLaser.** The RedLaser shopping app compares online and offline prices of products at thousands of retailers and tells you your distance to the nearest store (iPhone, Android).

8. **Goodzer.** When you're buying electronics and don't want to buy online, use the Goodzer app to find store listings and

* Source: Print, Lynn Truong, editor of Wise Bread's personal finance apps store (apps.wisebread.com); online, Lynn Truong, editor of Wise Bread's personal finance apps store and best daily deals newsletter.

the best available price on that product in your neighborhood (iPhone).

9. **eBay.** Use the eBay app to find the best auction prices on items. You can also use the bar code scanner to find what you need (iPhone).

10. **Consumer Annual Reports Mobile Shopper.** While this isn't a free app, it can give you access to trusted *Consumer Reports* ratings and product information, including prices (iPhone, Android).

11. **Coupons App.** This app provides real-time coupons and daily deals available in your neighborhood. It also tells you where you can find the cheapest gas in town (Android).

12. **Yowza!!** The Yowza!! Shopping app tracks down local coupons and deals. The cashier can scan bar codes right from your phone (iPhone, iPad, iPod Touch).

13. **WHERE.** This app gives users access to exclusive deals at their favorite stores. It is set up as a recommendation engine on which users can share insights about their favorite places (iPhone, Android).

14. **Groupon.** The official Groupon app helps you keep track of the deals in your town. It also includes Groupon Now! listings in real time (Android).

15. **LivingSocial.** The LivingSocial app helps you monitor the day's deals with location-based information (Android).

16. **Slifter.** Slifter provides information about local deals and online/offline promotions for more than one billion products. Users can create lists to follow items on their wish list (iPhone).

17. **SavingStar Grocery E-coupons.** This app links to your grocery store loyalty cards and keeps track of items you buy regularly. It offers paperless e-coupons that are redeemable at more than twenty-four million grocery stores (Android).

18. **Weekly Ads & Sales.** Use the Weekly Ads & Sales app to get information about sale items at your favorite stores. Browse ads for Walgreens, CVS, Safeway, and other stores with a quick city search (Android).

19. GoodGuide. This app lets you learn about your favorite brands so that you can make more eco-friendly decisions. Simply scan a bar code to get health, environment, and social ratings for products (iPhone).

20. FastMall. Use the FastMall app to locate the best deals at different stores in your local mall. It also has a "Where Did I Park?" feature (iPhone).

TIPS FOR USING MOBILE SHOPPING APPS

While shopping apps are great for comparison shopping and securing good deals, you still have to make smart decisions about your purchases. Here are some important things to remember when using any of these apps:

- **Resist paying extra at the store when you can buy the same item cheaper online. Don't let the lure of instant gratification stop you from saving money.**
- **Ask for a price match. Many stores offer price-match guarantees when you show them a lower advertised price.**
- **Don't forget to do research before you buy. Take the time to look at ratings and reviews of different items so that you know what to expect, especially when buying electronics.**

Consumers as Manufacturers: The Maker Movement

I've been talking in this chapter about how technological advances are turning consumers into merchants. In the case of the software company Autodesk, new technology is turning consumers into manufacturers—and designers, too.

Although Autodesk has long been a leader in 3-D design for engineering and entertainment software, now the company is giving away Autodesk 123D, free 3-D modeling consumer software that lets anyone design and manufacture three-dimensional objects such as statues and models.

This dramatic offering is right in step with the groundbreaking maker movement of people who love to "create, build, design, tinker, modify, hack, invent, or simply make something." That's how *Forbes* magazine contributor T. J. McCue describes the people who fall into the maker movement category. In fact, McCue is so inspired by this movement that he started writing a blog targeted to the concept. In *The Makers,* McCue says that he is "motivated and moved by the idea—the belief—that the people who invent and build and make things have the power to change the world. People who 'remix' something or 'hack a better way' are destined to make big differences in the buying and selling landscape of society." It is McCue's belief that the makers of the world, along with small businesses and start-ups, are, in fact, the answer to the world's struggling economy. I would recommend talking with an intellectual property lawyer if you plan to use your new remix in any way other than for yourself.

And so, users of Autodesk's 3-D design software are joining the ranks of tinkerers and hackers who are buying ready-made products and either tweaking them, customizing them, or even reengineering them to do something they were not originally designed to do. I read a *New York Times* interview with Carl Bass, chief executive of Autodesk. He, too, has a big vision on this topic and said, "We are entering a period where the entire act of making things, seeing how they are used and what the manufacturing process is, will change."

Through its apps for the iPhone, iPad, iPod, and Android, the company is making design technology accessible to professional as well as amateur designers, home owners, students, and casual creators. Whether it's a kid looking to build a new contraption, a seasoned pro sketching out a great new idea, or someone who just wants to amp up his or her creative output, Autodesk is taking technology originally built for engineers, movie studios, automakers, and architectural firms, and making it available to anyone who wants to create and share ideas with the world.

In the name of crowdsourced science, even hermit crabs are enjoying the benefits of the 3-D printers and the maker movement. Project Shellter invites MakerBot, a global leader in desktop 3D printing, operators, and digital designers to create 3-D printed shells for hermit crabs that have, apparently, been suffering something of a housing shortage. (You can't make this stuff up!) It's true. A global shell shortage has driven hermit crabs around the world to take up residence in everything from bottles to shotgun shells. Needless to say, the possibilities are endless.

Instead of buying an expensive model, today's hands-on consumers can now buy the technology that allows them to create that model themselves. Sketch-Book Mobile, a full-featured mobile-device drawing program that sells for 99 cents, has attracted seven million downloads to mobile devices in recent years, according to an article in the *New York Times*. Comparable industrial design software would run you about $4,000. The idea that you could design a model of something by photographing it from multiple angles with a smartphone was unthinkable just a few short years ago. What does it all mean? New technology is allowing consumers to grab the reins of design and production, turning the economics of the business upside down.

Virtual Grocery Shopping

Cynics say that smartphones are a source of daily distraction in our already frantic lives. But when it comes to helping us get our hands on essential products, innovative companies are finding ways to radically change the way we buy. For example, Home Plus, a South Korean supermarket chain, has developed a virtual grocery store that allows commuters to restock their kitchens—while they're waiting in the subway!

Home Plus filled subway stations with photographic images of groceries. Each item is accompanied by a quick-response code that encodes data, the product, and its price. The customer scans the code, and the product is automatically entered to a shopping cart. When the customer is ready to check out, she does so using her phone. The grocery orders are automatically routed to the store, which fills the orders and delivers them. Voilà! Groceries await customers on their doorsteps when they arrive home at the end of the day! Home Plus reported a 130 percent increase in online sales since the introduction of the virtual shopping system, and with more than ten thousand customers, it has been a huge hit.

Dr. Abel Sanchez, research lead at MIT's Intelligent Engineering Systems Laboratory, told *Technology Review* magazine, "For sure, your cell phone will be the graphical user interface to the shopping services. Think of the early days of the web versus today. In the early 1990s, the web was one way, like a paper book. Today the web is full of interaction; it's how we do our jobs. I think the supermarket will go through a similar transformation." Home Plus continues to launch this service in markets around the globe, on top of its online grocery stores and an app that lets customers choose the grocery items they want on their smartphones, and then pick up the orders at their convenience.

We've never been subject to more savvy marketing, the kind that inundates you every time you turn on your television, browse the internet, or step inside a Best Buy. So perhaps it's only fair that we've also never had access to so much smart technology, the kind that allows buyers to scan a QR code, compare prices, read customer reviews, ask more intelligent questions, and get the best bargain possible. For those willing to take the wheel, the era of the empowered buyer is in full throttle! And depending on where you're shopping, you might be able to conduct the entire transaction with a mobile payment system such as Google Wallet, which is poised to replace plastic altogether. But in the online era, you could also forgo money by logging onto an auction site that allows you to trade or sell goods using your smartphone. Today's shoppers are not only smart buyers but are also sellers.

INFUSIONSOFT VIDEO SERIES CASE STUDY
Model Train Hobbyist Uses YouTube and Database Marketing to Turn His Passion into a Thriving Business

Scott Griggs started selling model trains out of his parents' garage in 1975. More than three decades later, his business has grown into a company that employs twenty-five people and contains several warehouses full of model trains that he buys and sells all over the globe. Griggs attributes much of his recent success to the internet. After selling model trains on eBay early on, he started Trainz.com (www.trainz.com), a one-stop shop for new and used model trains, as well as parts and resources for hobbyists. He buys most of his products from collectors who have basements full of model trains, but he also buys from new manufacturers and defunct hobby stores.

The company also has tens of thousands of new items that are either in stock at its warehouse or available for purchase through affiliates. Trainz.com is unlike many online businesses, in that Griggs actually has inventory at his Buford, Georgia, headquarters. With that said, he also runs a slick online operation that relies on automated marketing software to keep his business lively and organized. In fact, Griggs noted, approximately 50 percent of his business is done online these days.

As Griggs taps into an industry that is estimated to bring in more than $1 billion annually, one of his biggest challenges is to continually grow his database, which he calls the "heart and soul" of his company. To do this, he must produce niche content that draws model train enthusiasts and other prospective buyers to his company's website. "We use some social media, and we upload a lot of videos on YouTube," he explained. "In fact, right now we have the most watched model train set video on YouTube, with more than two million views."

But the primary way that Griggs adds to his database is by producing a guide for selling model trains that can be downloaded on Trainz.com. According to Scott, once someone downloads the report after the required submission of an email address, it's a safe bet that this person wants to buy or sell a model train.

At that point, he noted, his Infusionsoft automated marketing systems take over, sending an email encouraging the site visitor to send Trainz.com an inventory list, which allows experts at the company to make the individual an offer. If the visitor doesn't take the offer right away, the system sends a series of emails designed to gauge his or her interest in selling. Eventually the visitor either sells the model trains or unsubscribes from the list. And Griggs told me that it seems to be working.

Watch the video here!
Scan QR code or go to http://www.wordofmouse.com/qr/18/index.htm.

Chapter Summary Points

- The educated buyer is the empowered buyer. Technology provides us with more opportunity than ever before to make smart purchases.

- The next big revolution in the way that money is exchanged will involve your phone, with mobile apps such as Google Wallet. Mobile payment systems are the future.

- Technology that changes the way we make purchases allows consumers to become merchants.

- Consult apps, customer reviews, and price comparisons to make sure you get the best deal possible.

- The maker movement, facilitated by consumer 3-D printers, will change the face of the economy.

- Trading is the new buying. Yes, the barter system is the earliest form of consumerism. But whereas money has dominated for so long as the preferred means of transactions, a heightened interest in saving money and/or going green has breathed new life into the old method of exchanging goods, and now trading for products brings a certain social cachet or buying status to the whole transaction. And consumers are using the internet and mobile devices to secure these very exchanges.

- Use a product like the Square to turn your smartphone into a cash register that accepts credit cards.

- Get ready to buy your groceries using your phone, just like the South Koreans.

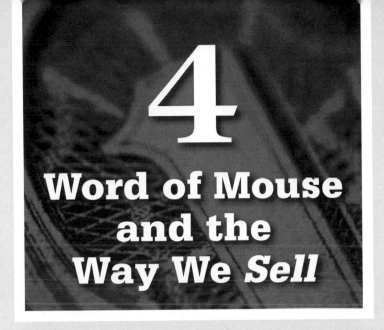

4

Word of Mouse and the Way We *Sell*

In the past, commerce was a one-way street. Sellers made the rules, and buyers followed them. A buyer who objected to those rules could take his or her business elsewhere, but more often than not, options were limited.

In the era of Google, Twitter, Yelp, and Facebook, this is no longer the case. Suddenly, choice is plentiful (if not altogether overwhelming), prices are negotiable, and the competition is fierce. Clearly, the balance of power has shifted toward the consumers, who are now armed with more information than ever before in the history of business, about the products, wholesale pricing models, competition, and even the manufacturing process. These days, consumers often expect transactions to be more like conversations—and with special pricing, too—all to make them feel unique. Long gone are the days when a seller alone set the terms of the commercial interaction.

Today buyers and sellers are empowered with something I will call "e-formation." Consider it the intelligence we get from the web. As a seller, I have more e-formation about the competition: who has stock, what's the wholesale price of a given product, and how cheaply I can get supplies. I also have more e-formation about who's buying my product, who's a likely candidate to buy it, and how much I should pay—on a per client basis—for a specific "click" or "lead" that could turn into a sale. I also have twenty different ways to attract a client to my site, as opposed to waiting for someone to walk into my store in the mall. It would not be a fair fight if one compared the two models: the online player would win hands down at almost every level.

> These days, consumers often expect transactions to be more like conversations— and with special pricing, too—all to make them feel unique. Long gone are the days when a seller alone set the terms of the commercial interaction.

In the old world, I had the store, I had inventory, I had a warehouse, I had employees, I had overhead, and then I had to advertise and pray for customers to come in the door. Now I don't need any of it! If I'm a seller, I don't need the overhead, I don't need the physical store, I don't need the manufacturing—in fact, I don't even need to own the product! Online, I can sell products owned and warehoused by others! This is all possible because of e-formation.

The only way to prosper in this ruthless marketplace is to adapt. Sellers need to rely on creativity and craft, offering high-quality products in an innovative fashion (or somebody else will). And they will do all of it on the fly, knowing full well that today's marketing strategy is tomorrow's old news. Much of it will be happening on smartphones that act as networked sensors, informing us about the world around us, no matter where we go. In fact, analysts believe that over the next few years, most online searches will migrate from desktop devices to mobile ones. Companies that are prepared to take advantage of this shift will be able to capture new customers and bolster their long-term prospects.

"MARC" MY WORDS Whether you're a buyer or a seller, the future of "staying close to the client" is via mobile! In some ways, none of this is new. The marketplace has always mirrored the natural world, with the better-adapted businesses thriving, while their less-equipped competition dies off. The difference, however, comes down to the speed at which all this is happening.

In the years to come, the speed of technological innovation will accelerate alongside the increasing intelligence of the consumer. This is what happens when people can access expert information on a networked smartphone or tablet whenever they want. If sellers hope to continue providing their customers with solutions, selling must evolve in lockstep with buying. And right now, buyers—peering out over a marketplace where they always have access to the best and brightest—are holding the reins.

"In hindsight, I'd say my first mistake was letting my competitors advertise on my website."

Renting Is the New Selling

In today's economy, it's the innovative seller who will come out ahead. Now, more than ever, finding "white space" in new market opportunities is what separates the winners from the losers. One way that marketers are getting creative is by opting to "rent," rather than outright sell, their products. This trend is taking off, with some industries paving previously nonexistent roads in this new territory.

APPAREL AND ACCESSORIES

A few years ago, I took my daughter Tracy to the Grammy Awards. While at the party the night before, she befriended singer and actress Jennifer Hudson. The next day, Jennifer walked Tracy into the awards ceremony. So it goes without saying that we are big Jennifer Hudson fans. And, as such, we watched the first *Sex and the City* movie, in which Jennifer plays the role of Carrie Bradshaw's assistant, Louise. In one scene, Carrie admires Louise's purse and asks her where she bought this highly sought-after designer bag—and, more important, how she could afford the high price. That's when Hudson's character plugs the company name Bag Borrow or Steal, which has since become the Netflix of purses. It was a big moment for the online store, which allows women to rent designer handbags and accessories by the week, month, or season, giving their closets a celebrity upgrade. When the customer has gotten her use from an item, she simply mails it back (shipping is free) and picks a new one. Customers keep the rentals, from Tiffany jewelry to Chanel handbags, as long as they want.

Launched by a former accessories editor at *Vanity Fair* magazine, Bag Borrow or Steal is one of the first businesses to harness the power of online renting. The business model is so smart and so simple! The flexibility of renting is made for the massive scale provided by the web. It also ties into larger trends of sharing everything online; not just downloadable entertainment like digital music and movies but also tangible goods.

One of the company's first advisers, Robert Burke, is the founder and principal of a leading New York City luxury products consulting firm, Robert Burke Associates.

Watch the video here!
Scan the QR code or go to http://y2u.be/rovPexkhFJA.

I recently watched a YouTube video of Burke speaking at a Columbia Business School conference about the Bag Borrow or Steal success story.

"When you think about vacation homes, there are a lot of people who go to places like St. Bart's who are never going to buy a home there, but certainly rent them and enjoy them," said Burke. "They want the experience without all the headaches of ownership."

Burke noted that more than three-quarters of the BMWs you see on the road these days are leased, introducing the luxury brand to customers who would not buy the vehicles. Early on, about 70 percent of Bag Borrow or Steal's business was in opening-price goods, meaning items $500 and under, Burke said. Now the majority of its business lies in renting handbags costing $1,500 and over.

"This business has seen increases, certainly with the current economic climate, in ways that they've never anticipated," Burke observed.

In this technology-driven era of selling, businesses that are flexible and creative have the best chance of excelling. Among the more innovative business models springing up are those that allow customers to rent items that we used to buy online. That's why I say, "Renting is the new selling."

RENTING A CAR— FOR TWENTY MINUTES?

Another one of my favorite businesses tapping into the rental trend is Getaround, a company that enables car owners to rent their vehicles to friends, coworkers, and neighbors, offsetting the expense of vehicle ownership through sharing. The cost is as low as $3 an hour. For not very much money, you can rent a nearby car by the hour, day, or week. The savings add up to hundreds or even thousands of dollars on auto payments, insurance, maintenance, and so forth. The car is outfitted with the Getaround Carkit, which combines GPS, Wi-Fi, and keyless remote technology to allow safe and simple car sharing, and is the first device designed exclusively for peer-to-peer car sharing. Coupled with an iPhone app, the Carkit makes it possible for users to easily conduct entire transactions, including reserving, paying for, and unlocking cars, using nothing but their iPhone! Getaround's peer-to-peer car rental marketplace can provide meaningful financial benefits to both owners and renters. Owners can pocket thousands of dollars each year for lending out their vehicles. Meanwhile, according to the research firm Frost & Sullivan, the average renter saves over $1,800 per year by using a car-sharing service over owning a car for the same number of miles driven.

The average renter saves over $1,800 per year by using a car-sharing service over owning a car for the same number of miles driven.

"There are over two hundred fifty million personal vehicles in the United States, and they sit idle an average of twenty-two hours each day," said Getaround founder and CEO Sam Zaid. "Getaround frees people from the burden of car ownership by turning an idle, costly, and underutilized asset into something that can generate revenue, and our Getaround Carkit and smartphone technology make car sharing safe and accessible to everyone."

Unlike services that require owners to surrender their cars to the fleet, Getaround lets car owners maintain complete control over their cars. Owners set the pricing and availability, and can optionally approve each rental request individually. Meanwhile, renters are given a broad selection of vehicles and pricing, and the ability to rent nearby cars instantly. In addition to the keyless remote technology, the Getaround Carkit ensures proper use of the vehicle through its tracking and reporting features. To further enhance the safety of its service, Getaround is also working with one of the nation's largest insurance groups to provide premium insurance coverage throughout every Getaround rental.

Here are two other businesses that are finding new ways to use renting to their advantage:

● Rent an expert! Want a professional chess player to teach you strategy? Curious about what a Nobel laureate thinks about US trade policy with China? Expert Insight, a company started by Brandon Adams, a PhD graduate of Harvard Business School, provides individuals and businesses with the chance to rent an expert. Whether you're seeking financial advice, sports coaching, or just plain counseling, you can find a variety of experts on the Expert Insight website who are ready to chat with you over the phone or through video chat, usually for a per-hour fee. Imagine a small business hiring a famed economist to gain an edge over a competitor. Or a young chess enthusiast who doesn't have time to attend an expensive camp forking over a few hundred dollars to hear from a master directly.

Considering how much we already pay for expertise—often while crowded into large lecture halls (think college)—hiring a one-on-one authority who is tailored to your needs is hardly a far-fetched idea.

> **True story:** I needed to know the answer to a trademark question recently, and I logged on to the Expert Insight website. Instead of hiring a lawyer who would have charged me an inflated hourly rate and required all sorts of paperwork, I found a lawyer through Expert Insight. I read his background, and it looked as if he fitted the bill. I submitted my question and was charged $60 on my credit card at ten thirty at night. Within fifteen minutes, my temporary lawyer had given me the answer I needed. We went back and forth with two other follow-up questions conducted over email, and he charged my card another $40 by the time we were done. In the end, I saved hundreds—if not thousands—of dollars and got my answers *incredibly fast.*

● You need a designer gown for a wedding or a onetime event, but you don't want to spend a bundle knowing you'll probably never wear it again. Rent the Runway is a web service that lets consumers rent designer gowns for only 10 percent of what it would cost to buy the gown. One of the strengths of this business is that it creates a win-win situation for everyone involved. Customers get to look good. Designers, meanwhile, get an opportunity to market their designs, building a brand following along the way. In the end, the gowns are available for sale at a discounted price. The site is full of useful options that customize the shopping experience the same way that a brick-and-mortar clothes shop might. You can enter your measurements, body type, size, color preferences, designer preferences, and budget preferences. The site even recommends outfits geared to your body type and style, and suggests accessories that complement each ensemble. From a woman's perspective, it's exciting stuff. From a seller's perspective, it's smart marketing and distribution.

The internet fosters P2P, or peer-to-peer, renting! Here's a list of other things that you can find for rent these days just by using your favorite search engine:

- Dogs
- Smartphones
- Bicycles
- Fitness equipment
- Party supplies
- Textbooks
- Camping gear
- Solar panels
- Homes
- Watches
- Tools
- Sports cars
- Celebrities (for special appearances)
- Wives
- Husbands
- Graphic designers
- Mechanics
- Caskets

I too questioned "caskets." Here's the scoop: a number of funeral service websites are facilitating requests for rented caskets. The rentable casket is specially designed as a shell suitable for public visitation that houses a simple inner container to hold the body. After the service, the funeral director removes the inner container from the outer casket shell. The inner container holding the body is then transported to the place of final disposition, while the outer casket is reused for a number of services.

It's actually *very* smart—and is eco-friendly!

Tall, Dark, and Handy

When I don't get things done around the house, my wife often says, "I need to rent a second husband." Fortunately (for both of us), I found www.rentahusband.com.

REAL ESTATE: CHECK UP ON CURB APPEAL FROM ACROSS THE WORLD

Surfing Homes on Phones

When I'm driving around my hometown, I like to check out real estate in different neighborhoods for potential property investments. In the past, this required hiring an agent or searching through listings in a local paper. These days, I can just turn on my smartphone and pull up an app called Real Estate, by Smarter Agent.

This app is truly revolutionary: it allows you to search homes for sale, recently sold homes, and even apartments for rent. Using Smarter Agent's GPS-triggered real estate search technology, it can pinpoint your location and find property listings in your immediate area with the touch of a button. You can also search by address, community name, city, or zip code. The app, which is free, is compatible with iPhone, iPod Touch, and iPad. Amazing!

REAL ESTATE APPS REVEAL THE FOLLOWING

- Price
- Square footage
- Estimated mortgage
- Taxes
- Interior and exterior features
- Interactive maps
- Number of beds/baths
- Pictures and more!

The Changing Face of Coupons

Remember how your grandmother used to bring home a fresh stack of coupons every time she went grocery shopping? Sure, they saved her money, but coupons required planning, were chock-full of confusing disclaimers, and needed to be processed at the register by another human being. All this made them altogether time consuming. And the deals weren't exactly eye-catching, either: 25 cents off a box of cereal here, 75 cents off some laundry detergent there. Apparently some folks (especially those on the TV show *Extreme Couponing*) still do this on a full-time basis.

But although paper coupons may soon become a thing of the past, discounts and deals are more popular than ever before, thanks to innovations in technology and rapidly changing consumer expectations. Today deals are sourced online and shared with friends via smartphones in real time. When you register at a number of sites, the deals *find you* and are sent to your smartphone! One of the newer technologies tells a retailer when you are in the area, if not in the store, and the appropriate electronic incentive is sent as a text to your phone!

These coupons and incentives are often personalized, creative, interesting, and, most of all, targeted to your buying habits. They engage the customer like never before. And—as many sellers already know—in the postrecession world, customers equate deals with status and sophistication. In the future, businesses that hope to survive will find increasingly novel ways to offer customers deals using technology, creativity, and maybe even transparency. Before forking over cash, the customer of the not-so-distant future will expect to know how the product is made, where it comes from, and what's used to make it—he or she may even want to see photos of the manufacturing process in action! I found that one high-end watch manufacturer posted videos on YouTube of the watches being assembled in Switzerland.

In the postrecession world, customers equate deals with status and sophistication.

Here's a list of statistics that show how much our approach to shopping has changed in recent years:

- Online coupons account for only 1 percent of all coupons distributed, but 10 percent of those that are redeemed.*

- 79 percent of smartphone owners use their phones for shopping-related activities, and of those, nearly half (48 percent) use their phones to look for or use discounts and coupons.†

- 53 percent of Chinese and 47 percent of Korean smartphone owners have used mobile coupons to purchase products in-store. Comparative figures for other countries are: United States, 22 percent; United Kingdom and Turkey, 14 percent; Spain, 13 percent; Germany, 11 percent; France, 10 percent; and Netherlands, 7 percent.‡

- 67 percent of mobile users agree that location-based coupons on a mobile device are "convenient and useful," while 42 percent say they have already used a mobile coupon of some kind.§

* Catalina.
† Google and IPSOS.
‡ Google and IPSOS.
§ Prosper Mobile Insights.

Imagine the not-so-distant future, when your phone detects what you want to buy and the appropriate coupons "pop up on the screen" when you go to the register to check out! Better yet, the phone knows what items you have on your shopping list, if not what items are already in the shopping basket, and prompts you not to buy Tide detergent this week because it will be going on sale later!

"MARC" MY WORDS The day of an advanced mobile coupon draws near. The next-generation mobile coupon will track where a customer is and what he last bought from any given store the moment he walks into that store. For any of these above scenarios, that customer will receive a specific texted coupon, created especially for him, from his favorite merchant, based completely on his purchase history and buying habits. *Very cool!*

Social Media and Word of Mouse Marketing

Social media is redefining how buyers obtain information and interact with brands. At its best, social media lets sellers direct connections between people who represent their businesses and potential customers. At its worst, social media, when done incorrectly, simply upsets clients and prospects, who end up disliking the marketed brand.

> ### In social media, just as in the real world, presence is *felt*. Prospects and clients need to feel a personal involvement with the firm, product, service, or brand.

For instance, any business can create a profile on Facebook. It's the way a business uses Facebook that provides customers with a sense of connection.

What's in it for me? That's what every buyer is thinking! Just because a seller is online doesn't mean that its presence is known or implemented correctly. In social media, just as in the real world, presence is *felt*. Prospects and clients need to feel a personal involvement with the firm, product, service, or brand.

Here's an outline of best practices to help guide companies, large and small, as they engage in social media marketing and communications:

Promoting Products Using Twitter

I recently read a short article on the site MarketingSherpa that explains how Woot, a discount online retailer, is using Twitter in an extremely innovative way by promoting *a deal a day*. The concept is simple and brilliant. Dave

Rutledge, creative director for Woot, and his team use Twitter to push sales of their deeply discounted products. Customers can buy only each day's featured product. When it's sold out, it's gone. A new product posts at midnight each day. Woot's one-deal-a-day model has attracted an impressive following of loyal shoppers. All the company needs is a way to get the word out for each day's deal. A short block of text does the trick. And Twitter is the perfect medium.

CASE STUDY
Mexican Restaurant Grows Business and Brand— Almost by Accident

We have already seen Dell computers and Zappos.com at work, strategically taking the social media scene by storm, building their tribes, and stimulating (massive) profit windfalls. Yet there are much smaller organizations, such as local food chains, that quietly start using social media to their advantage, one step at a time, and claim their online profit share. The perfect example is Chilango, a small restaurant that serves gourmet Mexican cuisine in London.

Count yourself lucky if you have had the chance to try one of its fresh, tasty burritos, but the real treat to experience is social media *à la Chilango*. Read on, and you'll understand how Chilango grew a brand and business, almost by accident. In short, what Chilango did was not only amazing, but also something that I believe any company, small or large, can do to generate Word of Mouse and get a frenzy of new customers—*without spending any money on advertising whatsoever.*

Here is how it all started. In 2010 Chilango donated a year's worth of free burrito meals as a raffle prize to support a local nonprofit organization. A young man named Richard FitzGerald won the prize and started to tweet about it. To cut the long story short, this campaign brought in a whopping 89,788 blog visits and pulled in hundreds of comments and Twitter mentions, and a lot of web coverage. Chilango probably never imagined what a single burrito prize could stir in the blogosphere. And it happened in less than a year. Without costing a penny for promotion. Here's what the winner had to say about how everything clicked and connected:

"One year ago I attended London Twestival [a gathering of people assembled via Twitter, usually in the interest of a social cause]. Almost hidden among all the people and tweeting, there were some girls selling raffle tickets to raise money for Concern Worldwide [a nonprofit focused on transforming the lives of "the poorest people in the poorest countries of the world"]. I purchased a couple of tickets and thought nothing more. The next morning I checked my Twitter account to learn that I had won a year's supply of burritos, courtesy of Chilango. It being a Twitter festival, people found out that I had won the prize pretty quickly and some began asking me for burritos. Realizing that eating all of the three hundred sixty-five meals myself would be both challenging and lonely, I decided, generously, to share the prize. The story of fifty-two burrito dates was born!" You can read about these burrito-dating experiences on 52 Burrito Dates (http://52burritodates.com) for a good "taste" of social Word of Mouse.

Back to business, though: the real success (besides the bump to Richard FitzGerald's dating schedule) showed up a year later. With a much heightened appreciation for the power of social media, the restaurant celebrated the opening of its fifth location on Cinco de Mayo by giving out free burritos. It announced the promotion with a single tweet: "We're getting set up! Free burritos all day today at Chilango Chancery Lane!" News of the giveaway spread like wildfire through social media, mostly Twitter. People appeared in droves to queue up for free burritos, forming a line that extended down Chancery Lane and around the block. Before long, street entertainment arrived to really get the party moving. And the tweeting frenzy exploded. People tweeted about the "*massive* queue" and the "insanely ridiculous street atmosphere on Chancery Lane," seeking "any update on the size of the queue outside Chilango."

Chilango has got it. In one year's time, the restaurant understood the Word of Mouse phenomenon, letting social media do the promotional legwork, then creating a "scene" at the event that would further propel the social media and make its brand live on long after the fifth of May as a place associated with good food *and* good fun.

From local shops to business-to-business (B2B) service firms, strategic marketing campaigns (or publicity stunts, as specialists call them) via social media can provide any business with more outreach, customers, and advertising than money could ever buy. And the main advantage is the long-lasting effect on the bottom line. Twitter is the right channel when used correctly. (Incorrect use of the medium includes hitting the audience over the head with multiple tweets a day that aren't relevant to them specifically.) That is why having perspective on how other companies leverage this social media phenomenon can help any company create its own game plan, revitalize (or create) its brand, and experience similar results.

Engaging the Mobile Shopper

Even people who aren't accustomed yet to making purchases using their phones will learn to adapt in the near future. Smart retailers are already implementing strategic mobile campaigns to engage the burgeoning mobile-shopper movement. Here are some examples of the mobile-sales explosion.

Four Trends in Mobile Shopping

1. Mobile phones can help you sell anything, from a latte to a new car. The shift is remarkable. People are taking their big-ticket-item purchases a lot more lightly, as they count on their mobile phones to handle the heavy lifting of hefty research. Conversely, we labor over the low-end purchases, such as where to buy a good cup of coffee, because mobile apps are being cleverly designed to engage and immerse us in a personalized shopping experience. Companies in the know are sure to develop apps that consider the broad range of shopping experiences, based on the products being offered.

2. **Shoppers shop anywhere, anytime, all the time.** Increasingly uncommon is the shopper who pencils a day on his or calendar to "do the shopping." These days, shopping is sprinkled throughout our days, filling in the whitespace moments of our lives as we wait in lines, in waiting rooms, in parking lots, wherever. Savvy marketers will jump to occupy this dotted landscape with mobile interactions that are relevant to their markets.

3. **Instant gratification is king.** Today's mobile shopper searches for a new outfit, orders takeout, and downloads the latest Lady Gaga album with just a few taps on his mobile device. To succeed in this fast-paced landscape, companies must provide value-added mobile apps and websites. To reach all types of mobile shoppers, companies should activate both mobile on-the-go and mobile in-store interactions. The expanding ways in which sellers will reach buyers via mobile in the near future are nothing short of staggering.

4. **Manufacturers and retailers unite.** More and more, we'll see these two entities working together to create a one-stop shop where mobile shoppers can collect discounts, as well as view product specifications and current inventory status. This comprehensive experience pulls shoppers through the purchase and may encourage a similar transaction in the future. William Rosen, formerly of Arc North America, has a lot to say on this topic.

"Mobile gives companies the power to market in a way that no channel ever has before by uniting the power of digital, promotion, retail, and database marketing," he says. "In addition, since people are always within arm's length of their mobile phones, sellers are reaching buyers and receive an instant response to a given deal, offer, or flash sale (a time-limited offer of high discounts)! From researching and browsing to buying and recommending, shoppers expect meaningful and useful mobile shopping experiences. The stakes are only getting higher as more and more shopping moves onto mobile."

"APPERVISING": THE NEW TREND IN SELLING

Let me say it again: mobile is everything. Whether we are listening to music on iPods, browsing the web via iPhones, playing games with friends on iPads, or reading books on an e-reader such as the Amazon Kindle, new mobile technology is changing the way that we connect with people and how we sell to consumers. If YouTube can be said to have turned the old television industry into interactive multimedia channeling, then mobile apps are sure to transform completely the way we sell and market.

We are not as dependent on the computer to access internet content as we were more than a decade ago. And, soon enough, businesses will be able to advertise their services and expand their brand awareness—all over the globe, on any mobile device—at lower costs than traditional media ever permitted.

This is the new phase of Word of Mouse advertising that I call APPvertising, a method that enables individuals and companies to reach more consumers and achieve more sales through mobile ad networks—faster, more cheaply, and with greater accuracy in targeting a prospect or client. With APPvertising, advertisers have the option to promote their offers within a phone or tablet application through banners, video ads, surveys, and so forth.

Harald Neidhardt, CMO and cofounder of Smaato (a company that helps mobile app developers and publishers make more ad revenue worldwide), talks about being "inside the tornado of the mobile industry," as he calls it in a slideshare presentation. "Mobile apps will continue to surprise the media. New smartphones and tablet PCs are enhancing our daily digital lives. With innovations like LTE [long-term evolution, a 4G wireless broadband technology developed by the Third Generation Partnership Project, an industry trade group], broadband bandwidth, NFC [near field communication] smartphones, and more relevant mobile ad formats, we will see a dramatic liftoff in global mobile advertising."

According to Smaato's *Mobile Advertising Trends* report, Asia is the leader in mobile advertising spending, followed by the United States and the United Kingdom. The group predicts that by 2013, mobile phones will overtake PCs as the most common web access device worldwide.

As of 2013, mobile phones have overtaken PCs as the most common web access device worldwide.

APPvertising is indeed the future, and with this new medium comes a new set of advertising guidelines. Businesses should consider these baseline rules for starters:

- **Avoid interrupting mobile users while they are playing games or listening to music. This kind of advertising never works and is the number one mistake that all APPvertisers should avoid like the plague.**

- **Permission marketing is wiser and more profitable in terms of conversions, sign-ups, and sales. Therefore, a company seeking to advertise during in-app interactions should request a mobile user's permission first. Otherwise it might get a lot of what only appear to be leads—as users click**

by accident or just to continue their game—but in the end, all those leads will leave the advertiser with a headache in abysmal lead conversions.

The web has changed. Marketing will never be the same, and selling is becoming transformed accordingly. What steps businesses take to enter this new Word of Mouse world will determine where they land in the competitive marketplace.

Retargeting and Relationship Targeting

The other day, I booked a plane ticket to the Amalfi Coast in southern Italy for a short vacation with some old friends. Afterward, the company I used to purchase the tickets sent me a confirmation email, which I opened and read. I then went on with my day.

A little later, I went back online and couldn't help noticing that the ad banners on one site after another—whether it was Google or the *Wall Street Journal*—appeared to be tailored to my trip. It was as if southern Italy had decided to visit me before I could visit it, offering me everything from rental cars to restaurant discounts.

It was as if my destination had decided to visit me before I could visit it, offering me everything from rental cars to restaurant discounts.

This is called "retargeting," and it's the newest front in the direct-advertising campaign. Here's how it works, as described by Dan Springer, CEO of Responsys (a marketing firm that is leading the charge), in an interview with the magazine *Fast Company*.

"We targeted you the first time when we sent you an email. Now we know you're interested, so we're retargeting you in a new location," Springer said. "That's just being a smart marketer."

In the beginning, according to a video on the Responsys website, "There was traditional display advertising, which is only based on website demographics (that's a start). Then we moved to Display Retargeting, which doesn't leverage behavioral or CRM [customer relationship management] data and isn't coordinated with your other marketing channels (good, but you can do better)."

Introducing "relationship targeting," which allows marketers to reach customers beyond the in-box, mobile phone, or social network, with display ads that are personalized, timely, and relevant.

"The average brand has less than 20 percent of its customers and prospects opted in to email or following it on Facebook or Twitter," according to the Responsys website. This means that marketers can now leverage their segmentation and targeting rules to reach all of their customers and prospects with display ads—wherever they are across the web—even the 80 percent who aren't opted in.

It may seem invasive to some, but as new technology continues to emerge, our contemporary conception of privacy will seem outdated and uptight.

> ## As new technology continues to emerge, our contemporary conception of privacy will seem outdated and uptight.

MOBILE CUSTOMER RELATIONSHIP MANAGEMENT APPS

These days, a salesperson is only as good as the tools in his toolbox. In the office, one of the most important assets is the organization's customer relationship management system: a combination of procedures, software, and internet mechanisms that helps the enterprise manage its customer relationships.

At my company, Razor Media Group, we use Infusionsoft CRM, an email marketing system, to manage our email list, contacts, customers, and leads. Razor Media has relationships with a number of affiliates, and we use Infusionsoft's affiliate reports to track interactions, transactions, and so on, with those entities. It's a powerful tool, and I have a sneaking suspicion that we're only scratching the surface of its potential.

Ironically, salespeople often lose access to this tool while they're on the road. Thanks to a host of CRM mobile apps and cloud computing, this is no longer the case. And there's a CRM app for just about every CRM system on the market.

> **If you have better metrics and information than your competitors have about your clients and their buying habits, you should be able to sell more, meaning you can pay more to acquire a client!**

Here's a sample of some of the best CRMs for customers on the move:

Name	Description	Device(s)
Sugar Mobile (**www.sugar crm.com/crm/ mobile-crm**)	Users can check reports, prioritize opportunities, set up meetings, and manage support cases. Updated email management capabilities make it easy to send follow-up emails from your mobile device, which automatically gets synced up with your SugarCRM system. Twitter Connector allows users to manage Twitter streams without having to leave the app. **Price: free** (with the Sugar Professional and Sugar Enterprise editions).	iPhone, iPod Touch, and iPad
Salesforce Mobile (**www .salesforce.com/ CRM**)	Users can access sales performance data, as well as critical account information, on the go. Because the app operates in the cloud, new leads are routed automatically to your mobile device, and any account changes or status updates made in the field get synced back to the system in the office, giving your team the most updated information. A mapping feature allows you to identify clients that are nearby, turning that potentially lost hour into an opportunity to make a sale. **Price: free.**	BlackBerry, iPhone, and Windows Mobile
CWR Mobility CRM (**www .cwrmobility .com**)	This app offers many of the same features and capabilities as its competitors. However, it stands out for its availability of deployment options. This application can be operated on nearly any mobile device. Users can access account, pipeline, and performance information from the comfort of their preferred smartphone or mobile device. **Price: free.**	iPhone, iPad, BlackBerry, Windows Phone 6.5, Windows Phone 7, and Android

Out-of-the-Box Thinking!

I've launched a number of businesses, and I'm always racking my brain to come up with new ways to integrate technology into the sales and marketing mix. Just when I think it's all been done, I find something mind-blowing and new—the kind of idea that makes you say, "Why didn't I think of that?" Here are a few of the more thought-provoking examples of innovative applications of technology to sales and marketing. They run the gamut, but all demonstrate the unlimited possibilities that technology can play in a business model or sales and marketing plan.

Facial recognition: Few sales tactics compare to the effectiveness of a face-to-face pitch. It's a little about the customer seeing the merchant as a person, not a corporation. But, more important, it's about the merchant seeing the customer: his physical, social, and personal traits, to which the most pertinent pitch can be applied. When the sales process moves online, the face time vanishes, along with the bricks and mortar. Enter facial recognition via software such as that from Face.com, an Israeli company. According to Gil Hirsch, its chief executive, various video chat sites were using the company's program to make sure that participants displayed their faces, not other body parts. During the editing of this book, Face.com was acquired by Facebook to facilitate its mammoth social network. But any facial recognition software like this also has retail uses, such as enabling a customer to upload a photo and then virtually try on eyeglass frames to see how they look on him or her. And how about makeup, hairstyles, and so forth?

Selling Fish via Twitter: Yuichi-kai, the Tobu fishing association in Japan, delivers fish straight from the ocean to its customers within twelve hours using Twitter and an online shopping site. Here's how it works: every morning, the fishermen post their catch. Customers can instantly check images and videos of the fish. Using Twitter accounts named after their ships, the fishermen update details and check orders. All of this is done via mobile phone, while the fishermen are still aboard their boats. As a result, they can immediately process orders the moment they get to port. It's not uncommon for an entire catch to be sold before the fisherman even returns to port.

The lesson here? Businesses will need to start thinking creatively—finding the white space in their markets—and use technology in a way that nobody else does. The market for the next few years is wide open, and a company's success may be unprecedented.

CASE STUDY
A Doritos and Xbox Game Campaign
Goes Viral

Marketing and advertising strategies often work 50 percent of the time, and the problem is that you don't know which 50 percent works until after all of the money has been spent! Marketing starts with the same basic principles of understanding one's audience. Knowing the nitty-gritty on target consumers will bring a business and its brand one step closer to the customers' hearts— and wallets. Chip maker Doritos, in its quest to engage and excite a large fan base, started an innovative viral campaign to build brand awareness and generate snack sales with an "Unlock Xbox" competition. Here's a breakdown of the campaign, from start to finish.

Marketing Challenge and Goal

Doritos knew that its customers (ages eighteen to thirty-four) loved to play video games, so the company was looking for a unique way to reach a large portion of this gaming audience and at the same time stir its main consumers in a provocative way.

Contest Details

Doritos released its Unlock Xbox contest, challenging fans to capture the essence of its snack in a live video game format. The purpose was to offer those with a video game idea, but no development skills, the ability to have their video games produced—and win a $50,000 gaming project with Doritos.

The competition attracted over 1,500 entries and pulled in plenty of great ideas. "We are always looking for new ways to connect with fans and give them unique opportunities to express their creativity in a way only Doritos and our partners can deliver," said Ann Mukherjee, chief marketing officer for parent company Frito-Lay, in a prepared release. "Many of the people who love Doritos also love gaming, and this innovative program gave our fans a chance to live their dreams [of seeing their video game ideas become a reality]." The Unlock Xbox's official website explained the contest results. First, an expert panel of judges selected the top eight. From there, the public voted to determine the top three semifinalists, who trekked to Microsoft headquarters in Seattle to make their last pitches.

Based on their pitches, two finalist games emerged, Doritos Crash Course and Harm's Way. These games were launched as free downloads on Xbox LIVE, with gamers voting on their favorite. The winner, Doritos Crash Course, became the fastest downloaded Xbox LIVE Arcade game in history, with over one million downloads in the first two weeks alone.

This campaign delivered high engagement and measurable results. Check out the numbers:

- **72 percent of users took action after seeing the Doritos ads on Xbox LIVE.**
- **Over 50 percent of those who saw the Doritos ad on Xbox LIVE clicked to find out more about the contest (and game entries).**
- **Over 40 percent voted for their favorite game.**
- **49 percent of respondents went out and bought snacks.**
- **24 percent told their friends about the Xbox LIVE contest.**
- **21 percent visited the Doritos website.**

Three Truisms to Take Away from the Doritos Campaign

1. Marketing is not about big-budget spending but about gathering the best facts and insights on a business's target audience with the least time, effort, and financial investment.

2. Brand awareness alone is nothing unless it connects with and engages the customer in a unique, exciting way.

3. A campaign will never go viral until it stirs consumers' imaginations to take action for a good cause or an enticing prize.

The age of merely selling to buyers is over. To be an effective seller in today's market, you need to connect with them. How do you create a "connection" if you're a seller? You need to be smart, deal oriented, socially connected, and most important, creative. The reason is simple: consumers can get the best of the best online, so sellers have to find new ways to stand out and build their brands. Maybe that means renting out an expensive product—such as handbags or luxury autos—that people are used to buying, building a market that was traditionally out of reach. Or maybe it means building a following by hawking discounted deals over Twitter in real time. Whatever you do, it has to be fast paced and app friendly, allowing your product or service to reach mobile shoppers whether they're in-store or on the go. As you'll learn in the next chapter, the same flexibility that makes businesses successful from the outside can be applied to the way they function internally as well. Whether you're running a company or freelancing on your own, before you can be an effective seller, you have to figure out how to be an effective worker.

INFUSIONSOFT VIDEO SERIES CASE STUDY
Building, Maintaining, and Updating Your Database of Clients and Prospects Are the Keys to Business Success!

For a business hoping to build an online presence, a database can be everything. This is what Laura Roeder, founder of LKR Social Media (http://lkr socialmedia.com), a company that helps small business use social media, tells her clients.

"When it comes to marketing, your database is really the only asset you have," she said. "It's great that you have thousands of followers on Twitter. But you don't own your Twitter followers or Facebook fans. People get their accounts shut down all the time—services come and go."

Instead, Roeder says, small-business owners should see social media as a means of driving people back to the company website, where their fans' email addresses can be captured.

"I think when you don't have people's email addresses, you're putting the impetus on them to come find you, to find your website, and to buy from you," she observed.

That's not to say that Roeder doesn't place a lot of emphasis on the importance of developing a coherent social media strategy. After all, the refreshingly candid businesswoman has more than fourteen thousand Facebook fans and over sixteen thousand Twitter followers with whom she interacts daily.

Roeder tells her clients that they need social media for two reasons. The first—as I already mentioned—is to collect contact information, which places you in charge of the relationship. The second, she said, is to begin the relationship-building process, which is essential for creating the trust that savvy buyers desire if they're going to make online purchases.

"The myth is that people come to your site and make immediate purchases, but that's not true online or in person," she said. "It's very rare we hear of a product and immediately go buy it. We like to read reviews and do research, so social media is a really effective way to make prospects feel like they can trust you enough to make purchases, whether you're selling online or you're a consultant."

Roeder uses the same social media strategy in her own business. LKR offers its clients video training programs to teach them how to do their own online marketing and blogging. Roeder has found that the videos are also a great way to attract prospective clients to her site when she advertises the programs through social media.

"These videos are sort of like digital footprints that you have all over the web," she explained. "As you do more webinars, more reports, or whatever you do, they add up, and you have twenty different ways that people can find you, get valuable information, and give you their email address."

She keeps track of her growing database with tools such as Infusionsoft's automated sales and marketing system. "We needed software that could handle all parts of our online business: taking credit cards, shopping carts and order forms, email marketing, and more," she said. "This system does all those things in one place, showing you all the emails your customers have opened, pages they've clicked on, and all the things they've bought—in one central database."

Watch the video here!
Scan the QR code or go to http://www.wordofmouse.com/qr/11/index.htm.

Chapter Summary Points

- In the era of Google, Twitter, Yelp, and Facebook, buying is no longer a one-way street—or even a two-way street. It's a chaotic bazaar where anything and everything is available if you just look hard enough.

- Sellers should not underestimate buyers. In the years to come, the speed of technological innovation will increase alongside the growing intelligence of the consumer.

- Thinking of creating a new online business? Don't forget that renting is the new selling. Find something people want to own but can't afford—or need only a few times—and consider renting it to others.

- Paper coupons are quickly becoming a thing of the past, but discounts and deals are more popular than ever before, thanks to innovations in technology. Today's customers demand deals!

- Instant gratification is king: to succeed in this fast-paced landscape, companies must provide value-added mobile apps and websites. To reach all types of mobile shoppers, companies should activate both mobile on-the-go and mobile in-store interactions.

- Businesses that are flexible and creative have the best chance of excelling.

- Social media are redefining how buyers get information and interact with brands.

- Sometimes all it takes is "a deal a day."

BONUS SECTION: WORD OF MOUSE
DRIVING TREND—DATA ANALYTICS

The Dollars Are in the Data!

Here is something you might not realize: every time you click your mouse, browse a website, pause on a photo, post on Facebook, make a purchase, or hand over your email address, your online behavior is being tracked, stored, analyzed, and, in many cases, sold.

Like a virtual Big Brother, today's intelligent companies are monitoring your decisions—both big and small—and tailoring their websites accordingly. With the help of intuitive software straight out of a sci-fi novel, their goal is to better understand the wants, needs, and whims of consumers just like you. Which Facebook ads elicit a response from you? How long do you spend on a given page? Which keywords pique your interest? What particular interval of marketing emails is most effective at getting you to open up your wallet? These are the kind of questions that online companies ask twenty-four hours day, seven days a week. If they don't have the data already, oftentimes they're willing to pay other networks top dollar for access to them.

To some, it's an invasion of privacy. To others, it's an example of companies catering to the increasingly nuanced demands of consumers. The idea is that smarter marketing leads to smarter buying. Wherever you stand on the issue, one thing is certain for consumers and creators alike: the future will be driven by data.

All this monitoring and analysis turn up a flood of data that the human mind could never hope to interpret. An entire internet economy has been unleashed to make sense of this for us; insiders call this information data analytics, or DA. It just might be the most influential industry out there. And remember, your computer is not the only thing generating data in the online age. Each day there are billions of texts, shared images, business transactions, phone calls, financial decisions, and more!

In fact, according to Wikibon, a professional community of practitioners, consultants, and researchers dedicated to solving technology and business problems through an open source sharing of free advisory knowledge, "the big data market is on the verge of a rapid growth spurt that will see it top the $50 billion mark worldwide within the next five years."

You've heard the expression "It takes money to make money." But this isn't the case anymore.

Yep, as I like to say, the dollars are in the data! But the big boys with the fancy software aren't the only ones who have access to dollars or data. You—

the consumer—do too. Whether you're a small-business owner with a product, a freelance writer with a blog, or a stay-at-home parent with an online hobby, it never hurts to know who is visiting your site and why. The more information you have, the more chance you have of giving your subscribers what they want and building your own customers—your own online community.

As far as businesses go, the old model was simple: if you owned a small or medium-sized business and wanted to get your name out there, you'd throw different marketing techniques at the wall and see what stuck. Some of us bought billboards, others shelled out cash for radio time. And still others dressed up their employees in goofy costumes and instructed them to hold up signs and dance around busy intersections. Let's face it: the old world of marketing was, in essence, a guessing game.

The lucky few were able to advertise on TV, which gave them access to the Nielsen ratings, allowing for a calculation of how many people would see an ad. Typically, only the big boys could advertise and get great information back, so they would know what worked and what didn't. You've heard the expression "It takes money to make money." But this isn't the case anymore.

Today we all can have the equivalent of Nielsen ratings on our desktops. They go by different names—Hadoop, StatCounter, Mint, Google Analytics— but they all do the same basic thing. They level the playing field between the big boys and the mom-and-pop operations, making us all smarter in the ways that we spend our marketing dollars. This time, it's not cost per *view,* but cost per *click.* It doesn't matter what you're marketing. You can pinpoint your target audience and tailor your message accordingly. That message starts with social media, blogs, and web campaigns. It ends with data analytics, which is akin to night vision goggles that help a business navigate through the murky world of marketing.

The prospect of diving into data analytics can seem daunting. That's why I've made this chapter a hands-on one, with a number of real-world case studies to help you understand DA in action. Break out your calculator. Put on your glasses. It's time to get techie!

PROTECTING YOUR DATA

As I mention throughout this section, the data you generate online are being collected, stored, analyzed, and even sold. Whether you think this new world of data collection is a road to smarter consumerism or an authoritarian invasion of privacy is up to you. Here's one group's take on things.

The Locker Project is an initiative that makes it possible for people to access and aggregate their own personal data for various reasons. What it means: Step 1 is to create the lockers that allow people to collect all their data in one resource. Step 2 is to enable application developers to build products on top of the personal data, creating a whole new data marketplace.

So what's a Locker? Here's how it's defined at the Locker Project website (www.lockerproject.org):

> *A Locker is a container for personal data, which gives the owner the ability to control how it's protected and shared. It retrieves and consolidates data from multiple sources, to create a single collection of the things you see and do online: the photos you take, the places you visit, the links you share, contact details for the people you communicate with, and much more. It also provides flexible application programming interfaces (APIs) for developers to build rich applications with access to all of this information. The Locker Project is an open source development effort, permissively licensed, and sponsored by Singly. Singly provides a personal data service based on this technology, and also welcomes its use by anyone for any purpose.*

For example, an individual could give her personal buyer or even interior designer—virtual or actual—access to her Locker in order to gain a complete understanding of her tastes and interests.

Data Analytics: Strapping On Your Goggles

When we think about the world's most popular websites, Facebook, Yahoo!, and Google come to mind. But behind the scenes of each site, a little-known software company is hard at work, helping some of the most successful on line companies access and analyze the vast amount of raw data turned up by the Internet. This particular company is called Hadoop. It was started a few years back by a man named Doug Cutting, who named his online venture after his son's toy elephant. The company makes it possible to break down massive amounts of data into small, digestible bites that are spread across thousands of computers. From there, technology makes it possible to mine the raw data for explanations and sometimes predictions of business and marketing patterns and relationships. A company could dig into a shopper's transactions, social stats, and geographical data to uncover how he or she is influenced by peers.

"You put access to huge amounts of data within reach of a large number of people," he said. "All of a sudden analysts and engineers can process terabytes of data and discover things about the company they didn't know and make the company smarter, better, and more profitable." Hadoop was designed to mimic Google's technology so that anyone could sieve through large data sets quickly and cheaply. Yahoo! and Facebook were among the first companies to implement Cutting's software, and the *New York Times,* the Walt Disney Company, Samsung, and hundreds of other firms have followed suit, often with similar software.

But what was once reserved for huge outfits is increasingly becoming mainstream. These days, start-ups, smaller retailers, and even individuals are developing easy-to-use versions of Hadoop or turning to programs like Google

Analytics for useful data about their websites. Take, for example, the California-based company Datameer, which created an Excel-like dashboard that enables regular businesspeople, not just data priests, to pose questions.

"For twenty years you had limited amounts of computing and storage power and could only ask certain things," says Datameer CEO Stefan Groschupf. "Now you just dump everything in there and ask whatever you want."

Let's say, for example, that Yahoo! wants to determine what kinds of stories hundreds of millions of its users prefer at certain times during the year. Or perhaps Facebook—which, by some estimates, manages forty billion user photos—wants to determine how closely you are linked to other people with whom you share photos. These analytics programs make very powerful, very specific searches that are accessible and user friendly. Most important, the programs are accessing staggeringly enormous amounts of data that are updated constantly for the most current perspective on the trends in question. For that matter, they also can access historic data, for a progressive study on how trends have changed over time. Hadoop even makes Excel obsolete for certain crunching purposes, because it provides users with insightful data that cannot be crammed into spreadsheets.

Amazon, the biggest online retailer in the United States, is known to analyze its data and site logs to see what items people look at before they buy a specific product, how long they stay online at a particular web page, and whether certain colors generate more sales. Then, all of this information is structured into real-time intelligence.

Different companies rely on different types of data analytics software, each with a specialized focus. In fact, the web is packed with intelligence tools and services that aid businesses in tracking and analyzing their data. These tools also help companies do the following:

- **improve their website designs**
- **send follow-up emails, based on a scripted marketing structure (for example, when people register as users on the website, an automated email thanks them for registering, and invites them to receive a weekly news digest)**
- **acquire customers**
- **develop upsell and/or cross-sell strategies (an example of "upsell" is when "people who bought this pink hoodie also bought these matching sweatpants"; an example of "cross-sell" is when a company sells an existing customer another one of its products, based on the idea that it's cheaper and easier to sell product B to a customer who has already bought product A than to sell product A to a new customer)**

The goal is to take the guesswork out of marketing and provide an accurate method of gathering customer data, building a profile of the target audience, and predicting consumer behavior.

"MARC" MY WORDS Data analytics is a perpetually evolving tool for businesses, regardless of their size. What it isn't, however, is a cure-all. Continual testing, tweaking, and reevaluating help determine what will make or break a business in both the real world and the virtual one.

Data analytics tools do the following:
- track, measure, and identify the weak and profit-pulling paths within a business to help predict consumer behavior
- enhance relationships with customers
- create more brand loyalty
- improve conversion rates

UNDERSTANDING HOW TO TURN YOUR DATA INTO DOLLARS!

The key to an organization's success with metrics is to have someone on board who is able to analyze and understand the company's data and then be able to make accurate predictions. Good training is a crucial part of the company's ability to get the most out of intelligence tools.

> The goal is to take the guesswork out of marketing and provide an accurate method of gathering customer data, building a profile of the target audience and predicting consumer behavior.

Google Analytics, now a free service, generates detailed data about a website's visitors. It is the most widely used web analytics program, currently in use on around 57 percent of the ten thousand most popular websites. And according to Alexa, a web information company based in San Francisco, Google Analytics is used at around 50 percent of the top one million websites. Its popularity is attributed to its simplicity and a number of advanced features that are perfect for curious amateurs and professional marketers.

At Blinds.com, one of the companies I co-own, we have a huge data analytics group that does nothing but run numbers all day and decide which advertising and marketing works, which doesn't, and how to test and keep testing in order to make our customers happier and lower our marketing costs.

CASE STUDY
Getting More Customers Using Data Analytics

Wayne S. Bell is a marketing consultant and avid believer in using metrics for a business's marketing gain. He's told me many stories about how his firm, TxtWorx, has employed this powerful tool with great success.

For example, a sports bar and grill restaurant owner in North Carolina contacted Bell about coaching him on the various ways that his establishment could leverage the internet to get more customers. The restaurant had a Facebook page, but it had caused his business more harm than good.

Of course, Bell was intrigued about the "more harm than good" comment. He was told that the owner asked the people in his church to Like the sports bar and grill Facebook Business page so he could create some buzz for his business. What he did not know was that several of the regular customers were having an inappropriate conversation inside the Facebook Business page wall for all to see. Needless to say, his church friends were not impressed! After a conversation about his business and what he expected from the internet and technology, he implemented the following.

QR codes: create a unique QR code for each section of town to conduct analysis to determine the best locations to advertise in the future.

Texting keyword: create a keyword to be used in radio advertisements and for in-house contests during the big games. The reason for this is to build the database of customers to get better analytics and send more targeted promotions in the future.

Mobile website: take the most important content from the desktop website and create a user-friendly mobile website that is centered on getting the customer to visit the location.

Social media accounts: create a Twitter account and a Foursquare app, and update the Facebook Business page for a professional look that carries forward the branding. Twitter and Foursquare were created to allow customers to inform their followers of their current locations and experiences there.

Updated desktop website: use the latest in HTML5 (HyperText Markup Language, the main markup language used to display web pages) technology to create a more engaging website for visitors to interact with the brand.

Analytics: understand and obtain analytics on all of the above locations to grab data, so he could analyze the most profitable paths for adding revenue to his bottom line.

At the three-month client-checkup meeting, Bell's client informed him that customer feedback on the restaurant's Facebook page had given him the idea to have a quiz night. He also indicated a 22 percent increase in business since implementation of Bell's service.

Good analytics is the foundation of making the internet, technology, and mobile devices work for any type of business or nonprofit organization.

In the above story, Bell was able to email the owner a report every Friday at two o'clock specifying the key areas he needed to tweak in order to improve business the following week or for the following campaign. Here are some of the insights that Bell's services revealed to the owner:

- **best performing marketing channel**
- **best paid keywords on search engines**
- **the site that is sending the most visitors to the website**
- **how much revenue is generated by social media**
- **the flow of actions the visitor takes while on the site, for future optimization**
- **the underperforming marketing channels, to reallocate those funds to a more productive channel**
- **updates to the website to be in line with the way that visitors are interacting with it**
- **the number of visitors who were using a mobile device and their screen size, for future optimization**

DATA ANALYTICS IN ACTION

The business world's cup runneth over with success stories that showcase the power of analytics.

CASE STUDY
Seton Hall Enrollment Grows via Facebook

As a private school, Seton Hall University relies heavily on tuition as its main source of revenue, which means it is crucial that the New Jersey university continually find new ways to connect with the source of that revenue: young people.

To do this, Seton Hall has turned in recent years to Facebook. Instead of trying to draw prospective students to the university's website, marketers decided to reach out to young people where they already spend much of their time: on Facebook. The hope, according to Coremetrics, an online analytics company that Seton Hall hired, was that Facebook would allow the university to reach students earlier in the recruitment process, increasing enrollment and revenue.

Instead of trying to draw prospective students to the university's website, marketers decided to reach out to young people where they already spend much of their time: on Facebook.

In the past, the university had generated traffic to its website via Facebook ads, but people who clicked through the advertisements did not necessarily engage with the website in a productive way. And while the university's marketing team still believed that Facebook might be leading potential students to the Seton Hall site through other channels, it didn't have a way to connect the two. The university decided to create a new Facebook campaign to increase enrollment for an upcoming academic year and to integrate that campaign with analytics from Coremetrics.

Over the course of several years, Seton Hall has turned to programs such as Coremetrics Impression Attribution and Coremetrics Social. These tools allow marketers to track the return on investment (ROI) of social channels alongside other channels, analyze the impact of referral visitors from social networking sites, monitor the downstream impact of social content impressions, and track real-time conversations on both Facebook and Twitter.

What were the results?

- **By midsummer, two months before classes were to begin, tuition deposits for the class of 2014 were 25 percent higher than those of the previous year at the same time.**
- **At this same time, enrollment was tracking at 13 percent ahead of the previous year's class.**
- **By the end of the enrollment period, Seton Hall had its largest freshman class in thirty years, with an 18 percent increase in net present revenue of $29 million.**

With the data acquired, Seton Hall can perform deep analysis on its own site, allowing administrators to make more accurate and better-informed decisions on where to invest their advertising budget and marketing efforts. The larger point is that marketing is no longer based on good old-fashioned guessing.

"Without the data, we would have seen Facebook as only obliquely connected with top-line enrollment and bottom-line revenue goals," said Rob Brosnan, senior director of strategic marketing for Seton Hall. "Because of the data, we can see that Facebook is a significant and subtly sophisticated new front in the development of markets for the university."

CASE STUDY
Double Sales with Data Analytics

Boden, a clothing store, is one of the fastest-growing direct-order companies in the United Kingdom and the United States. At one point, the company introduced a host of new features to its website. The challenge was to evaluate the impact of each new feature on an individual basis, in order to understand how it contributed to sales. Using data analytics, the company discovered that two features—the Shop by Trouser Fit tool and the New Arrivals area—were the most appreciated by customers. As a result, they were prioritized for additional investment.

With plans for the autumn collection launch, Boden was looking to find out if these tools had, in fact, supercharged the number of trousers or new arrivals sold in comparison with prelaunch sales. The company also wanted to compare online results against offline sales figures. Analysis showed that the most popular products were found lower on the page, leading to a page redesign that resulted in more product views and higher conversions. It allowed Boden to grasp how visitors navigated through the site from the Shop by Trouser Fit results pages and how their navigational behavior differed from that of other visitors.

"We wish we could ask our customers, 'How can we make our website work better for you?'" said an online manager of Boden UK. "But it would be impossible to canvass all of them! Now we are improving the website simply by watching our visitors walk around the store. It's like turning the lights on."

And what were the results? The Shop by Trouser Fit feature proved to have an outstanding effect on sales, with a whopping 160 percent increase in trouser orders on the website postlaunch.

PLUG IN:

Live Chats Improve Business

Ez Texting, a provider of web-based text messaging services, found that adding a live-chat widget (the embedded function that launches a chat box that pops up when you're visiting a website, usually initiating a real-time dialogue between you and a customer service representative for the owner of the website) helped increase sign-ups by 31 percent over the original design (without a live chat widget). Josh Malin, marketing director of Ez Texting, said, "I know that testing can contradict deeply held beliefs, but it is helpful every now and then to go through a test that confirms this. It makes it that much easier in the future to test other long-held beliefs. And, of course, it's always great to have solid data to explain the inclusion of some counterintuitive element on our front-end sales site to everyone else at the company." (Source: visual websiteoptimizer.com/split-testing-blog/live-chat-increases-signups.)

Every small business needs a competitive advantage! What's yours?

Did You Know?

You can test the effectiveness of different versions of your website simultaneously.

Split testing helps a website owner try out two versions of his page at the same time to determine which one is more effective. With this approach, a business can test two headlines, two order buttons, two prices, two money-back guarantees, two colors, and so on.

Multivariate testing, meanwhile, is split testing to the third power. Multiple variables can be tested with one campaign. Web optimizer specialists recommend that for split testing campaigns, a site owner should drive at least five hundred to one thousand unique visitors before he can draw a conclusion and have a valid campaign. For multivariate campaigns, one will have to drive up to three thousand unique visitors or generate anywhere between two hundred and three hundred sales (if orders are what the businesses is tracking with its optimizer tool).

A US Hair Salon Franchisee Improves Cross-Sales Conversions

Mindshare Technologies is a company that provides brands and firms with the feedback-capturing tools required to monitor their customers' experience, on a daily basis. For instance, a US hair salon franchisee implemented an automated survey technology from Mindshare to get immediate daily input from customers.

The point-of-sale receipt for each customer incorporated a printed offer to call a toll-free number and collect an incentive. Customers called the number, answered a few questions via the telephone keypad, and obtained a redemption code valid for their next service. In addition, customers could also leave a voice recording of their feelings about the service.

Of particular interest to the salon was calibrating stylist recommendation of hair-care products. Individual training and coaching sessions were held on a baseline measurement. Once goals were set, additional focus was placed on increasing customers' perception of how many times a stylist suggested add-on products.

Each month, the management team used the month-end and week-end reports, reviewing, training, and setting goals with frontline associates.

RESULTS

- Hair care product sales grew from 3 percent to 8 percent within two months, after remaining stagnant for eight years.
- Survey responses to the question "Did the stylist suggest products?" rose from 46 percent to 55 percent in the same time period.

CASE STUDY
American Express Uses Analytics to Evaluate Facebook's "Link, Like, Love"

The merging of social media sites and commerce is well under way. I'm often surprised by how seamless the transition has been. Take the Facebook Link, Like, Love program. Here's how it works: you link your American Express card to your Facebook account. Then American Express delivers deals and offers based on your Facebook activity—pages you like and share—as well as the actions of your Facebook friends. With a single click, you can attach a discount to your account. And if you make the related transaction using your Amex card, you get a discount, too.

A strategic communications firm called Beyond the Arc helped American Express evaluate the program's effectiveness. Its team of social media analysts sampled up to two million posts on Facebook and Twitter over a two-month period. Through text analytics and business intelligence, the team members distilled the high volume down to twenty-one thousand relevant posts. By examining the raw data, they gained insights into the customer experience, from acquisition to retention.

Most customer comments were generated during the registration and usage stages (for example, "How does it work?"). American Express even acknowledged that privacy concerns arose during the registration phase, when users had reservations about giving the Facebook app permission to work with their American Express info. They asked questions such as, "Is this a scam?" or "If real, is this secure?"

The American Express Facebook team said that it worked with some of these reluctant users. The Facebook page notes: "This is a secure American Express page. Your card account information will remain private, protected, and will not be shared with Facebook."

In the end, merging these distinct yet complementary mediums appears to have worked on both sides. The platform made it simple for users to get deals they wanted and share them with their friends, leveraging the social network to build engagement and business growth. The news and discussion generated on American Express and its innovation (mostly positive retweets and shares) also raised awareness.

There were five "general" offers geared to motivate repeat usage:

1. Merchant discounts
2. Travel
3. Food
4. Events
5. Specials or freebies

In the final phase, advocacy, the analytics team found that satisfied users shared the program and also included links to attract new customers, concluding that Facebook looks like an effective platform to increase user sharing and generate business.*

DATA ANALYTICS AS A TOOL FOR MEASURING PEOPLE'S ONLINE INFLUENCE

How many Facebook friends do you have? That's a question I've heard my daughters ask over the years when they discuss their social media selves. But the answer to this question is actually becoming more and more important. According to Klout, a website that measures people's online influence, "Our friendships and professional connections have moved online, making influence measurable for the first time in history."

If you're a member of the media or a new business owner, a little bit of clout can go a long way. New users can create accounts or log in with their Twitter or Facebook accounts. The way Klout works is simple: it measures your influence, on a scale of 1 to 100, based on your ability to drive action to social networks. Each day, the site provides your account with a new score that is measured through one of the following actions:

- **Twitter mentions and retweets**
- **Facebook comments, wall posts, and Likes**
- **Foursquare tips, to-dos, and dones**
- **Google+ comments, reshares, and +1s**
- **LinkedIn comments and Likes**

Although it feels fantastic to have a ton of connections, what really matters is *how* people engage with your social media content. You'll be better off with a small, engaged audience than with a large inactive network. If you aim for a high Klout score, then focus on creating the best content, something with which your network will want to engage and share.

THE FUTURE OF DATA ANALYTICS

According to Gartner Worldwide IT Spending Forecast (the leading indicator of major technology trends across the hardware, software, IT services, and telecom markets), by 2014, almost one-third of analytic applications will use proactive, predictive, and forecasting capabilities. We will also see growth in the use of social listening platforms and sentiment analytics tools. WordPress .com (WordPress is a free and open-source web-design and blogging tool, and a dynamic content management system) defines social media listening platforms as "solutions that gather data from various social media outlets and news sources by monitoring millions if not billions of conversations and generating text analytics based on predefined criteria. They can also determine the sentiment of a speaker or writer in regard to a topic or document/file."

Here are some of the services that social listening platforms can offer a company or brand:

- **Track reach and spread of any communication (email, press release, Twitter, Facebook)**
- **Handle emergency situations**
- **Monitor conversations 24/7**
- **Identify and reach out to key bloggers and social media influencers**
- **Spot emerging trends, discussion themes, and topics***

Social media intelligence tools that integrate offline and online data will become the standard for the years to come and will help e-commerce, information technology (IT), retail, banking, and other sectors develop more insight into their consumers and customers than ever before. Before you shell out a bunch of cash for an expensive analytics package, however, remember that services such as Google Analytics, Flurry Analytics, and MapMyUser are free.

WHAT DOES DATA ANALYTICS MEAN TO YOU?

As we go about our daily lives, we create vast oceans of personal data. But data is more than mere information. Collectively, it makes up your online identity and all the decisions, purchases, relationships, interests, and behaviors that come with it. There is a multibillion-dollar industry flourishing behind your computer screen, with a goal to collect that identity and make money by anticipating its next step. Whether you want to take part in that industry or not, it's important for you—as an internet user and as a citizen—to know that it exists.

I hope I've made it clear that you don't have to be a businessperson to understand the importance of data analytics. You might be an aspiring photographer who sets up a website and wants to figure out a niche. You might be the creator of a popular YouTube channel who wants to find out what topics generate the most interest online. You might be a small-business owner who needs to start shifting business online. Or you might be an activist who wants to fight for people's online privacy rights. Whoever you are and whatever you want to do, data can help.

---

* PracticalAnalytics.WordPress.com.

Case Study: Data + Members = An Engaged Organization

My friend John Perry, director of information technology at NACE International, has managed to "up the ampage" on the Houston-based nonprofit organization's use of technology to deliver meaningful information and services to its membership. He has tapped into the magic of metrics to ensure that the leaders' decisions are in line with members' expectations, and I find his story to be very translatable to any organization. So I asked him to write a brief case study on the topic of NACE's use of CRM, database marketing, and data analytics. Here's the story, in John's words:

NACE International, a nonprofit organization focusing on corrosion mitigation, had a bit of a communications problem. We really had no way of knowing how much interaction each member was actually having with staff, and this uncertainty tended to distance the organization from its members in a very real way. We had to find a way to smooth the communications, both inbound and outbound, so that members could interact with NACE meaningfully, effectively, and efficiently.

NACE members run the gamut from academic and management professionals, who are highly technically savvy, to field applicators, who are less likely to carry smartphones or use the internet extensively. As with any marketing effort, the challenge was how to communicate the right message in the right medium.

To help us get the equation right, we created fun apps that let our members update their data and created prize-based systems to encourage them to do so. Our clients carry a wealth of information about NACE's history that we had not anticipated they would want to share with us. At the end of the day, we gained a lot, and our clients now feel like they are an instrumental part of the process—which they are. We continued to grow the level of information our members had access to and allowed them to share various levels of that access with other members as a way of building their personal brands in the industry. CRM gives us the unique ability to identify market segments via profile update information and to measure our effectiveness in attempting to reach them through various mediums.

The profile information is clearly important to us, but the real value to the business is the transparency of how our members are participating with NACE.

Our next area of focus is on trending: aggregating the social media buzz in the corrosion industry to help us establish short-term radar for product development.

Bonus Section Summary Points

- Everything you do online creates data, which are tracked, stored, analyzed, and, in some cases, sold. Internet users should be aware that their data are being used, whether they accept that fact or not.

- Data analytics is the method or system that helps individuals and businesses gain better insights from their current data, learn new things about their customers, predict behaviors, and make better marketing or advertising decisions.

- There are innovative products and services on the market that help decipher data analytics, including business intelligence tools, website analytics services, and split testing and multivariate testing software.

- Before a website owner obtains analytics, it's important that he or she increase the page views. This starts with an innovative approach to social media and online marketing.

- Trends to watch for in the coming years: social listening platforms and sentient analytics tools, programs that measure online influence, and social media intelligence tools that integrate offline and online data.

Your thoughts are important!
Please rate *Word of Mouse* on Amazon.com!

Hate change? Most of us do. My dad used to say, "If you keep doing what you've always done, you'll keep getting what you've always gotten!" These days, that may be true only for weight loss (eat less, work out more). In our Word of Mouse world, others are changing, getting faster, smarter, and more efficient! So if your business doesn't change, falling behind is inevitable!

5

Word of Mouse and the Way We *Work*

Few industries, if any, have been untouched by the changes imposed by digital technologies in recent decades. Whether it is music or news (Napster or the Huffington Post*), diplomacy (WikiLeaks), or global finance (internet banks), the increasing speed of information continues to transform some industries and kill off others.*

But destruction breeds creation, and with it comes a new ecosystem of never-before-seen jobs that promise to revolutionize the world economy. Many people now earn their paychecks in an environment of connectivity driven by increasingly sophisticated mobile devices, social networks, and cloud computing that keeps coworkers, management, and employees in constant communication.

The Network Effect

Rob Paterson, the cofounder of the Queen Street Commons, works as a consultant who helps organizations use networks. His take on the emerging workforce model is based on how technology will ultimately affect tomorrow's workforce, something that Paterson refers to as "the end of the job." The way I see it, this "end," like all endings, will yield winners and losers. Understanding the changes, in both technology and environment, helps position people "in the know" to benefit from such changes. So, *in the end,* the end of a job translates to opportunity.

"I'd like you to do a presentation on business ethics. If you don't have time to prepare something, just steal it off the internet."

Here's a little history to put this statement into perspective. In 1900 most businesses were small and localized. Their connections were usually confined to the community of which they were a part. Over the next century, this model was supplanted by one with a monolithic scale based on the machine.

The way Paterson explains it, the internet is taking us "back to the future." Now a small business can be connected to anyone and everyone in the world via the "network effect." This connection allows the skilled artisan to compete with the big-box retailer, only now the artisan has access to a global network that offers more customers than her corporate competition ever had before.

Just as technology is taking away some jobs, it is also generating new ways to make a good living. Over the last few decades, unemployed people have been given tools that allow them to be more productive than those with traditional jobs. What's more, a successful small business can now afford tools that were once reserved only for large firms. It all comes back to how well we deal with change and network, or provide strength in numbers.

Adapting to a New, Social, Interactive Workforce

Technology has created tectonic shifts in the workplace over the last decade, and companies across all industries are still learning how to adjust. To put it simply, the hierarchical system of organizing labor, which compensated employees for manning a cubicle for eight hours a day, is already a vestige of a bygone era. Unfortunately, many companies don't know how to adapt.

Artisans - Hierarchies - Networks

~19th C   +/- 20th C   21st C

Graphic courtesy of Harold Jarche, *Life in Perpetual Beta* (www.jarche.com).

"MARC" MY WORDS In the near future, a new generation of wired young people will reconfigure the way that employees engage with one another and with organizations of all kinds. In the meantime, things are going to get a bit chaotic!

The Concern

Amid the chaos of the evolving workplace, professionals who have spent entire careers working in a hierarchical structure in which the focus was on the external customer find themselves ill equipped for the change. The new workplace is social, fast paced, interactive, and open to constant change—often brought about by new technologies, apps, and easier access to information about the competition. Not understanding how to collaborate and adapt in this new era of customer interaction—particularly when it comes to social media—can feel foreign and frightening. I predict that age will form the basis of a coming digital divide that will leave many companies at a disadvantage. Just like individuals, either they "get it" or they don't. While individuals can often skate by without a specific knowledge or understanding, our free-market economy and a very aggressively competitive landscape force businesses to either understand and embrace technological changes or risk being outsourced—if not disappearing altogether.

The Solution

One of the ways that companies can address their own digital divide is by taking advantage of business models such as coworking (explained on page 135) and crowdsourcing, both of which have become popular ways to incorporate innovative solutions to the problems quickly and efficiently. Companies such as InnoCentive (an open network of millions of problem solvers who connect using a cloud-based technology platform to innovate, problem-solve, and facilitate research and development) hope to mobilize "vast pools of productivity and intellectual capacity" through mass participation, according to the InnoCentive website. And they're finding the perfect professionals for the job instead of making do with what they've got. Crowdsourcing is letting the freshly lean businesses of today invent, reinvent, and market their inventions with a slim and trim employee base and millions of dollars in profits.

IN THE MEANTIME

The new workforce will not wait for companies to accommodate its needs. Instead, workers will embrace alternatives such as coworking, which will allow them to market themselves and hook up with clients at a lower cost, ultimately threatening larger, slower companies in the process. From this collaborative model, which is project based and adaptable, talented young professionals will find new niches in which to create start-ups that emphasize sharing and flexibility, while their larger, slower competition dies off.

CASE STUDY
The Rise of Guru.com

Guru.com, an online workplace and one of my absolute favorite websites, was launched almost a decade back for those who were tired of their routine nine-to-five jobs. Currently, it's arguably the world's biggest marketplace for hiring freelance workers. Let's have a look at what the guys at Guru do differently, which allowed them to gain so much mileage in such a short time span. Other firms, such as oDesk and Elance, have similar business models, but we'll focus on the Guru.com model here.

Back in the day, online work was more or less restricted to data entry and typing jobs, and there was a lot of doubt over the authenticity of these sites. In addition, there were B2B schemes that involved selling a product to an audience or survey sites that would pay you a measly amount for your opinion. The big problem was that these services failed to capitalize on individual quality. These sites were a dime a dozen, with an increasing number of them requiring an initial down payment for beginning the required work. Many of them started spamming users and robbing them of their money by providing false information about the job requirements. The term "online workplace" was an utter lie. In any new market, no one knows who will win or lose. The big issue here is that there are many variables moving all at once. With all of the changes going on in markets, technology, broadband, internet, apps, social media, and smartphones, let's just say that a lot of business models are thrown against the wall—and only a few of them stick.

By contrast, Guru.com simply requires its users to upload their portfolios or interests. Employers post projects, and, based on their requirements, freelancers can apply. No money exchanged, no complicated procedures, just a simple proposal. Once the freelancer has been chosen and the work completed, employees transfer the predetermined amount to the user's account, a small percentage of which is taken by the website (7.45 percent or 11.95 percent, depending on the profile's membership level).

The main reason that Guru.com succeeded was that neither employers nor freelancers needed to pay a registration fee. The fee was incurred only once the project was successful. So there was little or no risk involved from the very beginning. Also, the fee both parties incurred was minimal.

On rare occasions, employers have asked freelancers to submit a sample piece from their chosen topic. The idea is to ask a handful of freelancers to write sample articles free of charge, and you've got half your project ready without paying a dollar. All you need to do is thread the various articles together. The website is trying its best to fend off adversaries by keeping stringent control over posts and identifying employers to be banned. But if its success rate increases tenfold in the next year, so will the spam rate. Also, Guru.com has created a virtual class system, with a divide between those paying to use Guru and those who use it free. The registered freelancers do get more preferences, which translate into better chances of being awarded a project. However, this service can be taken up by anybody, so, to be fair to the company, it has created an ecosystem where online working can flourish. Fees for membership can be paid monthly or annually and vary, depending on the freelancer skill type ($9.95 monthly for administration support to $34.95 for database and programming and lots of skill categories in between) and membership type (from Basic to Guru Vendor).

CASE STUDY
Collaboration Is King!

In the past, the top-down managerial styles of big companies were suited for big office buildings that centralized oversight and regulation. To create a product or offer a service, often on a strict deadline, companies needed to be highly organized and efficient. But in today's information economy, professionals are increasingly mobile and much more self-sufficient. In cities across the United States, these so-called laptop professionals—graphic designers, writers, software developers, and artists of all kinds—are turning to a collaborative style of work in which people share a common space.

Known as coworking, this new style of work allows like-minded creative professionals to limit costs and share ideas among themselves—often getting answers and input much faster than before. In the past, when a software engineer or project manager closed down at five o'clock, he would pick up where he'd left off the next morning. Now, with coworkers in other countries and time zones working, say, three eight-hour shifts in the same day, a project can get done much faster. Imagine the competitive advantage a firm has when implementing a coworking strategy so it can complete a project three times faster than its competitors.

> **Imagine the competitive advantage a firm has when implementing a coworking strategy so it can complete a project three times faster than its competitors.**

Coworking thrives in big cities that have an abundance of independent professionals, but it isn't restricted to urban areas. In fact, coworking office spaces can be found in communities across the country, especially in small towns that have a history of trading resources and working closely with neighbors. What truly makes a coworking community strong is diverse membership. At the same time, many rural communities have limited capital and a lack of infrastructure, which make coworking a viable alternative. A typical coworking space might allow a graphic designer to interact with someone who runs a small nonprofit, or a photographer to hook up with a web designer in search of original content for a client's page. Coworking spaces draw from a wide spectrum of professionals, attracting holistic health professionals, part-time lawyers, and small-business owners. An effective coworking space allows communities large and small to come together to share expertise and create opportunity.

Attracting Talent in the Future

One thing that excites me about the future is that survivalist companies will have to find new ways to recruit and retain talent. Not only will markets become more competitive but also employees—empowered by their access to information and ability to market themselves on a large scale—will become more demanding. Consequently, existing workplaces will be more horizontal than ever before. I like the way author, activist, blogger, and consultant David Bollier of the Aspen Institute (an educational organization based in Aspen, Colorado) puts it in his 2011 report *The Future of Work: What It Means for Individuals, Businesses, Markets, and Governments*:

> *When talent is highly fluid and moving in and out of organizations, access to talent becomes a serious challenge. So how to assure reliable access to talent? Trust and* transparency *(full, accurate, timely disclosure of information) are important in attracting the best workers. Clarity of mission and purpose are becoming important in galvanizing people to contribute their best.*

Did You Know?

Firms are turning to video to find new employees.

I've owned and operated twenty different businesses in my lifetime and hired hundreds of people to work for me or with me. On average, I would receive twenty-five to thirty résumés per open position. So, in all, I've enjoyed the mind-numbing task of trudging through hundreds of résumés. Once I sifted through them all, I faced the joys of first-round interviews, only to discover—and rediscover, again and again—that too many job candidates sizzle on paper and then fizzle in person. That's because résumés rarely capture that intangible mix of charisma and confidence that makes someone an attractive hire. There's a reason that employers pay headhunters big bucks to track down talented folks with strong interpersonal skills and a great résumé.

These days, firms are also turning to services such as Take the Interview, a job-interview service that adds a video component to a job-candidate screening. Instead of screening numerous people in person, employers post questions electronically, and candidates record their answers via their computers' video cameras. A video interview allows firms to flip through candidates quickly, picking prospective hires out of a daunting pack of applicants. And potential employees save the time they would have spent stressing over a lengthy first-round interview, as well as the travel time and the expense of having to travel to the company or to an outside agency for an in-person interview. Employers, meanwhile, can save resources instead of committing to a forty-five-minute interview or hiring a recruiter, which is often a large expense—especially in a bad economy saturated with underqualified candidates as well as overqualified candidates. The service costs between $45 and $300 per month, depending on how much a company plans to use it. The concept has been a hit. Within three months of launching, Take the Interview won more than 350 customers, including Boston University and Living Social. While the concept has taken off, the people at Take the Interview are not resting on their laurels. They're quickly adapting their business model to match expressed needs of current and potential clients. The company is considering collaborating with another company to crowdsource skill tests appropriate for specific positions and will be beefing up the service's five-star rating system with more elaborate scoring features to help employers manage information from and correspondence with their favorite job candidates.

Collaborating in the Cloud

The contemporary workplace encourages collaboration and discourages hierarchy. As a result, it's important for any employee to be able to communicate freely, and new technology is increasing these possibilities. Take "the cloud," for example. The cloud basically refers to any computing resources that are delivered over the internet. One of the emerging online ventures taking advantage of this need is Huddle, a website that provides companies with a new way to share their work with project collaborators online. Huddle bills itself as the number one alternative to SharePoint (another business collaboration platform) for enterprise collaboration and content management in the cloud, and it is used by more than one hundred thousand businesses globally (source: huddle.com).

A secure online environment where companies can share within their business ecosystem, Huddle replaces email as a de facto standard for cross-firewall collaboration (sharing work between protected networks). Users can also access documents on mobile devices such as the iPad and Android. It's a solution that is perfectly suited for the modern workplace, most of all because it lets employees operate independently, while sharing information on a large horizontal scale.

Yammer is another collaborative environment that I like a lot. The company boasts many stories of global companies that are using Yammer's business-networking tool to collaborate, share knowledge, and crowdsource ideas. Consider, for example, Lingo24, a global translation-services provider based in the United Kingdom. The firm employs 150 people across three continents, supported by a network of over 4,000 professional translators. They use Yammer for just about any kind of collaboration, but the way they crowdsource ideas is truly innovative.

Lingo24 was embarking on the task of designing a new website and used Yammer to crowdsource ideas for the graphics to be used. Yammer assembled the entire Lingo24 workforce for a companywide brainstorming of sorts. The effort resulted in suggestions and posted samples of artwork from individuals throughout the organization, and ultimately inspired new designs on the website. It was a truly collaborative exercise that engaged the entire company, thereby offering a more honest representation of the people who work there and the spirit of the organization than would have come out of a single marketing department.

CASE STUDY
Brand Consistency in Marketing

Kia Motors Corporation uses Huddle to disseminate information and maintain brand consistency in marketing activities across 70 dedicated PR offices, more than 40,000 global employees, and numerous external agencies. From its humble beginnings as a manufacturer of bicycle parts more than sixty-five years ago, Kia Motors has emerged as the driving force behind the South Korean automotive market. The company boasts an ever-expanding product line that is sold through a network of more than 4,000 dealers, 20 sales subsidiaries, and 141 distributors, covering 172 countries around the world.

With such a large number of focus markets and so many people with whom to communicate, Kia Motors was faced with the challenge of communicating consistent marketing messages across borders, languages, and cultures—safely and securely. The company wanted to ensure that the messages conveyed to customers during special events and press junkets, and through television and print advertisements, matched their expectations in Kia Motors's showrooms and dealerships. Brand messaging also needed to be consistent globally, yet embrace cultural differences. To enable the effective dissemination of information across all internal and external teams, Kia Motors turned to Huddle.

Pamela Muñoz, the auto manufacturer's assistant manager of international communications, explains in a prepared statement on the Huddle website: "At Kia Motors, we think globally. We're a very global company, but we incorporate a lot of our local initiatives into our products, communication strategies, and marketing campaigns." So the teams needed a tool that would enable them to communicate information in a timely, secure, and relevant way. It was especially important that information coming from Kia's Seoul headquarters be shared with local teams and spokespeople as soon as possible.

Kia Motors produces a wealth of content on a regular basis. For example, the monthly external newsletter alone is translated into seven different languages, and key messaging is distributed quarterly to the global network. This educates employees on new technology that has been released, new product launches, and updated communication strategies. Social media guidelines, as well as corporate standards and statements, also need to be shared with the company's network.

Before using Huddle, a lot of Kia Motors' messages and confidential photos were being leaked to the press, and the company couldn't identify the origin of these leaks. In launching integrated marketing campaigns worldwide, retaining version control and incorporating local feedback into marketing materials were also challenging.

Huddle has given Kia's public relations team the ability to retain a tremendous amount of control over what messaging is released to the public. PR campaign coordination has also improved. "As a small central team, we sometimes struggled with the huge number of queries received in response to a piece of collateral," Muñoz reports on the Huddle website. "When documents were distributed via email, we'd often get more than fifty emails back with numerous questions, different viewpoints to consider, and multiple comments from people in the same region. Huddle has enabled teams to participate in discussions and help each other."

A Social Media Network for Business Referrals

Referrals are arguably the number one source of new clients for small businesses. And the internet provides the perfect platform for providing those referrals, at a cost that's affordable to even the barest-budget start-up.

In the case of Referral Key, the cost is nothing. A business referral network, Referral Key helps small businesses create their own private referral networks to generate more sales leads. In a nutshell, you set up your free account, and then reach out to your friends and associates with an email inviting them to join your network. By joining, they are simply agreeing to keep you in mind as a business to recommend to *their* friends and associates for appropriate business needs. When a member of your network does refer someone to you, and that referral leads to business for you, you reward that member with a gift: anything from cash to a filet mignon from Omaha Steaks.

This is how business referrals traditionally work. The internet model just makes the whole concept more effective by helping you build out and manage your network. The idea makes a lot of sense, provided that members don't haphazardly start referring business in their excitement to win that filet mignon. It's a serious tool intended to nurture trusted referral relationships and should be treated as such, or the whole thing can easily turn into just another source of spam.

When we talk about work in the internet era, we tend to focus on three words: connectivity, collaboration, and creativity. These words summarize the way in which the traditional workplace is transforming. For the first time, almost everyone is connected at all times via social media and smartphones, whether we're talking about coworkers to bosses or businesses to consumers. The new pace of work has led many companies to turn to freelancers who specialize in collaboration. In turn, the collaborative era has led many young people to turn to alternative work styles such as coworking, which is cost efficient and fosters an environment that breeds more of my third word: creativity. Successful workplaces understand the importance of creativity in the internet age. Whether you're attracting talent or looking for solutions to new problems, creative thinking is one of the best investments that can be made in the workplace. Speaking of creativity, it's also one of the driving forces changing the ways that we play.

Your list or database is THE most important asset any business has! Build it. Protect it and do NOT overuse it!

Seven Apps for Employee Productivity

Keeping in step with the idea that "mobile is everything," businesses are turning to apps for solutions that will keep their employees productive even when they're not sitting at a desk. Here are a few of my current favorites (all costs are subject to change):

Scan2PDF Mobile: Tired of sitting on a wallet that's busting at the seams with receipts and business cards? This app, by Burrotech, lets you use your phone's camera to scan such documents as full-color PDFs and email them to your desktop. **Cost:** $14.99.

Documents to Go: What good does it do to get that important email you've been waiting for, if you can't read the attached report and spreadsheet? DataViz lets you create and edit Word and Excel files and PowerPoint presentations, and view PDF documents. A free version lets you view Word and Excel documents. **Cost:** $14.99

Bump: It's like a disco dance for phones. Tap your Bump-enabled phone with another Bump-enabled device, and you will instantly exchange your contact information, including name, address, phone, and photo—whatever you want to exchange. **Cost:** free.

textPlus: Say good-bye to the mahogany conference room. Say hello to textPlus, an app that lets up to twenty people conference via text message. It's convenient, it's mobile, and it's cheap. **Cost:** starting at $0.99 ($3.99 per year to have ads removed).

Seesmic: So, you're truly embracing the internet, and have gone all out and hired a social media coordinator to pump up marketing and PR efforts. Your next step is to help him or her organize all those Tweets. Seesmic neatly groups all your Twitter timelines in one screen, and will alert you when specific tweets are posted. **Cost:** free.

WaveSecure: These days, a person's smartphone is his or her life. What's priceless is not so much the phone itself, although these phones can be rather pricey, but, more so, the data in the phone. WaveSecure lets you remotely lock your phone if it's been lost. You can also track the SIM card, and back up any data. **Cost:** About $7 for every 3 months, $21 for one year.

6666Locale: When in Rome, do as the Romans do. Locale uses GPS to automatically switch your phone settings (wireless/networks, call and sound, display, apps, and so on) when you enter certain preset areas. **Cost:** $9.99.

INFUSIONSOFT VIDEO SERIES CASE STUDY
Online Service Helps Subscribers "Escape the Cubicle"

Today's employee faces a faltering economy, the ever-present threat of lay-offs, and a job market that feels strangely familiar to Depression-era grandparents. So there has never been a better time to think about starting a "side hustle," which is how Pamela Slim describes an activity you do during your "off-hours."

Slim would know. A former corporate manager and an entrepreneur for more than a decade, and now a business coach and successful author, she has a blog, *Escape from Cubicle Nation,* which is among the most popular career and marketing blogs on the web. Today she is one of the top one hundred women on Twitter, based on her Twitter Grade, which is determined by a person's influence and power using the medium (number of followers and number of tweets).

The thrust of Slim's message is one of liberation. "The internet has changed everything," she said. "I have sat in far too many conference rooms where people were let go and were completely unaware. The online world is one way to create a safety net or an entry point to building an amazing business."

When Slim dropped out of the corporate world in 1996 (she used to be the manager of training and development at Barclay's Global Investors, a $300 billion investment management firm in San Francisco), she entered a new entrepreneurial phase. In recent years, her entrepreneurial spirit has migrated online, where she relies on a bevy of tools—including a content-rich blog, a slick website, data analytics, and database marketing with Infusionsoft—to grow her business and promote her brand.

Apart from her business-coaching profession, Slim is a prolific writer and author of *Escape from Cubicle Nation,* a book that offers readers step-by-step advice on how to leave their jobs and pursue their passions. "My blog was really what attracted the book deal," she said. "When I wrote the book, I pulled content from my blog posts. The first time that you create something—like a post or a podcast—it's great if you can repurpose it."

Slim has designed the home page of her website to attract subscribers and increase the size of her online database, which is managed using Infusionsoft's automated marketing software. Slim has even found ways to capture people's subscription information via text when she's doing a live talk. In the past, a speaking engagement in front of a crowd of five hundred might land her fifty business cards to add to her database. Today, she noted, almost everyone has a cell phone.

"So I can be delivering a talk and say, 'If you want an e-book, I've prepared some follow-up materials for you. Whip out your cell phones and text to this number.' Immediately, people can get access, and, of course, I can get that connection with them. To me, that's revolutionary." This technology is called a five-digit short code.

Slim and her team look at her website's analytics each quarter and make necessary tweaks, though she expects that process to increase in frequency. Tailoring her content to the evolving needs of her subscribers gives her brand a personal touch that builds customer loyalty, which is the key to eternal freedom from the cubicle nation.

Watch the video here!
Scan the QR code or go to http://www.wordofmouse.com/qr/13/index.htm.

Chapter Summary Points

- The increasing speed of information continues to transform some industries and kill off others.

- In our wake lies an old model of work, one that is outdated, inefficient, mired in hierarchy, and based on forty-hour workweeks and top-down decisions.

- Many people now earn their paychecks in an environment of connectivity driven by increasingly sophisticated mobile devices, social networks, and cloud computing that keeps coworkers, management, and employees in constant communication.

- We need to break from century-old workplace ideals that promote standards, enforced cooperation, and management control of the same. Instead, new methods must be put in place—methods that enable creative work in an interconnected economy.

- Companies can address their own digital divide by taking advantage of business models such as crowdsourcing and coworking.

- In today's workplace, collaboration is king!

- Résumés rarely capture that intangible mix of charisma and confidence that makes someone an attractive hire. Implement video interviews instead.

- Companies should invest in collaboration. Look at sites that promote sharing, communication, and cooperation, such as Huddle.

- Relax! Your company is not the only one struggling to adapt to the tectonic shifts in the workplace.

- Unhappy with your career? There has never been a better time to embark on a career shift!

BONUS SECTION:
WORD OF MOUSE DRIVING TREND— CROWDSOURCING

The secret weapon for the smaller player, the entrepreneur, the small business that wants to compete with larger companies or major corporations, domestically and internationally, is to (1) understand, (2) know how to access, and (3) utilize crowdsourcing and outsourcing in *every way possible* within your enterprise. Avoiding fixed costs such as salaries and turning to costs that are variable in nature—*that you pay for only when you need them*—is almost a requirement for success in today's competitive business environment.

In the Word of Mouse era, individuals and firms are able to collaborate and compete on equal ground more than at any previous time in history. The little guys, such as the entrepreneurs working from home, can now compete with the large companies and major corporations. I credit this dynamic to a number of factors, with crowdsourcing leading the pack.

The concept we know as crowdsourcing has enjoyed many monikers over the years: from the stodgy "mass collaboration," to the folksy "tapping the wisdom of the crowds," to the techie "open sourcing," and the economical "wikinomics." In its current form, the term "crowdsourcing" was coined by writer Jeff Howe (also a professor of journalism at Boston's Northeastern University) in a June 2006 issue of *Wired* magazine. He defined it as "the process by which the power of the many can be leveraged to accomplish feats that were once the province of a specialized few." Two years later, Howe updated the definition:

"Crowdsourcing is the act of taking a job traditionally performed by a designated agent (usually an employee) and outsourcing it to an undefined, generally large group of people in the form of an open call."

Despite Howe's insight, the crowdsourcing concept is hardly a new one. Companies have been tapping into the power of crowds for decades. For instance, in 1916, employees of Planters Peanuts launched an open contest to create a logo for the ten-year-old company. What is cutting edge about modern crowdsourcing, though, is how it is being fused with new technology; or more precisely, how crowds are being integrated with the latest web software and social media channels. When you are backed by the power of the internet, it is incredibly easy (and fast) to crowdsource just about anything. Bestselling author James Patterson wrote the first and last chapters of his "chain thriller," *AirBorne,* and then opened up the remaining twenty-eight chapters to be written by the public.

The right strategy and tools are all it takes for a business to harness the influence and power of its audience, using customers to inspire priceless ideas and feedback more easily than ever before. Although many think of crowdsourcing in terms of idea generation, it's impossible to overstate the importance of gathering good ol' customer feedback using this new medium. Here's what Dell chairman and CEO Michael Dell had to say about the topic at the launch of Dell's IdeaStorm (a website created by Dell in 2007 with the intent of gauging the public's most important and relevant ideas): "We listen, learn, and then improve and innovate based on what our customers want. It's one of the real advantages of being a direct company."

Few people realize the pervasiveness and popularity of crowdsourcing today. For example, take Wikipedia, which is among the most innovative crowdsourcing initiatives the web has ever produced. It's also an ideal example of how crowdsourcing really works—and why the concept has taken on an integral and permanent role in big-idea development for organizations of every size and nature.

Outsourcing has long been accepted as a viable way to accomplish a project that a person or organization does not have the time or skill set to complete in-house. In the outsourced model, the business would seek out bidders, "testing" their skills on a trial basis. Eventually the job would be awarded to the best candidate, but not before the company had exhausted a large number of hours, much research, and much effort in the process.

Crowdsourcing takes outsourcing to the next level. In terms of cost savings, it helps users bring together a wide group of individuals with similar skills and talents, enabling organizations to obtain and implement new ideas and generate feedback throughout the working process more quickly and efficiently.

GAIN A COMPETITIVE ADVANTAGE TODAY VIA CROWDSOURCING

Anyone who wants to get up to speed on crowdsourcing—and stay there—should bookmark the website Daily Crowdsource. It's stuffed with the latest news of, trends in, research on, and uses of crowdsourcing, and is extremely well represented with data, infograms (graphic visual representations of information, data, or knowledge), and guest bloggers.

The folks at Daily Crowdsource are driven to fine-tune and promote the field of crowdsourcing via the development of best practices, common methodologies for problem solving, and a unified front to the public. They have identified the need to categorize the concept as an important first step toward this end.

The group has proposed a taxonomy of crowdsourcing and has illustrated the categories in a graphic, which I have reprinted here, with the permission of the folks at the Daily Crowdsource (dailycrowdsource.com).

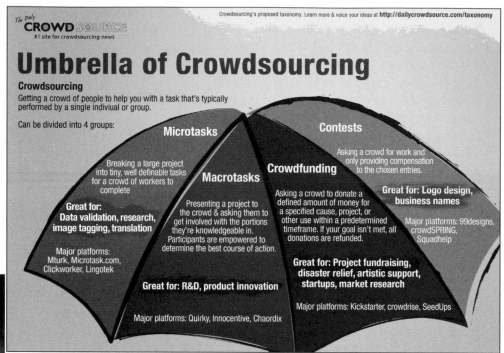

"These categories are defined by the relationship of the worker to the work and to those that control the production process," explains David Alan Grier, author of *When Computers Were Human* and crowd leader (a crowdsourcing industry leader) for the Daily Crowdsource. And, in the spirit of crowdsourcing, Grier invites the industry to discuss these categories and submit ideas on the scope of definitions, so that a stable document can be produced, and crowdsourcing can graduate to a more mature level of implementation.

The Cover Graphic of My Previous Book, Get Rich Click!— Was Crowdsourced

That's right. I turned to 99designs, put up a $750 reward for the best graphic, got over seven hundred proposals for very cool book covers, and finally chose one. In the old days, I would have worked with one graphic designer and chosen three to five options. I got more for less in not even half the time! This book was published by Simon & Schuster and its wonderful graphic artists came up with the cover you see on page 213.

CASE STUDY
Peperami's $10,000 Contest Generates Ad Campaign Ideas via Crowdsourcing

One of the revolutionary benefits of social media is that large companies and organizations can engage directly with their consumers. These days, it's not uncommon for companies to bypass their creative teams or in-house agencies and engage with those consumers directly when they want help creating new products or are testing out new ad content. For example, when Unilever wanted to generate ideas for an ad campaign for its pork sausage snack food Peperami, the company launched a contest, offering $10,000 to whoever submitted the best idea.

"We believe Peperami is a brand that deserves radical creative solutions and are confident that taking our brief out to thousands rather than a small team of creatives will provide us with the best possible idea and take our advertising to the next level," Peperami marketing manager Noam Buchalter told the UK-based newspaper the *Guardian.*

Since Peperami was already a well-established European brand, crowdsourcing was a logical solution for this project. But when it comes to creating long-term brand ideas from scratch, you will probably need copywriting professionals, not just consumers. However, if you're looking for a way to understand your consumers' needs and desires better than ever before, crowdsourcing is a great place to start.

"Today's consumers are looking for new levels of brand engagement, and this experiment shows that for the right brand, such as Peperami, crowdsourcing can be an excellent vehicle for creative consumer interaction," said Matt Burgess, Peperami managing director, in an interview with Daily Crowdsource. The company saved 60 percent in costs by forgoing the traditional model.

ISSUES TO CONSIDER BEFORE IMPLEMENTING CROWDSOURCING

Although the appeal of cost savings is hard to ignore, organizations should understand both the risks and the rewards of using crowdsourcing before they take the leap.

In most countries, crowdsourcing is not legislated. In the United States, a bill called the Entrepreneur Access to Capital Act would amend the Securities Exchange Act of 1934, allowing crowdsourcing for equity up to $10,000 per investor. In essence, if passed, it will let small commercial enterprises, such as individuals with ideas or small businesses, use the internet for crowdfunding by selling nonpublic securities to the public through "social media solicitations." The enterprise requests money in exchange for some promise of return at a later date. As of this writing, the legislation has been passed by the US House of Representatives and a different version was passed by the US Senate.

Putting aside the possible legal implications, which are yet to be determined, several business issues should be addressed at the onset of a crowdsourcing effort. Bill Johnston, director of Global Online Community at Dell, wrote an article for *Business Computing World,* an IT leadership blog, called "How to Make the Most Out of Crowdsourcing." The piece lays out some excellent points on this topic. I've excerpted some of it here, with *BCW*'s permission:

Eight Tips for Successful Crowdsourcing

1. The key to crowdsourcing is to find a way to solicit customer ideas directly, evaluate them efficiently, and implement the best ideas that make sense to the business. In the past, companies have approached this through suggestion boxes and online forms; however, these approaches fall short due to the fact that there is no open dialogue about the ideas, and the process doesn't scale easily.

2. The submitted content needs to be heavily scrutinized and backed up with valid factual references to ensure that the quality and reliability of the content are of a good standard. Wikipedia does this by managing its crowdsourced content, using editors to check the accuracy of the community's submissions.

3. Businesses must understand their "crowd" (aka their community). Businesses need to think about who makes up their crowd, what topics the crowd is knowledgeable and passionate about, and what its level of expertise is with the product, service, or industry.

4. If businesses do not think about who their crowd is, then the reliability and quality of information will suffer. There is no point in putting a subject out there that the crowd does not have any expertise or knowledge in.

5. It is also critical that the business sets the context and boundaries for ideas and discussion; otherwise the community will experience a decline over time. Signaling the topics or issues that the business wants to hear about directs the topic of conversation, encouraging productive ideas and suggestions from the community that the business can respond to.

6. If businesses have no intention of acting on the feedback and ideas the crowd provides, this type of activity can be a liability instead of an asset. Before embarking on any sort of crowdsource strategy, businesses must understand the implications of opening the door to this type of feedback, and be willing to act on what they hear, knowing that many things will challenge the status quo.

7. Having team members present and attendant in the community drives activity and engagement, as they can provide feedback on the ideas proposed by the community and identify ideas that will benefit the business.

8. The circumstances for a crowdsourcing initiative are ideal when the business is at a high state of readiness to receive input, reacting to and implementing feedback. It is critical that businesses signal to the community the topics they would like to discuss, attracting the appropriate members of "the crowd" to engage in conversation, and then acting on key findings.*

In short, it goes back to what my mother always used to tell me: "If a job's worth doing, it's worth doing right." Such is the case with crowdsourcing. A business that fails to strategize, with the above points in mind, is setting itself up for a failed project and, quite possibly, a damaged reputation within its community. That being said, a carefully considered and sound effort can deliver many times over on time, effort, and expense.

CASE STUDY
Crowdfunding: Author Raises $24,000 in Thirty Days with Kickstarter

Craig Mod is the coauthor of *Art Space Tokyo: An Intimate Guide to the Tokyo Art World,* a how-to guide chock-full of hidden galleries and museums. The writer was looking for a way to fund an updated edition of his book. After hearing about Kickstarter, he saw the site as an opportunity to create micro-seed capital (levels that are smaller than typical venture capital investments) and dove right in.

Before he put his project online where the community could engage with it, Mod started researching the top twenty to thirty highest-grossing Kickstarter campaigns to date.

The average pledge was around $62.50; most people were happy to pay $25 or $50 to fund these projects.

Mod recommends avoiding lower tiers—for example, under $25—and instead going for $100, $250, and up to $500 tiers. He recommends that you set for a maximum five tiers. Anything more than that, and you will leave supporters with paradoxical choices, with lower tiers potentially cannibalizing higher-tier engagements.

To cut the long story short, here are Mod's five-week campaign results with Kickstarter: He placed six tiers: $25, $65, $100, $250, $850, and $2,500, each with a different benefit. For example, $25 pledges would receive the *Art Space Tokyo* book in PDF format, while the $65 pledges would also receive the physical book format. Most individuals took the $65 option. He received a total of 262 pledges (mostly for $65 and $100), which translated into $23,325 in US currency. The financial goal was hit only sixteen days into the campaign.

Lesson Learned

Mod realized that the $25 tier allowed contributors to feel they were a part of the community while they supported the project. And this sense of belonging is a key issue to consider. With crowdfunding, a business is not only raising

---

* Business Computing World, www.businesscomputingworld.co.uk.

money but also building a base of loyal fans who will support it throughout the fund-raising campaign, and possibly future ones as well. The key to any organization's crowdfunding success is explaining in clear terms how the business will benefit from contributions and then tailoring those profits to the audience's needs and desires. Here's how Mod articulated his approach:

> *The $250 tier might have done better had I explained what the* tenugui *reward was earlier. And $850 was a perfect catchall for lovers of Takahashi-san's work, or those who have the means to give a project such substantial support. I didn't sell any of my mind-blowing bike/café/museum/architectural/culinary Tokyo day tours at my crazy rate of $2,500. But then again, that was there to make Takahashi's print look like a good deal, more than to turn me into a tour guide.*

Shortening the campaign from five to four weeks would also have been a better idea, Mod decided, helping him avoid the down days when he received fewer pledges.

Mod and his coauthor, Ashley Rawlings, promoted his Kickstarter project using three main methods:

1. Twitter and Facebook updates.

2. Personal mailings to a vast database of contacts in the art and design world that they had gathered over six years in the industry. Emails were sent in blitzes at the start and the end of the fund-raising period. Throughout the middle of the campaign, he provided progress reports that featured recent media coverage.

3. Online media: a number of top art and design blogs and magazines were targeted for postings. "My strategy for promoting projects is simple," Mod said in his website, craigmod.com. "I find a number of key, influential sites with topics that overlap with what I'm looking to promote. I then write emails specific to those blogs, magazines, and newspapers, highlighting the aspects of the project I think they'd be most interested in. Oftentimes, I'm writing to blogs that I've been reading for years, so for me, referencing older posts of theirs and personalizing these emails is trivial, and fun."

Looking back at the project, Mod advised setting higher financial goals to generate maximum dollars from the audience.

Here are a few other lessons worth mentioning:

• Think in terms of microseed capital and not one-off money (single transactions); having a long-term strategy is key.

• The fewer tiers, the better, to avoid confusing fans and to attract more pledges.

• Take advantage of all offline and online contacts, resources, and assets.

• Promote smartly: focus on high-quality, targeted community coverage.

• Dare to push pledge goals to the edge.

Note: I would also strongly suggest contacting a lawyer *before* you think of crowdfunding a project, to make certain that you are following all local, state, and federal laws that are in place to help consumers avoid fraudulent issues.

CASE STUDY
CloudSponge Increases Conversions by 33 Percent Using 99designs

CloudSponge is a company that helps website owners manage and share their customers' address books using web-based software. As the company's website explains, "Allowing people to import their webmail or desktop address books and tell their contacts about your service or connect with their friends on your website is an easy way to help your content or service to go viral." Founder Jay Gibb was looking for an outsourcing design alternative after realizing that conversion rates of his existing sites were not promising. He turned to 99designs and wrote a brief posting that went out to the 80,000-person community. Jay received 189 unique designs to choose from, and the winning design helped increase the new website conversion by 33 percent.

Time spent on the project: ten days.

Total investment in the campaign: $1,388 (single payment).

In a testimonial on the 99designs website, Gibb said, "The new design has dramatically increased my conversion rate, and I really enjoyed the whole 99 designs process. The price is right, the delivery timeline is predictable, and the artists are all eager to please. I'll definitely use it again whenever I need design work done."

CASE STUDY
Six Good Project Candidates for Crowdsourcing

The list of ideas that can be crowdsourced is long, to say the least. Businesses that want to dip their toes in the crowdsourcing waters may want to consider the following efforts:

1. Logos and web design: Long gone are the days when an organization had to pay thousands of dollars to a single graphic artist for a web design or logo. Sites such as 99designs, Logo Contest, DesignCrowd, LogoTournament, and Crowdsourcing Logo Design offer virtually unlimited potential to find the best talent, enabling crowds to create a company's dream logo—cheaply and fast.

2. Creative media (music, films, documentary): Amazon Studios, a division of Amazon, offers an ideal platform for novice and amateur filmmakers and screenwriters to showcase their potential movies or scripts to real studios. Their work is shared with a global community of fans and filmmakers that can provide feedback and suggestions. The best projects, as determined by Amazon Studios' story department, are rewarded with monthly cash prizes and move to the "Development Slate," where they are further refined with visitor feedback and primed for production into major Hollywood movies. Amazon Studios has a first-look deal with Warner Bros. Pictures, which means that it will be presenting its top projects to Hollywood's biggest studio for consideration as theatrical feature films.

3. **Book creation and promotion:** The book *Enterprise Social Technology* by Scott Klososky, which discusses how best to make use of social media to build an efficient business, is an early example of crowdsourced book production. From its cover design and content to its distribution and marketing, this book was developed via crowdsourcing. It serves as a model of how social tech and publishing can be mixed and exploited ethically and profitably.

Klososky discovered that crowdsourcing enabled him to create a book that was "richer in content and insight than a book produced by a single author or an editor working with a group of preselected contributors." The book was produced quickly and economically. Klososky applied the traditional publishing model of selling the book through retail locations and using traditional distribution methods.

Klososky generated buzz for his book by offering $20,000 worth of cash to individuals willing to take the risk and spread the word about it, according to a handful of creative crowdsourcing guidelines. For example, the first person who created a viral video about the book that received at least ten thousand views, providing a screen shot as proof, would win $1,000 in cash. But there's more. The person who managed to get 250 people to wear T-shirts emblazoned with the title and take a high-resolution group photo would win $5,000.

4. **Advertising campaigns:** Zooppa partners with firms to bring members exciting opportunities to create winning ads for major brands. Companies develop a creative brief describing their brand's attributes, target audience demographics, and campaign goals. Community members are then invited to produce ads in various formats: viral videos, print ads, scripts, and so on. Once members submit their entries, clients can select and award the best content or allow community members to vote on content submissions in order to determine additional award winners. Zooppa awards cash and distinct prizes, from publicity on the Zooppa website to a brand-new Kia Soul, to ad creators based on feedback received from the client, the community, and the Zooppa staff. Its motto: "Mutual interest creates mutual success!"

5. **Education:** A frustrated former teacher named Alex Grodd, looking for a solution to his experience with limited instructional content, launched BetterLesson. The online platform is designed to help teachers find high-quality lesson plans and classroom resources. Teachers can join the community of educators, where they can build and share innovative curriculums.

There are many types of education, ranging from academic to recreational to lifesaving. Because recent statistics show that one in five college women reports a case of sexual harm, the US Department of Health and Human Services (HHS) submitted a crowdsourcing challenge on the problem-solving platform ChallengePost. The site led to a smartphone application that aids young women in escaping a potential sexual assault.

6. Funding: For any investors looking to change the world or simply to make a difference in their community, there are plenty of crowdfunding websites out there as well. Here are just a few:

- A person wanting to fund a start-up company or idea can go to SeedUps or visit appbackr, the first crowdfunding marketplace for mobile applications. In return, the website says that investors can profit anywhere between 25 percent and 50 percent for every app sold.
- Investors inclined to help techie enthusiasts can hop over to Fundageek.
- For supporting movie initiatives, Kickstarter may be your best bet, considering that it is most well known as a source of funding in cinematic circles.
- Music fans who want to support new artists can benefit from a trip to ArtistShare, where they can fund artists' recording projects. In exchange, investors gain access to the creative process, limited-edition recordings, VIP access to recording sessions, and even credit listing on the CD.
- Redesignme attracts product manufacturers to participate in "RDM Challenges," where they pay to showcase new product concepts and ask the site's more than three thousand members for feedback. In exchange, members are rewarded with RDMs (Redesignme's online currency), which can then be exchanged for products such as MP3 players, game consoles, and gift cards.

The Crowdsourcing-Crowdfunding Connection

Putting it plainly, crowdsourcing and crowdfunding have a symbiotic relationship. If you're not sure how to see the synergies and put them to their best use, several products and services can help. Here are some examples:

- **WordPress.com "plug-ins":** The crowdfunding platform IgnitionDeck enables WordPress users to raise money on their own terms. No need to give away any cut of the funding, and the posting individual or organization has total control over his or her project. The platform is integrated with PayPal to accept funds worldwide and MailChimp and AWeber for email marketing campaigns.
- **Web-based services:** ChipIn is similar to IgnitionDeck because it integrates with PayPal and offers the opportunity to display the related widget in a sidebar on a blog or a web page, where others can see the project's progress. It is a web-based service that simplifies the process of collecting money from groups of people, and it is subject only to PayPal transaction fees.

CROWDSOURCING AND
CROWDFUNDING TRENDS

A telltale sign that a trend has gone from fad to staple is the emergence of subtrends within that trend. With crowdsourcing, the subtrends are past the point of germination and are well into development. Here are a few I've spotted:

● **Curated crowds**: Since anyone can request to join the crowd, it is hard to get more experts, rather than generalists, to participate in a project. Sites such as GeniusRocket are shifting to a curated model of crowdsourcing, which requires members to prove they're talented by providing links to a demo reel or portfolio, for example, before they can take part in projects.

● **Idle sourcing**: The easier it is for the community members to vote and pledge money, submit ideas, and offer their skills, the higher the success of the campaign seeking this input. Enter the age of idle sourcing, defined by Trend watching.com as "products and services that make it downright simple (if not effortless) to contribute to anything, from pinpointing roads in need of repairs to finding signs of extraterrestrial life."

With the help of smart sensors on mobile phones, 24/7 GPS, and accelerometer-enabled phones (which detect acceleration), the wave of individuals broadcasting data about their locations and activity is tsunami-like in nature.

Take, for example, Street Bump, an Android app that gives government agencies a real-time map of Boston road conditions. It uses the sensors and built-in GPS technology of the smartphone to register and report potholes automatically, with little help from the user.

I expect such usages to spark a slew of privacy concerns, as people's concerns catch up with the various uses of collected data. But that's the subject of another book.

● **Crowdsourcing standardization**: Since crowdsourcing is still in the early-adoption phase, one that appears to be increasing in popularity by the day, it's becoming increasingly hard to regulate. Plans to create a trade association and an official taxonomy, among many other things, will ensure its long-term usage and growth.

● **Taking self-publishing to the next level**: In the old days, if you wanted to write a book, you had to either have a big name or use your talent to attract the attention of a literary agent, who shopped your work to traditional book publishing companies in search of a deal. Increasingly, that model is becoming obsolete, thanks to crowdfunding and the proliferation of ebooks. Authors are beginning to launch their works by harnessing the power of crowds, and with no advertising expenses. While the hardest part of book publishing remains the actual research and writing, crowdsourcing platforms provide self-publishing authors a new option to showcase their work and fund their ideas.

For example, author Scott Berkun used Kickstarter to raise $5,832 for his book *Mindfire: Big Ideas for Curious Minds*. (For another example of publishing via crowdsourcing, see the case study in this section.) Can you imagine generating income from a book even before it's published and without relying on publishing contracts and agents? For writers willing to hustle, it's a dream come true.

● **Equity crowdfunding**: In the classic crowdfunding model, funders are rewarded with products, services, and preferential treatment, but not with a financial payoff. The project starters keep 100 percent of the intellectual property and their equity. Crowdcube, the first crowdfunding platform for businesses to raise equity in the United Kingdom, proposes a new way to invest, one in which UK-based entrepreneurs and businesses raise money by tapping into a "crowd" of like-minded individuals willing to invest smaller amounts of cash in exchange for rewards and a stake in their business. Through Crowdcube's platform the Rushmore Group attracted 143 individuals to invest in its fourth members-only bar in London, for a total of 10 percent equity. The average investment was 7,000 euros per person. This effort not only demonstrated consumer demand for another private club locally but also helped the company build a raving fan base on its opening night.

Darren Westlake, cofounder and CEO of Crowdcube, was quoted on its website as saying: "Raising £1 million for a single business on Crowdcube is a fantastic achievement but not a surprise to us. We firmly believe that raising finance using crowdfunding will transform the way businesses raise capital in the future. With over £1.4 million successfully raised on Crowdcube for British businesses since July 2011, we are bucking the trend and proving that there is now an alternative way to raise business finance in the UK."

There is no shortage of crowdsourcing and crowdfunding websites to get your business idea, creative work, or microtask off and running—without all the overhead of hiring full-time employees. Here's a sample of what you'll find if you start digging!

CREATIVE TALENT CROWDSOURCING WEBSITES

● **Advertising:** Poptent (www.poptent.net)

● **Brainstorming/feedback:** Kluster (www.kluster.com)

● **Business innovation:** Chaordix (www.chaordix.com)

● **Data cleansing and entry/content creation:** Amazon Mechanical Turk (www.mturk.com/mturk/welcome)

● **Images:** Flickr Creative Commons (www.flickr.com/creativecommons)

● **Logo design:** 99designs (www.99designs.com)

- **Product design and manufacturing:** Ponoko (www.ponoko.com)

- **Product naming/branding:** NameThis (www.namethis.com)

- **Product redesign:** Redesignme (www.redesignme.com)

- **Software and usability testing:** uTest (www.utest.com)

- **Writing:** Textbroker (www.textbroker.com), Guru.com (www.guru.com), Elance (www.elance.com)

- **Crowdfunding:** Kickstarter (www.kickstarter.com), Go Get Funding (gogetfunding.com), Early Shares (www.earlyshares.com)

Bonus Section Summary Points

- Crowdsourcing is the act of taking a job traditionally performed by a designated agent (usually an employee) and outsourcing it to an undefined, generally large group of people in the form of an open call.

- Since crowdsourcing is still in the early-adoption phase—one that appears to be increasing in popularity by the day—it's becoming increasingly hard to regulate it. Plans to create a trade association and an official taxonomy, among many other things, will ensure its growth. Initial categories include microtasks, macrotasks, crowdfunding, and contests.

- Like all the other crowd business models (data gathering for research, citizen engagement for nonprofits, and so on), crowdsourcing and crowdfunding are synergistic and tied to the same breakthrough approach to understanding, developing, learning, and accomplishing via the power of many.

- There is no limit to what individuals and companies can crowdsource, from advertising to creative products to funding. If you have a problem and want to challenge a group of people to try to solve it for you, try the "crowdsourcing" platform ChallengePost.

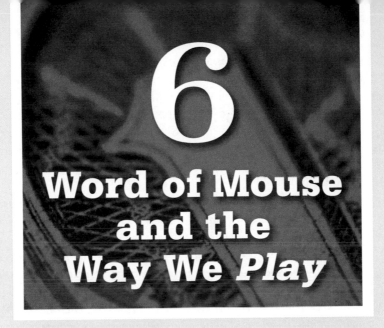

6

Word of Mouse and the Way We Play

When I think back to my childhood, one of the first things that come to mind is all my toys: G.I. Joe, Frisbees, the Rubik's Cube, LEGOs, Hot Wheels, and, of course, the Slinky. Most of these have remained remarkably popular over time—but maybe not as popular as technology-based toys, such as Nintendo, Xbox, and Leap Pads.

I don't mean to imply that Barbie dolls are destined for extinction. But whether you're five years old or fifty, the way we play is changing—or has changed—and is entering new technological territory, creating unknown possibilities and consequences. How fast is this happening? Here's an example from Sara Stephens, the editor working with me on this book. Sara has two daughters, and here's what she has to say:

> *For my daughter's sixth birthday, we got her a Barbie Dream Townhouse, with some Barbie dolls, clothes, and accessories. Only a year later, for her seventh birthday, all she wanted was a Nintendo 3DS. What a difference a year makes. Not only in her tastes but also in the technology available. Her favorite thing to do used to be going to see 3-D movies. I would take her, dragging my own feet, as I detest wearing the 3-D glasses. Now she gets to watch 3-D movies via Netflix*

on her handheld device at home, on car trips, waiting in the doctor's office—no 3-D glasses required!

Wow! Talk about a change in the way kids play! When the family is in the car, Sara added, and her girls are seeking entertainment, technology is not just a way to play—it's a parent's best friend. She and her husband used to keep their kids occupied with backseat movies. Now they just hand over their smartphone, laptop, or iPad.

She continued:

Whoever doesn't get Daddy's phone (which is usually more up to date with the latest and greatest games) gets to use the iPad, which is also loaded with games, Netflix, and so on. My three-year-old tends to prefer the iPad—although she is an Angry Birds master, mind you—because the larger screen lets her really wax artistic using the loaded paint programs. No longer am I packing coloring books, which inevitably get torn, or crayons, which invariably melt. It's all about the digital art. When the one kid starts to have iPad envy, I suggest that she start recording a photo journal of our trip, using the phone's camera. She is again a happy camper, taking pictures from the car window, or recording reporter-like videos of interviews with all the car's passengers. Once again, peace reigns in the family car; plus we have a nice collection of digital media (drawings, photos, and videos) to add to the family photo album on Flickr.

When the family is in the car, Sara added, and her girls are seeking entertainment, technology is not just a way to play—it's a parent's best friend.

But kids aren't the only ones changing how we play. Remember when you were a teenager, playing used to mean a night of bowling, ice skating, miniature golf, or a movie? Times have changed. Whether it's using technology to connect with your favorite musician, starring in your own online gambling tournament with friends you may have never met, using apps to make new guy friends for pickup basketball games, or creating virtual worlds with multiplayer online games, *playing* has been infused with a new degree of revived creativity and mental challenge. Perhaps even more important, you never have to *stop* playing, regardless of your age.

My wife, Beverle, used to be an avid Scrabble player. The ability to get a triple word score on *benzoxycamphors* (don't ask me what it means) tickles her more than a shopping spree. Well, almost as much. But Bev has retired her wooden Scrabble tiles and now sharpens her linguistic skills playing Words with Friends, a popular social mobile game that challenges players to create the highest-scoring words while competing against family and friends. She can now humiliate players in up to twenty games at once *and* chat with the players during the games. I, for one, am thankful to have been removed from the Scrabble hot seat. And Bev is happy to be challenged by more worthy opponents.

"I'm too young for Facebook.
I'm on Head-Shoulders-Knees-and-Toes Book."

When it comes to senior citizens, it's unlikely that they will ever give up the dominoes or card games that showcase skills they have built over their lifetimes. And I don't see them dropping out of the bingo night social scenes at local churches or community centers. These pastimes play an important role in their lives. But technology has afforded new recreational options to add to their day, which has more room to be filled than that of any other age group. Catering to a need and desire to challenge memories and draw on experiences, DVDs such as the movie trivia game Scene It? offer versions based on classic films. And to inject more physical activity into their days, some seniors and senior citizen centers engage in online sports tournaments for tennis, bowling, baseball, and other games using Wii or Xbox Kinect gaming systems. These activities let seniors be social and be active, overcoming the obstacles presented by playing outside. The AARP, the nonprofit organization for people ages fifty and over, even offers free online games on its website (www.aarp.org) and publishes a seasonal review of "video games for grown-ups"—a must-read for any senior who wants to get engaged in the brave new world of play.

In this chapter, I will give you a host of ways that people play in our new Word of Mouse world and show you how the digital world has breathed new life into the games of yesteryear.

Keeping Active in a World of Digital Play

Physically interactive games are great not only because they promote aerobic activity but also because they tire out your kids, zapping that excess energy that keeps them up late. They offer a fantastic alternative form of entertainment to vegging out on the couch, killing zombies with a controller in one hand and a can of Jolt Cola and a bag of potato chips in the other. I couldn't resist talking about some of my favorite physically interactive games.

The Konami title Dance Dance Revolution made a big splash when it was introduced in 2001. Within a few years, it had sold more than 1.2 million copies in North America, so it shouldn't surprise you if your kids are familiar with it already. One of the more popular contemporary games is Revolution, which is compatible with Sony PlayStation 2 and Microsoft Xbox. I like this game because it's physically engaging, allowing users to dance to energetic music by stepping on special footpad controllers. If you really want to break a sweat, try Dance Dance Revolution Extreme. The game combines the original Revolution with the EyeToy, a camera attachment that tracks hand and body movements. Over the years this gadget alone has been responsible for a new wave of physically demanding games, most of which can be controlled with the wave of a user's hand. Furthermore, if you live in a city like Houston or Phoenix, where going outside is a bit of a challenge due to the heat and humidity, such games really fill the need for physical activity at any age. For example, EyeToy: Antigrav allows players to control a hover board using their whole body. If your kids are into martial arts, or you just want to keep them active, check out EyeToy: Kinetic, which includes personal trainers who teach kickboxing, aerobics, and even yoga.

Now, if you really want to exhaust your little ones, strap on the sensor armbands that come with Tek Tag (www.wildplanet.com/tektag), which track the number of times somebody has been touched. If you thought the game of tag couldn't get any more sophisticated, you might also be surprised by I-Toy's latest incarnation of hacky sack. Using an electronic footpad that counts the number of kicks it has received before recording a score, the game can get a bit addictive. Last, but not least, even dressing up has gone tech with Get-Ups, (www.bigboing.com), which are basically animal and fairy costumes for younger children. But unlike conventional dinosaur costumes, these make sounds that are triggered by the child's movement. I wish I'd had something like that when I was growing up!

FUTURECASTING: WHY FANS WILL BECOME THE MOST POWERFUL PLAYERS IN THE SPORTS WORLD

We already visit the websites of favorite teams, check our smartphones for scores, listen to games in progress (sometimes multiple games at a time), order tickets online, browse sports blogs, and enter chat rooms to dissect the latest results and gossip. Using your smartphone, you can track a sporting event as it's happening—anywhere in the world! Physical newspapers are disappearing, but online sports journalism is thriving.

And don't forget social media. Sites such as Facebook, MySpace, Twitter, YouTube, and Flickr have opened up new opportunities for sports news and discussion. These sites take us beyond mere reportage, linking fans to one another as well as to professional athletes, allowing everyone to share opinions, ideas, and photos in real time all over the globe. At my house, when one game is on my television, it's not uncommon for another to be streaming on my computer, allowing me to watch my alma mater (the University of Texas at Austin—Hook 'em, Horns!) play football while I keep tabs on my daughter's school in another time zone across the country. It's brilliant!

But the interactive feel of fandom is only just beginning. In fact, you ain't seen nothin' yet. In the future, the battle for your attention will make *you* the new player. Amid the fight to win over customers, media corporations will offer consumers exclusive data and entertainment packages with amazing features.

"MARC" MY WORDS Being a fan in the future will blow your mind! Sports and entertainment will become completely interactive. Do you recall the robot R2D2 showing a 4-D holographic video message from Princess Leia in *Star Wars*? This, too, is about to become a reality. We're already enjoying "live" performances by deceased artists, such as the cameo of rapper Tupac Shakur, served up via hologram at the 2012 Coachella Music Festival. And you can expect more to follow, as the estates of Jimi Hendrix and Elvis Presley have already begun the process of thrilling fans both old and new with the experience of seeing these classic artists "perform" virtually on a physical stage.

We will watch sports and entertainment in full 3-D and 4-D and walk around the stadium that's projected on the floor of our home theaters. At some point, the internet will allow us to design our own sports and entertainment packages by choosing select camera angles, announcers, instant replay on demand, and interviews with our favorite player or coach. The future has much to offer. Just wait and see!

When "Pay Per Click" via Google is such a VITAL component to growing your client list, you'd better know the value of a prospect and client . . . because your competitors certainly do! If they are outbidding you for keywords, they know more than you do!

CASE STUDY
How to Start a Playful Meme!

According to Wikipedia, a meme is "an idea, behavior, or style that spreads from person to person within a culture." A meme acts as a unit for carrying cultural ideas, symbols, or practices from one mind to another through writing, speech, gestures, rituals, or other imitable phenomena. What makes memes fascinating is that they act as cultural "genes" that identify a culture, self-replicate through that culture, and mutate in response to the influences of that culture. Catchphrases are an excellent example of memes, and they generally catch on because large audiences watch the same movie or television program where the phrase was originally uttered. Viewers start dropping the phrase into conversation as a shared form of metaphoric speech. Eventually the phrase makes its way into conversations even with those who never heard its original mention—and, therefore, don't understand its original context. But by now, they have a complete understanding of its meaning, based on how it has embedded itself into cultural vocabulary. A good example is the expression "Show me the money," which comes from the movie *Jerry Maguire*.

Another example would be what has occurred with Tim Tebow, the popular professional quarterback and an evangelical Christian. He has been praying in public since his college football days at the University of Florida, where he won two national championships and the Heisman Trophy. But it wasn't until Jared Kleinstein, a twenty-four-year-old Denver Broncos fan living in New York City, turned Tebow's faith into an internet phenomenon that it became the talk of the sports world.

It began improbably, in the celebratory moments of a Tebow-led comeback victory in week seven of the 2011 NFL season, when Kleinstein noticed the quarterback kneeling in prayer as the stadium erupted around him. "We were at a bar in Manhattan," Kleinstein said in an interview with the *Houston Chronicle*. "I look up and see Tim kneeling down quietly while everyone was celebrating, and it caught my attention."

Kleinstein had a friend snap a photo of him imitating the pose, in which one knee is placed on the ground and a fist is placed near the face. He posted the photo to Facebook a few hours later, and pretty soon the comments began adding up. By the time he got up the next morning, he'd created the phenomenon that is now known as "Tebowing."

Kleinstein purchased the domain name Tebowing.com for $10 and sent an email to friends asking for photo submissions. The concept, as defined by Kleinstein's website, was incredibly simple: "to get down on a knee and start praying, even if everyone else around you is doing something completely different."

The site had 785 views the day it launched. The number shot up to 10,000 the second day and more than a quarter million twenty-four hours later. Kleinstein's site has had about 16,000 photo submissions from eighty countries so far, and countless more have appeared on Facebook and Twitter. Several months later, he was still in a state of shock.

"I was stunned," Kleinstein told the *Houston Chronicle*. "But that was just the beginning. Now we've had around 1.8 million unique visitors and more than 16 million page views. It's crazy."

The media took notice, and soon after, Tebowing was all over television and the web. It was featured on Fox, CBS, CNN, and the *Huffington Post*. Since then, Tebow has appeared on the cover of *Sports Illustrated*, been mentioned at the December 2011 Republican presidential primary debate in Iowa, and been mocked in a playful *Saturday Night Live* skit. (The last has become an internet meme all its own.) With more page views came more photo submissions to Kleinstein's site. He even began selling T-shirts, hats, and other gear, the production of which he'd outsourced to an online company.

How far do the Tebowing website's tentacles reach? At one point, according to a story in the *Houston Chronicle*, the site had submissions from seven of the eight new world wonders (including India's Taj Mahal, Rome's Colosseum, and the Great Wall of China), missing only Machu Picchu. Kleinstein offered a free shirt to anyone who submitted a photo of him or herself Tebowing at the ancient Peruvian site. Within a day, he had three.

"It's popular because it's simple, fun, easy to do, and it appeals to people on many different levels," Kleinstein observed. "I think one of the most important things is how simple it is. That's what gives the fad its currency."

Even Tebow is all about Tebowing, telling CBS News not long after the website went up, "It's not my job to see what people's reasons are behind it. But I know, like, a kid that tweeted me with cancer and said, 'I'm Tebowing while I'm chemoing.' How cool is that? If that gives him any encouragement or just puts a smile on his face or gives him encouragement to pray, then that's really awesome, and that's completely worth it for me."

Kleinstein said the pose doesn't have to be considered religious in nature. For Broncos fans who found something to unite under (before Tebow was traded to the New York Jets just months later), Kleinstein compares it to New York Yankees slugger Babe Ruth's iconic "called shot" during the 1932 World Series.

"If you're Tebowing, you can be expressing a lot of different things," he said. "It's perfect for an online audience because it applies to all sorts of people."

As of this writing, Tebow just got a trademark on his name and Tebowing, so only time will tell what happens next.

To "Play" Is Also to "Consume"

My daughter is a big fan of the singer Josh Groban. One day she asked me to help her purchase tickets to one of his upcoming shows. When I logged on to his site to learn more about him, I was struck by a startling discovery: these days, fan sites are being created because the fans are treated as the best consumers of the artists' music and other consumables.

Being a consumer means a lot more than merely downloading a few of your favorite tracks on iTunes. The whole consumer experience has become enriched by additional products and services that surround the purchase through various media, long after the original transaction.

If you join Groban's fan club, for example, you receive "first access" to his best seats; insights into his new artistic endeavors, background, and upcoming shows; and more. The goal of his marketing team is to create a terrifically informed and intimate consumer. If it succeeds, the artist can count on support and revenue from fans like my daughter for years to come.

The trick is finding new ways to build intimacy with your fans. On Groban's site, you can watch YouTube videos of him backstage, connect with other fans in his online community, download fan photos, follow his regular status updates on a number of social media sites, and follow his blog posts.

A $20 membership package sweetens the deal with discounts to Groban's online store, access to exclusive contests and music, and much more. Groban's music is part of his allure online, but there are times when it can feel secondary to connecting with his brand, which encompasses far more than his art. This is the power and allure of savvy marketing. And in the age of the internet, narrowcasting (the dissemination of information to a narrow audience, not the public) marketing can be awfully powerful. It's also how artists and fans "play" and "feel they are a part of the artist's entourage" in the online era.

Looking for Some New Buddies?
Try Bromance!

When you think about using your smartphone to meet people, the first thing that comes to mind for many young adults is dating apps. These days, single adults with busy careers and long to-do lists turn to all forms of new media to find mates—without a second thought. But what if you're a busy guy looking for other guys with whom you can shoot hoops, grab a beer, or catch the game? You might turn to Bromance, an app for straight guys who want to "play," and I do mean play (like sports, for instance), with other straight guys. The app is aimed at males between the ages of twenty-one and forty who are "looking to get up, get out, and be active in both social and physical events," according to the company.

Why do straight men need an app to meet other straight men? Good question. According to the app's founders, in today's transient world, meeting "bros" requires lots of effort and can be fraught with humiliation. One example is Jeffrey Canty, who collaborated with three other developers to create an app after graduating from college and discovering that connecting with other guys (for the sake of hanging out) was downright difficult. The idea of Bromance came as a result of this challenge. "I am the perfect candidate for this application as I get used to the area. I moved to Chicago because this is an up-and-coming tech mecca, not to mention the city is alive—with people in the parks, riding bikes, running races, working out, sailing, and going out to the bars and nightclubs," Canty said in a 2011 interview in the *Houston Chronicle*.

In the same article, Geoffrey Greif, a professor at the University of Maryland School of Social Work and the author of *Buddy System: Understanding Male Friendships*, confirmed the need for such an app. According to Greif, men are accustomed to being rejected by women, but experience feelings of acute vulnerability at the idea of being turned down by a man. This is largely because competition comes more naturally to men than does the notion of befriending. Men also are leery of being perceived as stalkers, Greif continues in the article. Activities serve as the backbone of male relationships, but it takes a lot of face time before a man is comfortable engaging in activities with another person.

The Bromance app steps in as a middleman, if you will, letting users create a short "brofile" for other men to view. Nearby events are listed and can be filtered to match "bros" with similar interests. An email can then be generated to resulting matches for appropriate events or activities.

CASE STUDY
Staples Center Transforms a Fan's Experience with Technology

When the Los Angeles Lakers play at the Staples Center these days, fans are treated to an entirely new and interactive way of viewing the action. Cutting-edge custom digital video technology connects fans more closely to what's happening on the court, while providing a wide array of information about onsite amenities and services available to them.

Owned and operated by AEG, the Staples Center is one of the premier sports and entertainment venues in the world, hosting four major sports franchises, more than 250 events, and four million visitors annually. AEG recognized a need to upgrade the site's electronic capabilities to better serve its increasingly tech-savvy fan base while creating new revenue streams for the site, sponsors, and partners. The makeover has resulted in one of the most innovative facilities in the world.

One of the most noticeable changes is the addition of a digital video and content distribution system that centrally controls and delivers targeted high-definition video and highly relevant digital content to guests. More than 375 high-definition video displays located in the luxury suites (including 175 full HD 3-D screens), at refreshment stands, and around the premier level give fans an immersive multimedia experience. For example:

- In the luxury suites, the video system personalizes the event experience by allowing fans to customize their views of the live game or switch to other channels of premium HD content by simply changing the channel via the touch screens. In the future, fans will also be able to order concessions and team merchandise for delivery to the suites by using the touch screens on their phones.

- Any sports arena is faced with the challenge of constantly changing games, teams, and events. At the Staples Center, the venue's entire color scheme, content, and branding can be coordinated and affected with the push of a few buttons. In the concession stands, dynamic menu boards can easily be updated with new menu items and pricing.

CASE STUDY
Playing the Odds:
Handheld Gambling Devices Hit Sin City!

Las Vegas keeps a tight grip on yesteryear, with its famous Strip casinos the Flamingo and the Tropicana evoking memories of the Rat Pack days. But this doesn't mean Sin City isn't open to change. With an impact that rivals the announcement of the Mirage Hotel in 1989, gambling devices such as the Pocket-Casino have hit the city by storm. The handheld gaming device allows gamblers to wager on almost anything, including live sports, with bets such as whether NBA basketball player Luis Scola will score thirty points in the first half of a game or if LeBron James will make the next two free throws.

PocketCasinos are tablet-sized devices provided by casinos to their guests. In short, these gizmos give gamblers everything they could possibly want or need to indulge in their vice of choice, 24/7/365, as long as they are on the casino's property. Using PocketCasinos, gamblers can:

- place bets from anywhere in the casino—bars, restaurants, even swimming pools—without waiting in line at the betting counter
- enjoy a bigger betting market, with opportunities to bet on everything in sports from the first down to whether a kicker makes or misses a field goal
- make smarter bets, gauging every set of odds with fingertip access to all the same information available at the counter, from lists of bets to odds to game information
- make bets as the game is unfolding without ever leaving their VIP seats

These devices embody the development of a technology that does everything just as the "old way" could, but with significant advantages. The benefits are so compelling that old-school gamblers are evolving into technology-savvy gamblers before you can say "Sammy Davis Jr." Betting with your mobile device can't be far behind!

CASE STUDY
Playing via Twitter to Create Art

We often talk about social media in terms of how they have revolutionized communication. But one important aspect of social media that doesn't get highlighted enough is how they harness so much creative energy. Here's an example of what I mean: Christof R. Davis, a thirty-year-old composer in the United Kingdom, recently asked Twitter users to contribute lyrical suggestions with the hashtag #BSong for him to employ as a source test for a new choral work he was writing. Though a seasoned composer with musical, feature film, and commercial experience, Davis had never composed via social media.

Over the last few years, for those who tweet, Twitter has taken the world by storm and reached into every aspect of our lives. A staggering number of creative types are already generating poignant and poetic content on the social network each and every day. Davis's project, called Project Birdsong, was designed to bring together these short tweets to create a brilliant piece of choral music that not only reflects the zeitgeist of 2012 but also lives on as a collectively created musical work.

For a tweet to be submitted to the project, it had to be hashtagged #BSong. Submissions remained open for several months, with all the correctly formatted tweets being presented on a website for a public vote. The best lyrical tweets (as voted for by the public) were then used as the text for the choral composition. The composer collaborated with the selected tweet authors throughout the creative process.

As of this writing, composition was still under way. By press time, however, I'm certain that you will be able to find the world premiere performance of the completed work online. It is intended that this premiere will be financed through crowdfunding, which is also in keeping with the collective/social ethos of the project. Davis also plans to have the finished work written for vocal soloists, SATB (soprano, alto, tenor, bass) choir, and chamber orchestra.

You can find more information about Davis's efforts on the project blog: http://projectbirdsong.blogspot.com/. Davis's Twitter username is @cdavismusic.

CASE STUDY
Creating Music:
Los Angeles Philharmonic Loses Out
to Outsourcing, Prague Wins!

I recently sat on an airplane next to a composer who is in charge of creating music for a major movie company. He said that he was in charge of hiring the LA Philharmonic to create musical scores for each of the studio's movies. When his budget was sliced, he thought he would try outsourcing the music. He tapped into the creative talents in Prague, of all places. The results, he said, were shocking in every respect.

To hire the LA Philharmonic, he said, he had to have a "minimum number of musicians," and each had to be paid so much per hour, with so many minimum hours per day. His costs were something along the lines of $40,000 for the music he needed to have created. So, in true Word of Mouse fashion, he turned to the Prague Philharmonic Orchestra. For approximately 10 percent of the cost, or $4,000, the Prague Philharmonic created the exact score he needed for his movie. The amazing part: he didn't even need to travel to the Czech Republic. He directed his music by logging onto Skype and listening to the score as it was being arranged, and he then oversaw the recording session from the comfort of his own home.

CASE STUDY
Music for the Masses?

Considering that music is in the ear of the beholder, I offer another example of Twitter's entry into the world of musical arts. Sonic artist and programmer Daniel Jones and composer Peter Gregson joined forces with the Britten Sinfonia chamber orchestra to create the Listening Machine, a program that listens to the Twitter activity of five hundred people in the United Kingdom and uses algorithms to translate that into music. The "participants" were selected from varying fields, including the arts, sports, and technology. Updates posted by the participants were analyzed for sound and meaning, and then recorded as individual musical cells. The Listening Machine's generative software then recombined the cells into a musical composition. The resulting piece was said to present a musical interpretation of the mental and emotional traffic occurring in the UK population. It was a six-month living composition, made available online for listeners to enjoy the live, musical vibe of British sentiment, as the Listening Machine adjusted its responses to social patterns expressed via tweets with new musical output.

If you're a parent, you know how hard it is to keep your kids entertained. And while I'm not suggesting that you use your iPad as a babysitter, educational apps and games mean technology can be a parent's best friend. I'm not talking about plopping your kid in front of a computer, either. If you live in a part of the country with a long winter—or if you want to keep your children healthy—a variety of video games such as Tek Tag and I-Kix are designed to keep your kids active and engaged.

And there's no need for adults to feel left out. If you're hoping to improve your social life or jump-start a new fitness routine, guess what, there's an app for that! The point is that playing is not just for kids anymore; now it's a life-long hobby. Before you download a social media app in hopes of meeting some new friends, make sure that you're aware of all the new ways people are communicating.

INFUSIONSOFT VIDEO SERIES CASE STUDY
Personal Branding in the Age of Social Media

Stroll through an airport bookstore, and you are sure to find any number of titles about how to unleash your inner artist. But Samantha Bennett was never interested in writing one of those. Instead, she penned *The Organized Artist Book: A Success Book for Creative People Who Want to Be More Organized and Organized People Who'd Like to Be More Creative* (a work in progress as of this writing).

"I wanted to do something for those of us whose inner artist is plenty unleashed, almost to a fault," she explained. "How do we stay on track? How do we manage our time and money? How do we manage the rest of our lives?" This book was followed by the establishment of her small business, the Organized Artist Company (www.theorganizedartistcompany.com). Bennett is also a senior facilitator at Sam Christensen Studios, a company that specializes in personal branding and identity definition.

"Let's start by admitting that the phrase 'personal branding' sounds awful," she said, laughing. "But the idea behind it is not just good, it's *essential* for someone who wants to create and put their work out there. You need to be communicating a clear, authentic truth about who you are, what your values are, and how you operate.

"Other people who vibe with you and like what you do will find you, and they will tell their friends, and you'll have this wonderful tribe of customers and clients and fans and readers of whatever it is you're doing," Bennett continued. "But when that message is muddied, insincere, or confusing, you hamper your own success."

The first tool that Bennett uses to build her brand is social media. "It's an incredible opportunity to express the truth of who you are," she said, noting that this tool allows her to attract new clients and get referrals by keeping in touch with everyone she's ever known. "Maybe that person I grew up with in

Chicago is the editor at a magazine," she said. "It's perfect for marketing, and it's an amazing way to keep putting out that clear, consistent message of who you are."

The second tool is technology; specifically, Infusionsoft. As a one-person business, Bennett doesn't have a large budget for marketing. After someone has signed up on her website, she says she has only two or three days before people forget why they are there. To create a connection, she takes an unconventional approach and sends them a poem, sometimes humorous, sometimes inspirational, sometimes a combination of both.

"There's not a business book in the world that would tell you to write poems to potential customers," she said. "But by the time someone gets two or three of these, people think I'm their sister."

How creative!

Watch the video here!
Scan the QR code or go to http://www.wordofmouse.com/qr/15/index.htm.

Chapter Summary Points

- Whether you're five or fifty years old, the way we play is changing and entering new technological territory, creating countless possibilities and consequences.

- If you're a parent, technology can help your kids express their creativity and learn about the world around them.

- If your kids play online, make sure they incorporate games that require physical activity.

- Sports fans of the future will get to interact with their favorite teams, players, and journalists using technology.

- Need new friends? An app can help you widen your social circle.

- Apps are one of the best ways to stay in shape, tweak your diet, or receive workout tips from your favorite athletes.

- Social media aren't just for socializing; they're also a way to express your innate creativity.

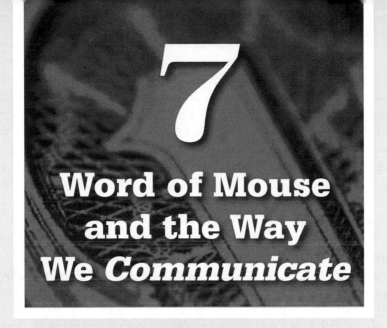

7

Word of Mouse and the Way We *Communicate*

We are living right in the eye of the storm of change. This is a time of imminent confusion. Evidence of transformations abounds, and surviving the torrent means adapting, learning, and, for many of us, relearning.

At the epicenter swirls a mix of new communication media: digital vehicles for the expression and dissemination of information and ideas. They are shockingly different and faster than any communication tools of the past. They are increasingly replacing the tools we used just a few years ago. The changes and innovations are emerging on every front. As always, being aware of and fluent in these new media not only empowers people but also ensures their professional survival.

Imagine this: you are a rising young star in the National Basketball Association who has been tapped as the future of your franchise. A week before the season starts, you are sitting on the team bus with your teammates, coaches, members of the dance squad, and some season ticket holders. Suddenly, their phones start to light up simultaneously with texts, tweets, and calls from agents, family members, and friends. A blockbuster trade has just gone through, breaking up the nucleus of the team and shipping you halfway across the country in the blink of an eye.

Still clad in your team uniform, you can't figure out why everyone keeps looking back at you uncomfortably. Then you check your Facebook page, where fans are already posting their heartfelt good-byes. You are floored. A phone call from your agent a few minutes later merely confirms everything that you already knew from Facebook, Twitter, the ESPN website, and every smartphone owner within ten feet of you. Talk about awkward!

Sound far-fetched? It isn't at all. Stories like this one can be found all across the professional sports landscape each season. Two decades ago, a player could expect to learn that he'd been traded when he received a phone call from his agent. He'd be the first to know, so he had time to prepare a statement and put on a smile before he faced the media or the fans. Not anymore. If news used to amble down a one-way street full of speed bumps and the occasional patrol car, now it rockets down an unregulated, intercontinental superhighway where speed limits have been abolished and traffic cops are permanently off duty.

Almost nightly, we watch celebrities being interviewed about the latest high-profile story. Invariably, they say, "I first heard about it from a friend" or "I got a text on my cell phone." Communication today is faster, quicker, smarter, better—and there's a lot more of it. From broadcasting to narrowcasting (dissemination of information to a narrow audience, not the public), advances in technology have changed the way we communicate, and it will continue to change for years to come. In the old world, you picked up the phone and talked to your kids. Now you text them or leave them a message on Facebook, and if you're lucky, they'll text you back. Because new forms of communication are the key to the future, knowing how to navigate them will play a large role in your success.

GLASBERGEN

"You changed your Facebook relationship status 347 times today. Want to talk about it?"

We no longer live in an hour-to-hour world—or even a minute-to-minute world. Thanks to the ubiquity of smartphones and social media outlets, society communicates at a pace that might best be described as second-to-second. And it's getting faster.

How We Communicate:
Oh, How Times Have Changed!

Our oldest daughter is out of college. When a storm was heading up the East Coast last year, we called her on her cell phone and said, "If you can't use your cell phone to let us know you are okay, be sure to find a landline and call." Her response was priceless: "What's a landline?" Ouch! That one really hit home! And yet her experience reflects the massive transformation that we, as a Word of Mouse society, have experienced and will continue to undergo—at an accelerated rate—for decades to come.

Let's take a closer look at these changes.

In the past, we communicated in person as well as via:

- **telephone (home, office, pay phone, cellular)**
- **mail**
- **voice mail and phone answering machines**
- **email**
- **fax**
- **newspapers**
- **magazines**
- **billboards**
- **television**
- **radio**
- **books**
- **speeches and events**
- **colleges and universities**
- **movies**

Now, in the Word of Mouse age, while we certainly have all of the above ways to communicate, an incredible shift has already taken place, and communication will continue to change in the foreseeable future.

In the present, we communicate by:

- **Skype, ooVoo, etc. (face-to-face)**
- **instant messaging**
- **texting**
- **social media (Facebook, Twitter, LinkedIn, and so on)**
- **YouTube**
- **smartphones**
- **websites**
- **videoconferencing (Skype, ooVoo, and so on)**
- **teleconferencing**
- **FedEx and UPS**
- **online colleges**
- **online and on-demand movies**

What happened between then and now? Let's examine further.

- **Telephone:** Home phones are disappearing as cellular phones take their place. Pay phones are all but dead.

- **Postal mail:** Dying fast.

- **Voice mail:** While still used, it's mostly on cell phones and in offices. Answering machines are gone, or they should be, based on the cost and fragility of tapes and machines, and the lack of clarity and manipulability of the messages.

- **Fax:** Quickly going away.

- **Newspapers:** Dying, losing readers to internet news channels.

- **Magazines:** Dying, losing readers to internet specialty sites.

- **Billboards:** Once static and generic, now going personalized and digital.

- **Network TV:** Now we have hundreds of cable channels, online TV, YouTube. Interactive TV is about to explode.

- **Radio:** The AM and FM bands are hurting. Online radio sites such as Pandora, SiriusXM Satellite Radio, Spotify, and so on are taking over. Traditional stations are geared to specific music types, but online stations take this format one step further, allowing listeners to specify a song, not just a genre, they like, and then serving up songs that have a similar feel. Beyond this, listeners can then design customized stations, built on a variety of narrowly defined desirable music choices. And for the purpose of listening to music, many people choose to build vast personal libraries and listen to their favorite songs or even audio books on their portable media players.

- **Books:** Hurt and dying. Going to ebooks.

- **FedEx and UPS have exploded.** The competitive nature and speed of work these days demand next-day delivery. For example, few offices would even think of dropping a contract in the mail.

- **Online colleges.** These have taken a respectable seat in the college market for a number of reasons (financial, ease of use, get the best of class in teachers, and so forth). Following suit, most traditional institutions are now entering the field of online education to offer students these same benefits and to remain competitive in the face of e-learning advantages.

In the future (it's closer than you think!), our communication will be based on:

- GPS-enabled smart mobile devices that do many of the communications we need—both one-to-one and one-to-many
- wireless everything
- smart appliances and devices
- holographic images
- virtual and augmented reality
- on-demand everything
- one bill, with most if not all bills consolidated into a central billing system
- language-translator implants
- internet-connection implants
- instant information
- one small mobile device that does everything
- phone implants (designed with a small chip housing a receiver and a transducer, with the receiver picking up mobile phone signals, and the transducer translating them into vibrations)

DWD:
Driving While Distracted

In this book, I write mostly about the positive disruptive influence technology has had in our lives. But the "all in moderation" principle applies to everything in life, including technology. And, as is the tendency with pastimes whose consumption we are forced to moderate in healthy, responsible doses, technology, too, beckons users with its temptress finger, resulting in the addition of yet another form of abuse: texting. While the act of texting in and of itself does not pose any particular physical threat (other than, perhaps, a serious case of eyestrain and tendinitis of the thumb, or "texting thumb"), when combined with driving, the habit is collecting kill points that are increasingly on a par with its substance-abuse counterparts.

In the past, driving was driving. You talked to your fellow passengers, raged at inconsiderate fellow drivers, pondered aloud, cursed the boss, and sang along with the radio, all with two hands on the wheel. The driving was your main activity, and your communications happened peripherally and verbally, with little impact on your concentrating on the task at hand.

But with the advent of cell phones, drivers invited additional conversations—and, thereby, distractions—into the car with them. Even the cell-phone-resistant among us eventually broke down and bought their first mobile devices for themselves and their kids, with the idea of using them as a safety measure. Like spare tires, jacks, and jumper cables, cell phones jumped into the essential driving toolbox as a means of getting help in the event of a vehicular mishap. But all it took was that first incoming phone call. Our response, akin to that of Pavlov's dogs, is to answer the ringing phone! We then had a conversation, did not wreck the car, and assumed (incorrectly) that this activity was okay. *Then we were hooked*. From that point on, the car became an extension of our living rooms and offices. We took calls and made calls wherever we were—in a car or, in some cases, in an elevator (no we do *not* want to listen to your conversation). The calls distracted us from focusing fully on driving. Still, at least our eyes were on the road during the conversations. Until texting came along!

Now we have texting—and a whole new level of distraction. Now we take calls, make calls, read texts, send texts, take pictures, and text pictures (complete with captions), all while driving, with frightening results. These eye-opening statistics tell the story better than I can:

Texting-While-Driving Statistics

- About six thousand deaths and a half million injuries are caused by distracted drivers every year.
- While teenagers are texting, they spend about 10 percent of the time drifting outside their lane.
- Talking on a cell phone while driving can make a young driver's reaction time as slow as that of a seventy-year-old.
- Answering a text steals your attention for about five seconds. That is enough time to travel the length of a football field.*

*National Highway Traffic Safety Administration.

A study conducted by the Virginia Tech Transportation Institute uncovered the following increased risks caused by cell phone usage while driving a commercial vehicle (a vehicle of 26,001 or more pounds, intended for transporting goods or passengers):

Risk Increases of Cell Phone Tasks by Vehicle Type

Cell phone task	Risk of crash or near-event crash
Light Vehicle, Dialing	2.8 times as high as nondistracted driving
Light Vehicle, Talking/Listening	1.3 times as high as nondistracted driving
Light Vehicle, Reaching for Object (Such as Electronic Device)	1.4 times as high as nondistracted driving
Heavy Vehicle/Truck, Dialing	5.9 times as high as nondistracted driving
Heavy Vehicle/Truck, Talking/Listening	1.0 times as high as nondistracted driving
Heavy Vehicle/Truck, Using/ Reaching for Electronic Device	6.7 times as high as nondistracted driving
Heavy Vehicle/Truck, Text Messaging	23.2 times as high as nondistracted driving

Three Ways to Save Your Teen's Life (or Someone Else's)

1. **Laws:** As of this writing, talking on a handheld cell phone while driving is banned in ten states (California, Connecticut, Delaware, Maryland, Nevada, New Jersey, New York, Oregon, Utah, and Washington) and the District of Columbia. Expect many more to follow.

2. **Cell phone carrier services:** Sprint's app to combat distracted driving locks the phone when the car is moving over ten miles per hour. It costs $2 a month and, as of this writing, is available on Android phones. DriveMode is free to AT&T customers. Rather than using GPS technology, the service requires users to enable or disable the function through a button on the phone before and after driving.

3. **Apps:** SafeApp is one of many emerging apps designed to cut down on distracted driving tied to mobile phone usage. Available on Android phones, SafeApp uses Bluetooth technology to shut down a phone's functions in the car. The app activates and deactivates automatically when the phone pairs to a Bluetooth device, sending a Do Not Disturb reply to texts and calls. The app is customizable and also has parental controls.

   There is no shortage of apps out there to prevent phone use in the car. By turning off the text chime or cell phone ring alerts, these systems have the potential to be a part of the solution, to help stop more people from getting into accidents. In the end, the responsibility rests with the driver. If you just can't resist using a phone while behind the wheel, choosing from a growing number of technical solutions might just save your life, or the lives of others.

How many domain names do you own? These days, for an extra $10 a year, why not get a new name . . . or twenty new names . . . and point all of them to your primary site? It's a simple and INEXPENSIVE way to increase traffic to your site.

How Groups Communicate Online

Many years ago, if you wanted to meet with a friend or a client, you would have to email or call her on the phone. That was back when Facebook and Skype did not exist.

Today businesses do not have to rely on door-to-door salesmen anymore; they can push the email send button and have hundreds of orders coming in, attach a message on their Facebook wall with a customer-only discount, or notify their LinkedIn groups about a $1,500 live seminar, and walk away with cash sitting in their PayPal account.

As the web expands and mobile apps find more adopters, we have a virtually unlimited number of channels and methods for reaching out and connecting with friends, colleagues, and clients.

HOW FRIENDS AND COLLEAGUES COMMUNICATE ONLINE
Email and Social Media

It looks as if more and more individuals, young as well as old, are starting to abandon the standard email and adopt Facebook, not because it is better but because their friends and colleagues are already there.

Social influence expert Robert Cialdini writes in his book *Influence: Science and Practice* that we are subconsciously influenced by those around us. We buy from people we like, know, and trust. We either go with the crowd or risk being left alone. When we want to buy a book, a house, or a car, we consult friends and ask for recommendations; we also look up online product reviews. Facebook, LinkedIn, Twitter, and other social networks bring us closer to our goal. Instead of relying on email or a Google search alone, we now reside in a world of multi-utility communications.

Email is founded on making one-on-one private connections, while Facebook goes way beyond this function. With Facebook, you know with almost 100 percent certainty when it is most appropriate to contact your friends or clients, and how to tie in the right message with what they are already doing, making this social network ideal for this reason.

Family/Personal Home Pages

It's fairly easy to build and host a website these days. Web design tools abound. They work pretty much the same as any word processing program; in fact, word processors pretty much have all the tools you need to create a web page. All you have to do is create a Word document and save it as an HTML (HyperText Markup Language) document. Then find a place to park it. Hosting services are dirt cheap, and in some cases, you can do it all for no cost if you're willing to place banner ads on your site.

Instant Messaging

When you absolutely have to talk to someone, and a phone call or texting is not an option, instant messaging is the medium of choice. Online messenger services let you see when your friends or family are online. You send them a note, and it pops up on top of whatever program they're working on, along with a reply box. I've had many nice "just catching up" chats with friends this way. These chats sometimes provide just the right short work break I needed. And if I'm on a roll at work and don't want to be disturbed, I just adjust my messenger settings so that people won't see I'm online. It's a tool that does its job remarkably well and fits nicely into the current scheme of communications.

YouTube and Flickr

Sites such as YouTube and Flickr represent another online communication form, centered on sharing, preference, and popular culture. Visitors can browse movies or photos, vote for their favorites, comment, and even upload their own work. Companies can now "search-engine optimize" their YouTube videos and bring more traffic to their websites.

Message Boards

These offer a great way to discuss various topics, generate feedback, and build community. The thread of any discussion is there for all to see, so you don't have to be in on the topic from the start. You can just search for the discussion of interest to you, find the thread, and follow it from there.

Blogs

Think of blogs as online journals. They range in topic from pregnancy diaries to logs of medical treatment, travels, you name it. Successful bloggers have a unique perspective on a particular topic, and they share their observations and musings periodically with a loyal community.

Twitter

Once you follow people on Twitter, you're likely to hear about any fleeting thought that crosses their minds. The definition of a tweet—"a short burst of inconsequential information"—pretty much says it all. Still, there are people with thousands of followers who hang on their every tweet. As far as Word of Mouse goes, Twitter probably represents the strongest medium for rapid-fire messages that can easily be distributed en masse.

© 2000 Randy Glasbergen.

HOW BUSINESSES COMMUNICATE IN THE AGE OF NOW

Businesses are using these same tools for the very same reasons that people are using them to communicate with family, friends, and community. This makes each medium an ideal communications vehicle for any marketing, promotion, or public relations effort. The internet and digital media forms have infiltrated businesses just as much as they have families and communities—and, in many ways, *because* they have infiltrated families and communities.

That being said, businesses still use email as their main source of connecting with clients, partners, and vendors. A survey from SurePayroll (a company that provides online payroll services) found that up to 80 percent of small-business owners believe that email is a key element in their business success.

Here are some of the other technologies that businesses are tapping.

Skype, ooVoo, and iPhone: The Benefits of Interactive Two-Way Video

All-in-one communications tools such as Skype and ooVoo transform web voice communication, making it easy to call, connect via video, or instant-message anyone else using these services for free, through any Wi-Fi-enabled desktop/laptop or smartphone device equipped with the service app. We used ooVoo to record videos of all the Infusionsoft Interview Series interviews in this book. The service allows for multiple participants, who can all see, hear, and text one another. You can even record these interactions in high definition. Scanning the QR code on any of these case studies will lead you to the resulting video files produced from ooVoo.

Small and large businesses alike can now do the following:

- schedule client meetings with ease
- train employees to perform smarter, using all the resources available to them for superior, more efficient work
- offer audio seminars and coaching programs
- create mastermind groups that act as think tanks and take their businesses to a higher level
- provide customer support and save on traditional long-distance calls

In essence, these capabilities have opened the doors for businesses to hire the best employees, regardless of location, and for people to find the perfect jobs for themselves, regardless of location. And once on board, they can do their jobs using resources worldwide—regardless of location. It's a global workforce and a global work market at everyone's fingertips.

GOOD AND BAD:
THE RUMOR MILL IS NOW ON STEROIDS

One of the by-products of faster, less-regulated communication is the increasing power of rumors. In the modern mediascape, it's a well-known truism in the field of public relations that a baseless rumor can be just as damaging—and sticky—as one based on truth. There has never been a time when rumors were so damaging and hard to dispel. They can live forever on the internet. It used to be that only public figures had to go to great lengths to manage their online reputations; today the vast majority of the internet-using public does as well.

Getting over a vicious rumor that is spread online is not easy in an age when social media and unending news cycles have increased the speed of information. Ask any PR professional, and he or she will tell you that it's almost impossible to get out ahead of a negative news story, thanks to Twitter, Facebook, and mobile media. But that's just the beginning. With hundreds of television shows and ravenous celebrity bloggers looking for new information to dig up, controlling a story is harder than ever, if not impossible.

If you think that the only people subject to this media nightmare are celebrities, you're wrong. With everyone from your kid to your grandmother spending time online—whether sharing drunken photos on Facebook or chatting about prescription medicines on an online health forum—it's clear that public figures are no longer the only ones vulnerable to privacy violations. That's why many people are turning to online reputation management companies to get rid of rumors before they can take root.

There are countless situations in which someone might turn to a company like this. Perhaps a photo of your child has triggered online bullying, and you want it removed for your family's safety. Or maybe your name has been wrongfully implicated in a news story that, when Googled, could harm your chances of landing a new job.

By understanding how to alter the results of searches on sites such as Google or Yahoo!, online-reputation managers make negative information more difficult to find. This can be done for as low as a few hundred dollars.

FUTURECASTING:
IF YOU THINK THINGS ARE MOVING FAST, JUST WAIT!

Fifty years ago, the tools we currently rely on to communicate were the stuff of science fiction. Today, with the aid of a smartphone, you can connect to the web, make calls, video chat, send images, and do things that your average science-fiction writer never imagined. New technology arrives so quickly that you can't help wondering what's next. In the short term, as smartphones grow in popularity and necessity, one-dimensional cell phones are likely to fade away. Increasingly, people will come to expect their phones to do everything from providing practical shopping information to downloading your virtual hotel room key, so you can bypass check-in.

It will take a matter of years, but the process will happen incrementally, as cutting-edge early-adopter consumers lead the way. They will be followed by others; almost everyone else will grow to embrace smartphones over time.

In the past, who had an audience? In most cases, it was whoever had the largest platform. More often than not, this was a public figure, such as a celebrity or a politician. It took an entire career to develop a platform large enough to engage a sizable audience. This is no longer the case. With the rise of the internet—and sites such as Facebook and Twitter—the bully pulpit has been democratized. If you have good ideas or products or talents, you will quickly rise to the top. You don't have to become a politician or a famous actor to get the world's attention anymore. Who knows? You might just have to be yourself. Whether that's a good thing or a bad thing is debatable, with fans of TV reality shows probably taking the former side of the argument and people who consider such shows time- and soul-sucking forms of talentless entertainment voicing the latter side. The internet will facilitate the exponential manifestation of such noncelebrities.

"MARC" MY WORDS We've already seen countless instances of the internet granting somebody sudden notoriety. In fact, it seems to happen almost daily, often for the wrong reasons (Octomom comes to mind as a good example of this phenomenon). But the internet's ability to grant fame could lead to dramatic changes in the way that we select our leaders, entertainers, and thinkers.

Sure, there are tons of trash online, but that doesn't mean that at its core the internet isn't a meritocracy, one that awards innovation and insight. Who knows, there could come a day in the not-so-distant future when a relatively unknown person harnesses the power of the internet to be elected president of the United States.

How About the Distant Future? Five Predictions

1. Language barriers will collapse as foreign languages are no longer considered foreign. Devices that translate languages in real time are allowing people from different countries and cultures to communicate without the need for an interpreter. Telecommunications firms in several countries are already testing real-time translation, so that when you are making a phone call to, say, China, you speak in English and the person at the other end hears it in Chinese—and vice versa.

2. The world will grow more interconnected, with faster speeds and new technologies.

3. Paper-thin displays and e-readers that update themselves in real time will become commonplace.

4. Augmented reality will enhance the way that we work and communicate.

5. Smart appliances will be the norm. They'll alert their owners and manufacturers when something needs fixing, or serve up recipes based on what the fridge has stocked, and so on.

Augmented Reality

The other day, I was watching an NFL football game on TV with my good friend and his twelve-year-old son, Matt. It didn't take long before Matt noticed a curious part of the game that most of us take for granted. He pointed to the yellow first-down line that appears on the field during each play.

"Is that line really on the field?" Matt asked me, looking puzzled. "No," I explained. "That's an example of a cool technology called augmented reality." Not surprisingly, Matt looked even more confused. I went on to explain—in twelve-year-old terms—that augmented reality (AR) allows TV viewers to see the line that the offensive team must cross to earn a first down. The real-world elements are the football field and players; the virtual element is the yellow line, which augments the image in real time. NHL hockey now shows the movement of the puck and the PGA shows the flight path of Tiger Woods's latest great shot!

Wikipedia defines augmented reality as "a live, direct, or indirect view of a physical, real-world environment whose elements are *augmented* by computer-generated sensory input such as sound, video, graphics, or GPS data. It is related to a more general concept called mediated reality, in which a view of reality is modified (possibly even diminished rather than augmented) by a computer. As a result, the technology functions by enhancing one's current perception of reality. By contrast, virtual reality replaces the real world with a simulated one." Think about some of the new technologies that let you use your photo to place a new hairdo or the latest Armani dress on the photo to see how it might look on you. Blinds.com uses a photo of your living room and allows you to place different blinds over the windows to see how they would look.

"MARC" MY WORDS Someday we'll be able to communicate by sending our thoughts through a network directly into another person's brain. Sure, we're decades away from such technology, but scientists are already working on brain-computer interfaces that allow people to transmit thoughts directly to a computer. I tested a game like this at the 2011 Consumer Electronics Show in Las Vegas, and it really did work (and it was a bit scary, too). Perhaps a century from now, maybe sooner, electronic telepathy will be a regular element of surgeries, relaxation, entertainment, and teaching!

Augmented reality (AR) is one of the most exciting technologies around. It could take the form of a handheld device such as a smartphone: some smartphones already have dozens of augmented-reality apps available. Or it could come in the form of smart glasses that allow wearers to see real-time digital information about the world around them.

Fox TV does the same, using AR techniques that are displayed during hockey games. In the past, the puck moved too fast to make for good TV, but Fox puts a "trail" on it as it moves across the ice, making it easy to follow on the screen.

I talked earlier in this book about an example of AR for restaurants, where you can stand in front of a restaurant and, through an augmented-reality system, read customer reviews or view discounts, specials, and information about ingredients without ever walking inside. But let's take it a step further. Several steps, really. What if you could glance at a stranger and see that person's name, Facebook profile, and Twitter handle—and if he or she is married or divorced, or whatever else he or she wanted to publicize? Sure, you might not want to broadcast that information in public. But what if you were at an academic conference or a convention designed for the purpose of networking? You would leave that event with meaningful contact information that far exceeds name, company, and phone number.

There's no question that AR devices will raise concerns about privacy, but there's also no doubt that this new technology will rewrite the rules of communication.

There's no question that augmented reality devices will raise concerns about privacy, but there's also no doubt that this new technology will rewrite the rules of communication.

Social Media = Social Restructuring

A recent study published by the Pew Research Center Internet and American Life Project reports that two-thirds of online adults (66 percent) use social media platforms such as Facebook, Twitter, MySpace, and LinkedIn. Let's take a look at what they're doing on these sites.

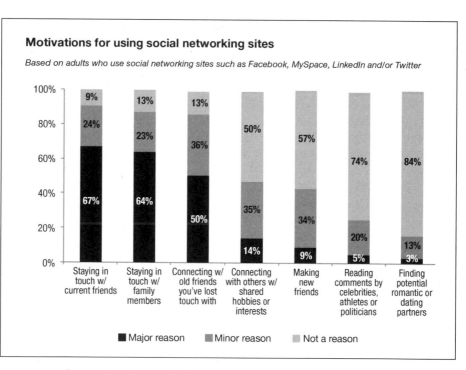

Motivations for using social networking sites

Based on adults who use social networking sites such as Facebook, MySpace, LinkedIn and/or Twitter

	Major reason	Minor reason	Not a reason
Staying in touch w/ current friends	67%	24%	9%
Staying in touch w/ family members	64%	23%	13%
Connecting w/ old friends you've lost touch with	50%	36%	13%
Connecting with others w/ shared hobbies or interests	14%	35%	50%
Making new friends	9%	34%	57%
Reading comments by celebrities, athletes or politicians	5%	20%	74%
Finding potential romantic or dating partners	3%	13%	84%

Source: Pew Research Center Internet and American Life Project.

Here are ten cool apps that already use AR:

Name	Description	Device
1. Golfscape GPS Rangefinder	This augmented-reality range finder for golf lovers covers more than thirty-five thousand golf courses worldwide. It displays the distance from the tee to the front, center, and back of the green for each hole.	Compatible with iPhone, iPod Touch, and iPad. Requires iOS 3.1 or later.
2. DanKam for iPhone	An augmented-reality application for those who are suffering from color-blindness. DamKam is experimental at this point, but it could have huge potential.	Compatible with iPhone, iPod Touch, and iPad. Requires iOS 4.0 or later.
3. Spyglass	This app turns your device into a spyglass. Shows you a compass, GPS info, and much more on the go. Very useful for outdoors.	Compatible with iPhone, iPod Touch, and iPad. Requires iOS 4.3 or later.
4. Panorama-scope	Gives you information about your surroundings: mountains (their names and stats), hiking trails (where they lead), and fishing spots (where they're located and how they're stocked). Great for those who are into outdoors, camping, and beyond.	Compatible with iPhone 3GS, iPhone 4, iPhone 4S, and iPad 2 Wi-Fi + 3G. Requires iOS 3.1 or later.
5. Cyclopedia	Adds Wikipedia information to your reality. When you move your device around, the app will automatically dig up encyclopedic information about what you're looking at and display it on your screen.	Compatible with iPhone, iPod Touch, and iPad. Requires iOS 4.2 or later.
6. Star Chart	Displays your very own virtual star chart on your device. Just point it at the sky, and Star Chart will tell you which stars and constellations you are seeing.	Compatible with iPhone, iPod Touch, and iPad. Requires iOS 3.0 or later.
7. SnapShop Showroom	A cool AR application that makes buying furniture or redecorating a room or house much more convenient and stress free by letting you visualize the furniture in your own home.	Compatible with iPhone, iPod Touch, and iPad. Requires iOS 3.1 or later.

Name	Description	Device
8. Augmented Car Finder	A fun car finder that takes advantage of augmented-reality technology to show you where you parked your car. It's not perfect, but it's one of the better ones on the market.	Compatible with iPhone 3GS, iPhone 4, iPhone 4S, and iPad 2 Wi-Fi + 3G. Requires iOS 3.1 or later.
9. Travel Guide	This travel guide helps you get around more conveniently in a foreign city, and it takes advantage of AR technology to help you get to your point of interest faster.	Compatible with iPhone 3GS, iPhone 4, iPhone 4S, and iPad 2 Wi-Fi + 3G. Requires iOS 4.0 or later.
10. SpotCrime	A powerful augmented-reality application that shows you what crimes have happened recently around your current location.	Compatible with iPhone, iPod Touch, and iPad. Requires iOS 4.0 or later.

Reprinted with permission from iPhoneNess.

TALKING TO YOUR KIDS VIA FACEBOOK

When it comes to staying in touch with the goings-on of our kids, my wife and I turn to Facebook. I'm pretty sure this is the case with many parents these days. It seems only fitting, as Facebook was born out of college students' desire to stay connected.

Facebook boasts around 150 million users in the United States, 28 million of whom are over forty-five years old, according to statistics from the website Inside Facebook. The fifty-five- to sixty-four-year-old age group make up 10.5 million, which falls only 4 million short of the thirteen- to seventeen-year-old age group. It's startlingly clear that this social media site can no longer be considered a plaything for the youth of our nation.

The website "Oh Crap. My Parents Joined Facebook" is a collection of parental Facebook faux pas. Some of the examples on the site are mortifying, but almost all are entertaining. In one example, a Facebook user's mother announces to the world that she's trying on a Harry Potter costume. In other, more embarrassing examples, parents divulge intimate family information, remind their kids they need to go to the dentist, or write messages to other people on their kid's wall.

No big deal, really, but this is certainly embarrassing stuff. And while your kids may not have a parental horror story about Facebook, there is a good chance you are friends with your kids online.

A 2011 survey from America Online (AOL) found that 76 percent of parents with kids on Facebook have friended their teens, but 29 percent of teenagers are ready to "Unfriend" their parents (block them from entering the teens' Facebook space). To make matters worse for mothers, teenagers are twice as likely to want to Unfriend Mom as opposed to Dad.

"Oh Crap. My Parents Joined Facebook" has nearly seven hundred Likes on Facebook. By comparison, the page "I Love That My Parents Are Cool Enough for Facebook" has around twenty.

Linda Fogg Phillips, a Facebook expert who travels the country educating parents about how to use the site, says she understands why most kids feel the way they do. The author of *Facebook for Parents: Answers to the Top 25 Questions*, Phillips teaches her adult pupils the basics when they attend her workshops.

- **Don't tag your kids in photos without their permission.**
- **Learn the difference between sending a private message and a public one.**
- **Don't post baby photos of your kids.**
- **Don't post belittling messages on their wall.**

Most parents can improve their understanding of the site relatively quickly. Sometimes it takes only one ninety-minute course to get up to speed, Fogg said. She reminds parents that in most cases it's not that their kids don't want to have an online relationship with them, it's just that the possibility of being embarrassed publicly by Mom and Dad is just too awful to contemplate.

"Son, I'd like us to spend more quality time together. Would you accept me as a Facebook friend and let me follow you on Twitter?"

"A lot of kids actually like having an online relationship with their parents," she said. "They like knowing that we care, and it can actually be good for the relationship, as long as there are healthy boundaries."

As Phillips noted, another benefit of friending your child on Facebook is that it allows you to monitor his or her behavior and interests from a safe distance. Remember, we're talking about teenagers in most cases here. They don't always know what kinds of photos are appropriate to tag themselves in, and they're not always thinking about how the photos might affect their college applications a few years down the road. That's where your wisdom as a parent is invaluable.

FAMILY CONNECTEDNESS

Family safety is an area where Word of Mouse promises the potential for absolute benefits, with very little cost and virtually no drawbacks. Here are some examples.

Life360°

This app, available for free on the Android and iPhone, lets families create private networks where they can see where their family members are. By clicking one button, children can send "check-ins" to their families, letting them know that they've made it to their destination safely. They can also send an instant panic alert that tells families exactly where they are and that they need help. In addition, the app points users to nearby safe spots such as hospitals, police stations, and so on.

For children without smartphones, the service works on feature phones (a mobile phone that is not considered a smartphone, but offers additional functions beyond standard mobile services). Life360° also provides a GPS device that can be slipped inside a young child's backpack or pocket. As of this writing, over six million families are using the app, so it's clear that parents are looking for modern methods of keeping their families safe.

PetHub

This company licenses to pet ID tag manufacturers QR codes and web addresses that point to web profiles about animals wearing the tags. When someone scans an enabled tag with a smartphone or types in the associated web address, a profile appears of the pet's medical history, dietary information, and emergency contact info. GPS data is extracted from the phone of the person who scanned the tag, and the pet's owner is notified immediately that someone scanned the animal's ID tag, along with the location of where the tag was scanned.

Amping Up Your Digital Communications

Did You Know?

Electronic paper will replace backlit panels.

When online newspapers began encroaching upon the territory of their paper ancestors, we lost the important feature of portability. This drawback was remedied with the introduction of e-readers such as the Kindle and the Nook. Tomorrow's e-readers will take things a step further. They will have wireless connections and be flexible and paper thin. So when you're done reading the paper over your morning coffee, you will be able to literally roll up the reader or neatly fold it and tuck it away for your afternoon coffee break.

Electronic paper and electronic ink compose a suite of display technology designed to mimic the appearance of ordinary ink on paper. Electronic paper differs from conventional backlit flat-panel displays in that it reflects light just like "regular" paper. What's particularly fascinating about these displays is that they can retain static text and images for indefinite periods of time with zero electricity. Images can be changed later.

Flexible electronic paper uses plastic substrates and plastic electronics for the guts of the display backplane (the functional core that actually displays the data). The "paper" is largely considered to be more comfortable to read than conventional displays, due to several of its characteristics:

- the stable image, which has no need to be refreshed constantly
- a wider viewing angle
- it reflects ambient light rather than emits its own light

I recently came across a video about Sony's Flexible OLED video screens that illustrates the future of "paper."

Watch the video here!
Scan the QR code or go to http://y2u.be/NcAm3KihFho.

Note to Parents on Texting Teens

The other day, I asked my daughter if she'd talked to her (identical twin) sister recently. She looked at me as though I was crazy before responding.

"No," she said. "But we've been texting a lot."

She went on to explain that this was a form of "talking" for people her age, and I listened politely. If you've got kids old enough to own smartphones, then you've probably had a similar conversation at some point. And while new technology may seem foreign, understanding it can give us a window into our kids and their worlds.

I have one friend who travels a lot for work. This keeps him away from his young son for weeks at a time, but no matter where he is in the world, he logs onto Skype every night so that he can see and talk to his kid before the boy goes to bed. In the long run, this technology will keep my friend close to his growing son.

The bottom line is that communication is faster, smarter, and more comprehensive than it's ever been. Understanding this can be the difference between success and failure. What do I mean by that? If you're a professional, learning how to navigate the world of social media, smartphones, instant messaging, video, and the web is critical to your success. Without these tools, you won't be able to keep up, much less land a job. The same goes for parents, who need to be able to monitor their kids' online activity to ensure their safety. Whether you want to keep tabs on your child, network with other professionals, or reconnect with old friends, learning how to communicate in the online era is the best—and only—place to start.

INFUSIONSOFT VIDEO SERIES CASE STUDY
Online Printing Taps Empty Mailboxes

A few years ago—if your mailbox was anything like mine—it was stuffed to the brim with junk mail each time you opened it. These days, my mailbox is less full, but my email in-box is always full.

I'm not the only one who noticed this shift. So did Nadine Larder, a savvy entrepreneur and the owner of Printer Bees (www.printerbees.com), a print marketing company that outsources small-business marketing needs, debunking conventional wisdom in the process. "For print marketing, there is no competition at the mailbox anymore—the door is wide open," she said. "What we do is use that avenue to combine print and online marketing for our customers."

One of the ways Printer Bees does this is through QR codes, which it places on clients' printed marketing pieces that end up in mailboxes. It turns a passive marketing piece into an interactive marketing piece—just like the QR code at the bottom of this story! When it comes to QR codes, Larder is an advocate, one who proclaims their value to whoever will listen.

"We add them for free," she said. "I tell my clients that QR codes are the fastest way for someone to collect their information and keep it. They're also the fastest way into a person's mobile phone, which we live and die by these days."

The self-proclaimed "technology geek" dove into the technology headfirst a few years ago, taking full advantage of a business coach and doing her own research to thoroughly learn her database marketing system. She considers this tool, paired with analytics utilities, to be at the heart of Printer Bees's customer relationship management strategy, which she has developed with the aim of personalizing her company for clients.

That's where Infusionsoft CRM came in, providing Larder with the ability to create a solid customer-service strategy. The software does this by helping Printer Bees hunt down leads, grow its database of clients, and manage them in the process. Here's an example of how it works:

When a prospective customer gets on the company's website and requests a print sample, he or she receives a series of emails from a Printer Bees employee named Nicole. She lets customers know that she's the main point of contact at the company and that print samples are on their way. From that point on, the customer will see Nicole's name in his or her in-box.

"The biggest mistake that companies make is that they take the person out of the company," Larder said. "I wanted our clients to have a name and somebody they could contact." Larder's customer-centric strategy seems to be working.

"We've increased our business by fifty percent, we've seen a growth of fifty percent in gross sales, and our staff has doubled in size, all thanks to our technology-based sales tools," she said.

Watch the video here!
Scan the QR code or go to http://www.wordofmouse.com/qr/17/index.htm.

Chapter Summary Points

- Communication today is faster, quicker, smarter, and better, and there's a lot more of it.

- More and more people are starting to abandon the standard email and adopt Facebook—not because it is better but because their friends and colleagues are already there.

- In the modern mediascape, a baseless rumor can be just as damaging, and sticky, as one based on truth.

- Increasingly, people will come to expect their phones to do everything from provide them with practical shopping information to seamlessly link them to large social platforms where their voices can be heard.

- Augmented reality will change the way we do everything from watching sporting events to reading a menu.

- Facebook isn't just for young people anymore. Whether you're young or old, social media are how people connect!

- To be an effective parent or professional, it's important that you master new forms of communication.

- Driving while distracted (DWD) is a serious threat to your (and others') safety, especially for new drivers.

- Don't buy an expensive phone plan next time you travel. Try Skype or Google Voice (a service that gives customers one number for all their phones, online voice mail, free US long distance, low rates on international calls, and many calling features).

8
(Bonus Chapter!)
As Word of Mouse Grows, So Does Cyber Crime!
Coauthored by James G. Conway Jr.

Five facts you may not know:

1. The US government sees fifteen thousand cyber attacks a *day*!

2. There are sixty thousand new computer viruses identified per *day*!

3. Thieves often gain access to a home by cloning a gate and/or garage door opener, and then simply letting themselves in!

4. Cyber attacks on our critical infrastructure will soon surpass traditional threats of terrorism as our number one national security threat.

5. When you open certain emails, you get a virus on your computer. But if you click on "No thanks," you can often still get hacked.

In any emerging market, especially the relatively new ones being created online, criminals are often the first players in the game, and they're adept at learning new and innovative ways to practice their trade! No discussion of Word of Mouse would be complete without exploring how the criminal element has infiltrated the internet and new consumer technologies. From the shady to the unethical to the downright criminal, morally corrupt schemers have tapped a wellspring of new ways in which to "work" the information technology system, unraveling the lives of unsuspecting victims who don't even know they've been targeted—much less how it happened or how it could have been prevented.

Just about every scam imaginable has graduated to cyberspace, giving crooks more access, more anonymity, and simply better odds. "Work at home!" scams, adoption scams, real estate fraud schemes, auto sales scams, and online romance scams continue to flourish and victimize people every day.

Maybe you think you're not one of these unsuspecting victims. Maybe you think you know all there is to know about the potential threats for cyber crime, and you're prepared to thwart any assault that comes knocking on your cyber door. To that I say, check the following list of facts. If you stumble across even one point that surprises you, you are not as informed as you thought you were. For every fact listed here, there are hundreds I haven't listed that pose as a cyber criminal's entryway into your life.

"The identity I stole was a fake!
Boy, you just can't trust people these days!"

Did You Know?

About these lurking dangers . . .

- If your mobile device has a working battery, the FBI can use a "back channel"—a microphone in your cell phone to hear everything going on in the proximity of the phone—even when the cell phone is turned off. Unless you take the battery out of the phone, the agents can listen in on everything that is said! That's 100 percent true.

- You will be hacked someday; it's just a matter of when and how much it will cost you!

- Cyber thieves gain incredible amounts of data from social media sites such as Facebook, Twitter, and YouTube. They even use photos you or your kids have posted to learn where you hang out. How? Many photos these days have location-embedded GPS data showing when and where the photo was taken!

- Cardiac pacemakers that use a specific wireless signal designed for easy adjustment are vulnerable to hacking, sometimes with fatal results.

- Free virus "protection" software is often the way the bad guys get into your computer system!

- Digital theft of gift cards is huge! Scam artists often scan gift cards. As soon as the cards are activated, the scammer wipes out the money on the scanned cards.

- Our current "smart grid" connects the power industry to the internet and, as a result, opens the door for anyone who wants to compromise the US power system.

This section of the book may actually scare you. It is shocking. The numbers are often hard to swallow. And the information, in general, can be overwhelming. But consider it required reading. The pill you'll swallow after being victimized by a cyber criminal is far more bitter. So on with the medicine!

To get the true facts on cyber crime and other internet-related theft, I turned to my close friend **James G. Conway Jr.**, president and managing director of Global Intel Strategies, a Houston-based firm that consults for, advises, and trains government agencies around the world, academia, and the media on terrorism and national security matters, as well as private sector corporations on security issues, counterterrorism measures, and risk mitigation. Jimmy, a retired FBI special agent, served his country with distinction for more than twenty-five years. For ten of these years, he served in a diplomatic capacity as the manager of international counterterrorism operations for the FBI in Europe and Latin America. James kindly cowrote this chapter of the book with me.

The Age of Cyber Crime

We live in a troublesome world that is witnessing a growing and massive wave of cyber threats at all levels of society and at all levels of technology. Unfortunately, this new world is evolving faster, and with more complexity, than we can even wrap our collective head around.

A US intelligence official recently summed it up best when he said that we are seeing a cyber environment in which emerging technologies are developed and implemented *before* security responses can be put in place. This, coupled with the sixty thousand new malicious computer programs identified each *day,* is costing us $400 billion a year in lost assets and time, according to security software maker Symantec-Norton (Symantec.com).

> According to a US intelligence official, we are seeing a cyber environment in which emerging technologies are developed and implemented *before* security responses can be put in place.

This cyber-heightened environment has an impact on each and every segment of society:

- **the grandmother who realizes when she opens her credit card bill that she has been the victim of a phishing scam**
- **the college student buying music downloads for his iPhone, who suddenly realizes that his identity has been stolen**
- **the giant defense contractors who spend millions to research and develop technology, only to have their intellectual property stolen and marketed by competitors in Asia**
- **US government agencies that realize the "bad guy" targets of their global investigations have compromised their communication networks and are eavesdropping on their strategic conversations with their law enforcement partners around the globe**

Experts are positioned to address these expanding and pervasive threats. Global federal police agencies, prosecutors, global intelligence agencies, and academics, as well as various sectors of the corporate environment that are losing billions of dollars to these cyber thieves, all do their part to serve and protect an increasingly technology-reliant world. But it's an endless game of whack-a-mole: as one threat surfaces and is addressed, another emerges that's even more pervasive and damaging than the last.

International Concerns

A few years back, Chinese hackers infected US power systems with software that would allow them to disrupt the entire power grid at will. The software was found and removed, but this compromise forced us to modernize and improve the reliability and security of our power grid through increased computerization. Now the grid can more quickly route power where it is needed and employ automatic controls to fix the problems. Yes, on the one hand, it initially will be more resistant to hackers trying to take down the system. On the other hand, it will be more complicated and, ultimately, because of its complexity, more vulnerable to hackers.

Smart Meters and the Smart Grid

Technically, a smart grid connects the power industry to the internet and, as a result, opens the door for anyone who wants to compromise the US power system, according to Dr. Stephen Holditch, a professor at the Texas A&M University Energy Engineering Institute (EEI). Electricity providers have installed thousands of smart meters throughout the country. The smart meters are a component of smart grids that use the internet and other information technology to monitor and control generation, delivery, and consumption of electricity. This allows consumers to better track their power use, and it improves the utilities' ability to identify and fix outages. Yes, these smart grids could save the United States and its consumers over $130 billion over the next decade, according to the EEI, but the Achilles' heel is the linkage to global communications systems that opens the door to potential hackers.

In 2012 FBI Director Robert Mueller told the Senate Select Committee on Intelligence that threats from cyber espionage, computer crime, and cyber attacks on our critical infrastructure will soon surpass traditional threats of terrorism as our number one national security threat. Mueller and his intelligence community partners testified that Russia and China run robust intrusion operations against both US industry and the US government sector on a daily basis. Although stopping another major terror attack on US soil continues to be the agency's top priority, he said, the threat from the cyber world will soon cut across and involve all FBI investigative programs.

Cyber Crime: It's Personal—and It's About You!

We know that cyber threats are affecting governments and businesses, but we're also seeing a huge increase in attacks against us, the individuals, in the form of identity theft, lost or compromised files, and the pilfering of our credit cards and bank accounts. Each and every one of us today most likely has been victimized—or knows someone who has been victimized—through exposure to the internet. The problem is exploding nearly beyond our capability to address it.

Five Facts That Will *Shock* You!

1. More than ten million people are victimized by a cyber crime of some kind each year, and the number is growing.

2. Businesses are losing more than $50 billion every year because of cyber crime.

3. Consumers are spending $5 billion every year to undo and "fix" the mess made by cyber crime.

4. The FBI's Internet Crime Complaint Center (IC3) receives more than twenty-five thousand complaints and referrals for investigation each month, and the number is climbing.

5. The most common method cyber crooks use to pilfer personal information is phishing: bogus emails that link to a rogue site into which the victim types private data such as name, account number, date of birth, and so on. The bad guys do their best to make the emails appear authentic by cutting and pasting to the message logos, mastheads, copyright marks, and even actual links.

Social media platforms such as Facebook, Twitter, LinkedIn, and Pinterest have exploded in number and purpose. These social networks are used not only by individuals to connect with old friends and exchange photos and videos but also by businesses looking to expand their markets. Cyber crooks are turning their attention to this target-rich environment because of the sheer number of potential victims. Facebook alone has more than 1 billion members, and many of them don't realize their vulnerability and, therefore, don't take the proper precautions to protect themselves.

Intelligence Obtained from Social Media

Social media really give the bad guys an edge. They are collecting intelligence on you, and because of the personalization of this genre, they've got a leg up with all the personal information posted on your Facebook page: where you live, work out, and go to school, as well as your likes and dislikes. Maybe they see that you have a million-dollar vacation home or have seats right behind the Boston Red Sox dugout. Now you're a more attractive target. They can even right-click on your photos and possibly identify where the photo was taken, giving themselves some valuable GPS information on your residence, your dorm, and Grandma's house, as well as your travel patterns and habits. Unless that feature on the camera is disabled, most photo locations can be identified by a simple right-click.

The FBI issued a warning recently regarding this topic. Most photos uploaded on social media platforms are taken with smartphones. What most people don't realize is that they are sharing more than just the photo. All sorts of details can be revealed through bits of information embedded in images taken with smartphones and the new digital cameras. This information, called metadata, may include the times, dates, and geographical coordinates (longitude and latitude) where the photos were taken. Imagine the doors these details can open for all kinds of predators, including stalkers, burglars, and pedophiles.

All sorts of details can be revealed through bits of information embedded in images taken with smartphones and the new digital cameras.

It's scary to think that kids going to their favorite food court at a mall may have been identified and targeted as frequenting this mall by someone wanting to do them harm—and that this person gathered and "clustered" the information online. Fortunately, some popular social media websites scrub metadata before photos are posted, and there are steps that can be taken with smartphones and cameras to disable this geotagging function.

Have You Seen This Photo of You?

Another trick the bad guys are using is to send you a message asking if you've seen a picture of yourself that has been posted on Facebook and to "check it out." People jump at this and immediately click on the link. This takes them to a Twitter or Facebook page, where they enter their account information. Unfortunately, both the email and the link are false, and you've been phished.

The crook now has your account name and password, along with control of your account. He may now also be able to hack into other accounts you have. There is some antiphishing software that can be downloaded, but common sense is most often the best advice. The same security measures we use in the physical world are those we should use in the cyber world. If you don't know who's knocking on your front door, you probably wouldn't answer it. Don't indiscriminately open the online door to crooks. People have also been duped in these online music IQ tests or surveys, which ask you to input your name and cell phone number. You may have just unwillingly subscribed to some service that *charges your cell phone* $9.95 a month.

The "Tweet for Cash" scam claims that folks can make large sums of money from home simply by tweeting. Victims end up providing a credit card number in order to receive a "Twitter Cash Starter Kit" for $1.95. Unfortunately, as is the case in many of these scams, the starter kit is only a seven-day trial, and the company ends up charging your credit card $50 a month until you realize what's happening and start the process of stopping the charges. With Twitter, one needs real-time protection against viruses and malware (also known as "malicious software," which is used to disrupt computer operations, gather sensitive information, or gain access to a private computer). By blindly clicking on URLs that appear all over Twitter, you never know where you're going, because the true identity of the full site is hidden. A click could take you to a real site or to one that installs all kinds of malware on your computer.

If you don't know who's knocking on your front door, you probably wouldn't answer it. Don't indiscriminately open the online door to crooks.

If you're going to ride the social media wave, implement some basic security measures.

Five Security Measures to Take on Social Media Sites

1. Check your privacy setting, allowing friends only. And be selective of your friends, because they can access any information viewable by friends.

2. Uncheck the box that allows sharing with search engines.

3. Beware of personal information that you or your children or their friends post.

4. Maintain some degree of anonymity. Stay away from using addresses, telephone numbers, and so on, and you may want to consider using an avatar (a graphical representation of you online) as an identifier, as opposed to using a photo.

5. Use your region, not your hometown, and consider using a Gmail or Yahoo! account instead of a more identifiable business account.

Many times over the past year, I have received nonsensical or illogical email messages from friends whose email addresses had been hijacked. In many instances, the message asked for money, stating that the sender is stranded or has a family member dying of a rare disease. Fortunately, in the instances where I received these calls for help, I had just recently spoken to the real people involved, so I knew they weren't in financial trouble in Africa or Asia.

Often these problems arise from just not having impenetrable enough passwords. We should all change our passwords often and with some degree of complexity, particularly if we use Wi-Fi with any regularity. Sometimes the bad guys that hijack these accounts will send out a shotgun email to everyone in the account's address book and attach a photo or video. The message turns out to be a solicitation for personal info or just a malicious dump of malware. If an associate or friend sends you an email that looks fishy, don't hit Reply. Instead, send the person a separate message and ask if it's real.

Generosity Exploited

Sadly, the cyber bad guys also exploit the good and generous nature of the human spirit. For example, after the 2011 Japanese tsunami and the Haitian and Chilean earthquakes the year before, scammers began flooding in-boxes with fake charitable causes. Unfortunately, many folks typed in their credit card numbers with hopes of helping. These numbers quickly landed in the coffers of the cyber crooks. People are getting wiser to these scams, and for the most part, many of the bogus emails are not that well done. The Federal Trade Commission (FTC) suggests you check for following red flags, which might indicate the charity email you're considering is a scam: cash requests; offers to send a courier or overnight delivery to collect your contribution; guarantees of sweepstakes winnings in exchange for a contribution; charities that suddenly spring up after a natural disaster, which more than likely do not have the required infrastructure to send donations to the affected areas (source: ftc.gov).

Facebook alone has more than 1 billion members, and many of them don't realize their vulnerability and, therefore, don't take the proper precautions to protect themselves.

It seems as though everyone in the world has received a request from a Nigerian "prince" who needs your bank account information merely to deposit his family's millions until he can work out some minor details, at which time he'll generously share a large percentage of his wealth for the kind "rental" of your bank account. FBI white-collar squads throughout the United States have files full of these emails and letters received and forwarded to them by citizens.

Scamming Our Financial Sensibilities

Around tax time, the phony IRS email scams start. A recent one involved what appeared to be an email from Intuit, maker of Quicken and TurboTax software. It appears quite legitimate and asks the recipients to visit a website to correct conflicting account details. Because the problem became so widespread, Intuit had to provide an address for reporting by consumers: spoof@intuit.com. People have also received spoof emails from the IRS notifying them that they are eligible for a "stimulus check," which, of course, will be provided upon receipt of the recipient's bank account information. The bad guys play upon their victims' greed, the common denominator in most of these scams.

Preying Upon Our Focus on Terrorism

The IRS is not the only agency of the federal government that has been used as a front for a cyber scam, and the bad guys know that a federal agency is a good front to legitimize a scam. We have seen in the past year fraudulent email messages allegedly from the FBI and the Department of Homeland Security (DHS). In one of these messages, Attorney General Eric Holder's name was used to advise the recipient that he or she was allegedly involved in money laundering and terrorist-related activity. To avoid prosecution, the recipient must obtain a certificate from the Economic and Financial Crimes Commission (EFCC) chairman at a cost of $370. The spam provided the name of the EFCC chairman and an email address from which the recipient could obtain the required certificate. The FBI and DHS *never* would send an email to individuals alerting or advising them of their role in some type of criminal activity. But, again, the bad guys are just playing the odds and need only a few participating victims to continue their criminal exploits in cyberspace.

In April 2011, one month before Al Qaeda leader Osama bin Laden was taken out by US military Special Forces, audio of a speech by him was being circulated fraudulently in emails. The speech was attached to an email titled "audio.exe" that went out claiming to be from the FBI and DHS containing the "new bin Laden speech Directed to the Peoples of Europe." What it actually contained for those who clicked on the attachment was malicious software intended to steal information from the recipients' computer.

Taking Advantage of Our Civic Duty

Recently the FBI received notice of spam email spoofing an nyc.gov address. The message was allegedly from the New York State Police and notified recipients that they had been issued a traffic ticket as a result of a moving violation. The email directed the recipients to print the ticket and mail the fine amount to a post office box address in Chatham, New York. Some of the recipients advised the FBI that their antivirus software indicated that the message contained malware.

An alarming number of other online fraud schemes are popping up in cyberspace every day, and the list and ingenuity continue to grow. Folks are receiving notices that they have won a lottery or prize sweepstakes, and all they have to do is send in the "processing fee," or they just have to pay the "taxes" up front before the money is sent to them. It's hard to believe that people would fall for these scams, but, again, the bad guys are banking on greed and just a very small percentage of recipients to respond, and they've once again disproven the idea that "crime doesn't pay."

Scamming Our Gift Cards

Gift card scams are becoming more popular, particularly around the holidays, when consumers are buying gift cards. First of all, *do not* buy gift cards from offers online or in classified ads. Buy directly from the retailer and don't provide personal data—it's not necessary. Also, when you purchase a gift card, have the cashier verify that the card is valid and for the amount you purchased.

What the bad guys are doing is scanning a group of gift cards off the rack *before* they are sold or physically copying down the serial numbers. Once someone buys and activates the gift card, the crook who has counterfeited the card quickly drains the gift card balance.

PIN codes are never needed for gift cards, but retailers are taking steps to avoid this scam in the future.

Scamming Job Postings

Some businesses have reported to the FBI that cyber criminals have engaged in a wire transfer fraud by responding to emails for employment opportunities posted online. Through the introduction of malware embedded in the email responses to the job posting, the cyber crooks were able to obtain the online banking credentials of a company employee authorized to conduct financial transactions within the company.

Hacking Your Parent's Pacemaker

While reports of hacking are commonplace, the stories that startle us most are instances when hackers have penetrated some of our everyday devices—those that we would never consider vulnerable or even of interest to the bad guys.

Hackers are targeting nearly every type of electronic device or information-storage medium, from video games to voice mail. Some of the targets may surprise you. The reason for hacking into these devices escapes common logic; what we do know is that the result of the hacking is sometimes deadly.

Medical implants such as pacemakers and insulin pumps are used to save lives and/or keep patients within a delicate range or balance of lifesaving drugs. Researchers have shown that certain pacemakers that use a wireless signal for easy adjustment are vulnerable to anyone with the right programming hardware. Doctors use these wireless programming devices to make subtle adjustments to these pacemaker "heart helpers" in order to avoid heart surgery. Unfortunately, the signal that is used is unencrypted (not encoded), so anyone who can get his hands on the signal for the device can literally manipulate that signal, possibly with fatal consequences. Insulin pumps are even more vulnerable. At a recent medical conference in Las Vegas, these devises were shown to be vulnerable to powerful radio signals from up to a half mile away, which could trigger a potentially fatal insulin overdose.

Baby monitors are popular with parents who want to maintain an eye and ear on their infants. They've been around for quite some time, and the new video-equipped units are in especially high demand. What parents don't realize is that the dozen or so wireless channels that these helpful devices use can often be picked up outside the home, giving anyone who has a similar device or wireless receiver an invisible window into your home. There was actually a 2009 court case in which an Illinois family sued Toys "R" Us when, after they purchased and used a baby monitoring system, a neighbor alerted them that he was picking up their signal on *his* system. The microphone in these units is so sensitive that conversations in the surrounding areas of the home could be picked up. Fortunately, the newer models have a "frequency hopping" technology that changes channels randomly. Just take note: the older and less expensive models are still out there.

Garage-Door Hacking

Are you afraid that someone will steal your car? You should be—now more than ever! Car thieves are climbing aboard the hi-tech train, and no longer have to resort to the old-school methods of breaking windows and hot-wiring a target automobile. Today tech-savvy bad guys can unlock your car, or even start it, simply by sending a few text messages. Many auto security systems, such as OnStar, use the same technology as that of a cell phone, and with a little trial and error, hackers can overcome some of the basic circuitry, gaining entry and access to your vehicle.

But you don't have to worry, because your car is safe in the garage, right? Wrong! Have you ever looked inside your garage door opener when you change the battery, and seen all those wires, contact points, and available code variances? Hackers can easily rig a garage door opener to accept a USB (Universal Serial Bus) port, and the software to modify how it operates is readily available on the web. Yes, there are tutorials online that happily walk a hacker through the process of hacking into your garage-door opener in minutes. Once he's in your garage, the happy criminal is just steps away from a single-key access to the garage door that leads into your home (unless your garage is detached).

Free "Protection" Software
Is Anything but Free

Okay, so we're all aware of these bad viruses and malware that could affect our computers. We all run some level of security on our computers, and the basic firewall and antivirus program is a fundamental protection for our computer as well as our wallet. Unfortunately, being online is a constant landscape full of landmines, and the bad guys never rest. They are smart, and they are innovative. They now realize that the antivirus and antispyware market is ripe for their criminal operations.

What the bad guys do nowadays is sell or even give away software offering protection to those who surf the net. In reality, what most of these programs do is infect and spread the very same malicious codes they claimed to block.

All of us have been confronted with those pesky pop-up boxes with the yellow or red triangle warning us that our computers are infected with a virus or are compromised by spyware. Many of us, trusting the pop-up and assuming the worst, think, "Well, it's great that I've been notified, and, heck, they said they just scanned my system and found this bug." Experts say that either way, they've got you. If you buy the program, they've really got you; and if you just click on the *X* in the upper right corner of the box to make it disappear, well, they still have you, but not as badly. You will continue to receive a rash of these pop-ups, and soon your computer may slow to a crawl, or you may not be able to open certain programs or files.

Many of us, trusting the pop-up and assuming the worst, think, "Well, it's great that I've been notified, and, heck, they said they just scanned my system and found this bug." Experts say that either way, they've got you.

These fake virus scams are run by scammers, hackers, or identity thieves. The scammer wants to sell you some antivirus product that most likely won't work and, in fact, may cause more problems than you expected. The hacker, of course, wants entry into your PC or computer system to either steal your data or just wreak havoc with your life, and the identity thief wants to steal your identity to use or sell to someone on the other side of the world.

From a technical standpoint, fake virus alerts are usually triggered by a Trojan that has found its way onto your system. These Trojans slip in the back door without your knowing it when you open an email attachment, download music or videos, visit fake or malicious websites, or click on a pop-up advertisement that automatically loads a virus onto your computer. Hackers can also access your computer through internet messaging services.

This cat-and-mouse game with the crooks will not go away, so we have to employ some basic but smart tactics to minimize our exposure. Those tactics include using a secure browser such as Mozilla Firefox, always having a firewall in place, and buying antivirus and antispyware software only from reputable companies directly off their websites.

Protecting Our Kids

Does your child quickly turn off the computer or change the screen when you enter the room? Has your child become inordinately withdrawn from the family? This often means that he is doing something that he knows he shouldn't be doing, and as parents, we need to be aware of what our kids are doing online.

When we talk about cyberspace and security, we have to address our most precious commodity: our children. Our kids today are totally connected, seemingly twenty-four hours a day, and child psychologists are studying the effects, both positive and negative. It was just ten years ago that a child could only make or receive a call on a cellular device. Today it is a minicomputer with the ability to text, instant-message, go online, and send and receive photos or other files. It also has a GPS installed.

While the internet and other technologies in our Word of Mouse society can promote socialization and open up a whole new world of knowledge and learning for our children, they can also leave our children vulnerable to the vermin that prey upon the innocence of a child.

Through education, community outreach, and an aggressive investigative and prosecutorial program, the FBI has vigorously addressed this most heinous of federal crimes. An investigation called Innocent Images has targeted internet child predators and has successfully identified, arrested, and prosecuted thousands of these online criminals. These deviants strategically seduce children through alleged kindness, gifts, or affection, communicating with them online and often representing themselves as other children.

Predators "fish the pond" for anyone who will respond. Many adolescent children have a natural curiosity about sex, and the bad guys will exploit this. In some explicit cases, the cyber pedophiles have been known to send and transmit sexual materials involving children and seek a positive response from a child. This is precisely why parental involvement in your child's internet use is critical.

Enjoy Word of Mouse marketing? Join WOMMA, the Word of Mouth Marketing Association.

Thirteen Ways to Protect Your
Child from Cyber Predators

1. Talk to your child about the dangers of strangers on the internet.

2. Never allow your children to post personal information such as full name, age, school, home address, cell phone number, or anything else that makes it easy to find and target them.

3. Review their computer history and see which websites, chat rooms, and other destinations they visit.

4. Look at instant messaging and texts. There are several ways to stay on top of texts. You can go through a service, like My Mobile Watchdog, which records text messages sent and received from your child's phone and allows you to review and print them. Or you can install an app on the phone, like Mobile Spy (undetectable by your child), which silently uploads data to your Mobile Spy account. Finally, you can check with your cell phone service provider to see what text-monitoring options it offers. For instant messages, check the messenger service. Some let you save message logs. One software package, iProtect You, features a monitoring system that logs instant message conversations for later review, lets you set up specific times during which messaging is allowed, and/or blocks this capability completely from the computer.

5. Ask your children if they know 100 percent of their "friends" on Facebook. Most kids accept friend requests from anyone and have no clue who is *really* friending them.

6. Spend time with your children online, explaining what can happen if they don't listen to your advice to protect themselves online.

7. Keep the computer in a common room of the house, not in your child's bedroom.

8. Use parental controls provided by your service provider and use blocking software.

9. Find out what safeguards are in place on the computers your children use during the day when they are at school, the library, or friends' houses.

10. Advise your youngsters that they are never *ever* to meet with anyone they met online.

11. Tell your children that they are never to upload pictures of themselves to someone they don't know.

12. Also make it clear to your children that they should never download photos from someone they don't know. If someone sends them something that seems inappropriate or makes them uncomfortable, they should advise you, the parent, immediately for referral to the local authorities or the FBI.

13. Advise your child of the harsh realities of life—that not everything people say online is true.

Finally, a few critical pieces of advice and red flags on this important and sensitive subject for parents to consider.

Three Red Flags That Might Indicate a Cyber Predator Is Targeting Your Child

1. Has your child received gifts or packages in the mail from someone you don't know? Online sexual predators have even sent kids airline tickets to Disney World and other places for face-to-face rendezvous.

2. Has your child received a phone call from someone you don't know, or does your telephone bill reflect long-distance numbers you don't recognize?

3. Is your child using an online account belonging to someone else? Online predators will often provide a separate account for their targets.

An immense and wonderful world of knowledge, culture, and entertainment is out there in cyberspace for our children, but the bad guys are lurking out there, too. We, the parents and guardians of our children, must assume the same responsibility to protect them online as we do to protect them each and every day in the real world.

Beware When You Travel

Finally, Jimmy said he likes to talk about a subject that he teaches his corporate clients: the vulnerabilities that confront us when we travel and how cyberspace and our cyber connections, even though they may be limited, may pose certain compromising and costly risks for us and our companies.

The financial damage to a company through the loss of a formula, a blueprint, a methodology, a customer list, a marketing plan, or a business bid or proposal can be inordinately costly.

SEVENTEEN FACTS TO CONSIDER WHEN TRAVELING ON BUSINESS

1. *All* information you send electronically—by fax, PDA (personal digital assistant, such as Palm, Pocket PC, or Windows Mobile), computer, or cell phone—can be intercepted, even if you've used a password.

2. Wireless devices are particularly vulnerable.

3. Assume that all your hotel room conversations on phones or in person are monitored.

4. Always meet business colleagues in public places with ambient noise to drown out any attempt to intercept the conversation. A coffee shop or busy hotel lobby works fine, as long as you don't mind exposing your contact in public.

5. Never leave your electronic device unattended or in the hotel safe. Files on devices can be exploited by good spies in a minute. Malicious software can also be introduced.

6. Never insert a foreign or unknown thumb drive (USB stick) into your electronic device. The big thing today is USB "gifts" given by companies or at trade shows.

7. Use a country-specific disposable cell phone upon arrival. These can easily be bought at airports or kiosks in most countries today. I always use fictitious information on the paperwork when I get one of these. If the seller requires ID, just show it in a cursory manner, and never let the merchant copy your ID, such as a passport or driver's license. If he insists, leave.

8. Never put your electronic devices in your checked luggage when traveling; keep them with you in a carry-on.

9. When you touch down in a country, secure all your electronic devices in a discreet carry-on before deplaning. Remember, there are less sophisticated thieves in and around airport and taxi stands who snatch laptop cases and other such electronic equipment.

10. Keep only software files on the hard drive of your laptop when traveling outside the United States.

11. Carry any sensitive proprietary information on your person at all times on an encrypted thumb drive and back up all these files before you travel.

12. Shield your passwords and computer screen from those around you. Also, use different passwords overseas, and then change them upon returning home.

13. Terminate computer connections when not using them and disable infrared ports and other features you do not need.

14. Clear your browser after each use and delete your history. Do not use the "Remember Me" feature when logging onto websites.

15. Avoid Wi-Fi networks if possible. In some countries, they are controlled by the intelligence services, and in almost all cases, they are not secure.

16. When you hold a sensitive business meeting, do it in a relatively secure physical environment.

17. Don't just turn off your cell phone; pull out the battery, too. Intelligence services can and do intercept your meetings through your cell phone, even when it's turned off.

Remember, the bad guys are still conducting the "world's second-oldest profession" and what they are most interested in stealing is America's hard-earned and valuable corporate secrets. They're not doing it the old James Bond way, with pretty blondes, fast cars, and false-bottom briefcases; they're doing it with the latest technology gadgets, in networks, and in cyberspace.

Ten Ways to Avoid Becoming a Victim of Cyber Crime

1. Never open an email attachment from anyone unfamiliar.

2. Never download music or videos from anyone or any website that you are not 100 percent sure is legitimate.

3. Never click on a link to a website that offers you something free. It is most likely a scam or a hacker trying to get into your computer.

4. Never click on a pop-up advertisement from someone you are not 100 percent sure is legitimate.

5. Change your passwords often. Once a month or every few months is not too often.

6. Know that when you take and post photos in this digital age, smart hackers can find encoded information that tells them where and when the photo was taken, alerting them to more personal information about yourself. If you just posted a photo from Maui, you just told the thief you may not be home for a few days!

7. Know that pedophiles and identity thieves are watching and monitoring Facebook and other social media sites to find their next victims.

8. Avoid Wi-Fi networks.

9. Make your social media pages, profiles, and posts as anonymous as possible: no phone numbers or addresses—and use an avatar for your profile picture.

10. Talk to your child about the dangers of strangers on the internet.

Marc Ostrofsky's Websites

Owned in Whole or in Part

Blinds.com

CuffLinks.com

eTickets.com

SummerCamps.com

GetRichClick.com

WordOfMouse.com

MarcOstrofsky.com

Marc Ostrofsky's Websites Coming Soon

MutualFunds.com

Bachelor.com

BeautyProducts.com

MortgageCompanies.com

InsuranceCompanies.com

HeartDisease.com

Photographer.com

Consulting.com

Expertz.com

MARCeting.com

APPortunity.com

Be Sure to Visit

GetRichClick.com

WordOfMouse.com

Start to Finish

We all start with questions . . .

From questions comes research.

From research come answers.

From answers comes knowledge.

From knowledge comes understanding.

From understanding comes
competitive advantage.

From competitive advantage comes
winning "the game."

Learn, understand, compete, and win.

Acknowledgments

No book of this nature is done by just one person!

First and foremost, thank-yous *must* go to my family. The most important person in my life is my wife, Beverle Gardner Ostrofsky. She has to be a real saint to put up with a passionate entrepreneur like me! Thank you, Bev! Then a thank-you to my daughters, Kelly Ostrofsky, Shelly Ostrofsky, and Tracy Ostrofsky; and my two stepdaughters, Madison "Maddy" Grieco and MaryGrace "MG" Grieco.

Of course, I never could have done this book without the love and support of my dad, Dr. Benjamin Ostrofsky, who is always a source of great advice—both professionally and personally. Not many people offer unconditional love, but both of my parents have always been there—through good times and bad. Thank you must also go out to Fani Zhishingo for taking care of Dad.

A big thank-you to the person who handled all the operations of my office: my former executive assistant, Kari Musgrove! Kari, you were a wonderful person to have around for your never-ending support and a sense of humor that is a certain necessity in managing my entrepreneurial fervor! A special thank-you for all of the professionals and great editors at Simon & Schuster! Especially my day-to-day contacts and editors Dominick Anfuso and Maura O'Brien. The other folks that helped make this book a reality include Martha Levin, Jennifer Weidman, Suzanne Donahue, and Carisa Hays.

I have to say that this book never would have been completed with the never-ending support of Sydney Tanigawa and Michael Szczerban at S&S and the managing editor of this book, my friend Sara Stephens! Sara, you are the best! I am so happy we reconnected for this, our second time around! Thank you to coauthor Jimmy Conway for his extraordinary chapter on cyber crime.

Next would be my network of lawyers, accountants, and other professionals, including Ken Browning, Michael Rubenstein, Harry Susman, Stan Toy, David Harris, and Robb Weller. Thank you to my sister, Dr. Keri Pearlson, in Austin, Texas, for introducing me to the internet in 1994, and to her husband, Dr. Yale Pearlson, and my niece, Hana Pearlson.

I want to thank Randy Glasbergen for the great cartoons that appear in *Word of Mouse* and in my previous book, *Get Rich Click!* Thank you to my network of friends who always seem to support me through the ups and the downs, including Andy and Wendy Bernstein, Jan Smith, Liz Kalodner, Albe Angel, and Joseph Fulvio.

Thank you to my business partners, including Paul Song, Michael Reese, Michael Goodwin, and our amazing staff at CuffLinks.com; Jay Steinfeld and Daniel Cotlar at Blinds.com; and Jackie and Moses Maestas at Summer Camps.com.

And, finally, thank you to the following groups, sites, and associations for their help and support: WOMMA (Word of Mouth Marketing Association);

David Fraser for his amazing technical support at ooVoo and for all of his help in conducting our video interviews; our friends at eMarketer.com for their great data points; and Trendwatching.com for great forward-trend data.

Also, to the staff at Wise Bread for its wonderful contribution of "Twenty Best Mobile Shopping Apps for Your Phone"; bloggers Harold Jarche and Rob Paterson for their prolific insights; the folks at Pew Research Center and their Internet and American Life Project research; Shama Kabani, the CEO of the Marketing Zen Group, for allowing us to reprint its article on ten ways to maximize Google+; and, of course, the entire senior management team at Infusionsoft—especially Jeff Mask and Clate Mask—who were gracious enough to write the foreword to this book.

I also greatly appreciate the time taken by the various professionals who participated in our Infusionsoft video interviews. They are: Dr. James St. Clair (TopDog Animal Health and Rehabilitation), Jeff Liesener (Topline Foods), Laura Roeder (LKR Social Media), Nadine Larder (Printer Bees), Pamela Slim (Escape from Cubicle Nation), Samantha Bennett (Organized Artist Company), and Scott Griggs (Trainz.com).

Thank you, everyone above. This book could not have happened without your support!

I want to again thank five people who were VITAL in making *Word of Mouse* come to life!

- Ms. Sara Stephens, the editor and my friend for many years. Sara worked tirelessly on this project. Thank you, Sara!
- Pete Holley, associate editor and creative contributor.
- Michael Szczerban, my editor at Simon & Schuster.
- Ken Browning, my agent and good friend.
- Beverle Gardner Ostrofsky, my wife and the one who puts up with my craziness on a day-to-day basis!

Thank you all for making *Word of Mouse* a reality!

The "A 2 Z" Rules of Online Success

by Marc Ostrofsky

Always ask Who, What, When, Where, Why, How, and How Much?

Build a business others want to buy.

Create *equity* versus *income*.

Develop a great management team = a large business versus a small business.

Exit strategy in place?

Forecast best-case, expected, and worst-case scenarios. Be able to survive the worst-case scenario!

Get a job or create a job? Only one of these gives you the freedom you want in life!

Hire your weaknesses and hire the person with the right attitude!

Information is king. The more you know, the easier it is to create competitive advantage!

Justify business decisions with a financial cost-benefit analysis.

Know what you don't know.

Learn more, earn more.

Mailing lists create equity. Build them. Protect them. Do *not* overuse them!

Networking is the key to growth—online and offline.

Outsource! Do it as much as you can, for as long as you can.

Partner with the best. Make less per sale but sell ten times as much!

Questions. Formulate clear and concise questions, so that you get the answers you need.

Research is the real key to success in business—and in life.

Social media = *free* marketing. Develop them. Interact with them. Use them strategically.

Teach. Prospects become buyers when they can answer "What's in it for me?"

Understand your market and be able to explain your competitive advantage.

Video is the key to teaching on the internet. Become an expert in front of the camera!

Win-win is the *only* way to play the game.

Xtra efforts = Xtraordinary profits! People notice the difference!

You are one person. Automate as much as you can and always hire the best you can afford.

Zap 'em if they aren't working out. Hire slow, fire fast!

My Secrets to Your Success

I've been involved in marketing most of my life, and along the way, I've learned some important "secrets." These perspectives are real. They are on target. They make all the difference.

Know what you don't know. So many people really can't tell you what they don't know—they don't have a clue. Find out what you don't know and bring in the best people who have the knowledge you lack.

Learn from the best (and never stop learning). Learn from people who are smarter than you. Learn from people who have been there, who have made the mistakes and know the tips, tricks, and secrets! Never stop learning. Just remember, it's smarter (and cheaper) to learn on their nickel!

KISS. Keep it simple, silly (okay: *stupid*). Don't get caught up trying to become the next Google, Facebook, PayPal, or eBay. These success stories receive all the publicity and fame but are the 1-in-1,000,000 exceptions. More often than not, the other 999,999 situations out there offer great *Get Rich Click!* opportunities, too. Think smaller ventures that make money, require little to no investment, and can be done over and over. The best ideas are often simple ones that are easy to clone or adapt to your situation.

Don't get caught up in "It's already been done" thinking. I hear this all the time: "If it's already out there, why should I do it?" or, "If someone else is selling it, why should I?" With this sort of thinking, there would be only one make of car on the market, one brand of computer, and one type of shoe. Very often, creating something new, whether it's a product, a service, or even a new business model, comes from recombining pieces that already exist. Add in an element of thinking outside the box, and you might find yourself coming up with the next site that makes money from day one and gets sold for $10 million!

Pay for the best person you can afford. Make that person part of your support network, whether in a business or as part of your entrepreneurial ventures. One $40,000 employee is often worth much more than two $20,000 people.

Hire the right attitude. When you come across those rare people who have a great personality, who are energetic and enthusiastic about life, and whom you immediately like and want to be around, hire them.

Hire your weaknesses. You can probably add and subtract, but a good certified public accountant (CPA) can often pay for himself many times over with efficiencies and strengths. And if you're not an attorney with expertise in that area, you'll need one, of course. Hire others who have the skills you may not have.

Do what you enjoy and stick to what you do best. When you pursue things that interest you, things in which you are accomplished, not only is life a lot more interesting and fun but also your riches will come in more ways than one!

Ask questions, cultivate contacts. I was the kid in class who always had a question. I've also developed incredible contacts from sources such as seminars, conventions, and conferences, and just from reading constantly. To be successful in business and stay one step ahead of the competition, you must never stop asking questions, researching your subject, and knowing all the players in the game.

If at first you don't succeed . . . The last principle comes from Albert Einstein, who said, "Insanity: doing the same thing over and over again and expecting different results." If one approach doesn't produce the outcome you'd hoped for, come at the situation from a different angle. As the nature of the internet is changing constantly, being creative, accepting change, and being flexible are huge assets.

I sincerely hope you enjoyed *Word of Mouse*! I would encourage you to use your Word of Mouse tactics to tell your friends and family about this book!

You can also tell me directly at WordOfMouse.com; https://www.facebook .com/wordofmouse; and at Twitter (@WordOfMouse or https://twitter.com/ wordofmouse).

Good luck in all of your personal and business ventures!

My Secrets

Index

229

Index

Index

235

Index

Index

About the Author

Marc Ostrofsky is the *New York Times* bestselling author of *Get Rich Click! The Ultimate Guide to Making Money on the Internet.* He is a futurist, serial entrepreneur, and domain-name investor best known for his world-record sale of the domain name Business.com for $7.5 million. His venture capital firm has created a number of successful telecommunication-, media-, and internet-based companies, including CuffLinks .com, Blinds.com, eTickets.com, and many others. Ostrofsky is a graduate of the University of Texas in Austin; is married to his wife, Beverle; and has five daughters.